The Civilization of the American Indian Series

Fire and the Spirits

Maker of Medicine, by Joan Hill. Reproduced through the courtesy of the Philbrook Art Center, Tulsa, Oklahoma.

Fire and the Spirits

Cherokee Law from Clan to Court

by

Rennard Strickland

FOREWORD BY NEILL H. ALFORD, JR.

University of Oklahoma Press : Norman

By Rennard Strickland

Speaker's Sourcebook Series (7 vols.; Fayetteville, 1965–71)
Sam Houston with the Cherokees (with Jack Gregory; Austin, 1967)
Starr's History of the Cherokees (editor; Fayetteville, 1967)
Indian Spirit Tales Series: *Cherokee Spirit Tales, Creek-Seminole Spirit Tales, Choctaw Spirit Tales, American Indian Spirit Tales* (Muskogee, 1969–74)
Language Is Sermonic (editor; Baton Rouge, 1970)
Hell on the Border (editor, with Jack Gregory; Muskogee, 1971)
The Cherokee People (with Earl Boyd Pierce; Phoenix, 1973)
How to Get into Law School (New York, 1974)
Legal Rights of Classroom Teachers (New York, 1975)
Fire and the Spirits: Cherokee Law from Clan to Court (Norman, 1975)

Library of Congress Cataloging in Publication Data

Strickland, Rennard.
   Fire and the spirits.

   (The Civilization of the American Indian series; no. 133)
   Bibliography: p.
   Includes index.
   1. Law, Cherokee. I. Title. II. Series.
KF8228.C505S7   340'.09701   74-15903
ISBN 0-8061-1227-1

For my mother and her Osage grandfather;
For my father and his Cherokee grandmother;

For my alma mater, the School of Law of
the University of Virginia, and her
faculty;

And, especially, for my mentor,
Jack Gregory, and for Mary

Foreword

Neill H. Alford, Jr.

The laws of American Indian tribes receive only fleeting recognition in most of the early accounts of the affairs of the English colonies in America and of the affairs of the new states following the American Revolution. We have the account by James Adair and those of a few others, but the history of the American Indian in the area of English occupation suffers from the lack of a highly organized and dedicated group of teachers and chroniclers such as the Jesuit missionaries in Central and South America. There was no Manuel de Nobrega and no José de Anchietas in the Carolinas. There was no Bartolomé de las Casas to plead the cause of the aborigine at the English Court.

The scholar who now seeks to explore the institutions of any Indian tribe or nation within the area of English occupation must deal with bits and pieces of evidence. The chroniclers of Indian "affairs" in the English settlements viewed those affairs as "troubles." William B. Stevens, who prepared the first history of Georgia of scholarly quality (*History of Georgia from Its First Discovery by Europeans to the Adoption of the Present Constitution in 1798*, 11 vols., 1847–59), wrote in his chapter "Settlement of Indian Affairs":

To give a history of these Indian difficulties the various turns in their treaties and negotiations, the skirmishing-like warfare so long kept up on the frontier, and the many harrowing details of massacre, cruelty and destruction, which were perpetrated in the white man's settlements, would require more space than can be given to such detail; and therefore much must be left untold, and much more must be left to the imagination, while the historian sketches a brief and confessedly incomplete outline of events connected with the Indian affairs of Georgia.

Lamentably this has been the pattern, and only a reader who recognizes the major obstacles a scholar encounters in his investigation of any aspect of American Indian culture will recognize clearly the monumental task that Strickland has so successfully accomplished in his study of the laws of the Cherokees. Combining his vast knowledge of the culture of this Indian nation, based not only upon his years of research but also upon his fieldwork among the Cherokees of Oklahoma, with his clear perception and firm grasp of the processes by which legal systems develop, Strickland presents a description and analysis of Cherokee law that will serve as a landmark for scholars in the future. In very careful detail he describes the impact of a European legal culture upon a society in which all legal institutions have strong overtones of religion and magic. The processes that he articulates have parallels today when European institutions and tribal traditions clash.

Much has been written in recent years concerning American Indians, and scholars have been particularly active in their study since the American Indian was identified as a member of an abused minority whose legal claims deserve redress. But among these writings Strickland's book will be recognized as a distinguished and concise treatment of the building of legal institutions by an able and intelligent group of true native Americans.

Preface

THERE is a widely held belief that the Cherokees dramatically broke with their ancient law ways and passed from a state of complete "savage" lawlessness to a highly sophisticated, efficiently operating "civilized" system of tribal laws and courts. Perhaps the most extreme statement of this idea, but one still representative of the concept of the instantaneous emergence of the full-blown Cherokee legal system, is found in a speech delivered to the Oklahoma Bar Association in 1910. William Thompson orated that the first Cherokee legal authority commanded, "Let there be light and there was light," and, "This fair land gave birth to a new system of jurisprudence in 1808 and lived its life and ceased to be in 1898, covering a period of ninety years."[1]

To anyone familiar with the development of legal institutions, this is obviously rhetoric of mythical proportions. Nonetheless, the myth of this miraculous birth of Cherokee law continues to prevail. The purpose of this book is to show that the Cherokee court system emerged not from a single act but by a gradual acculturation process fusing tribal law ways and Anglo-American legal institutions.

This book is about the legal aspects of the cultural phenomenon that twentieth-century man has come to call "modernization" and that the Jeffersonian called "civilization." Lon Fuller imagined a case in which "we are drafting a written constitution for a country emerging from a period in which any thread of legal continuity with pre-

---

1 William P. Thompson, "An Address Delivered Before the First Annual Meeting of the Oklahoma State Bar Association in 1910," *Chronicles of Oklahoma*, Vol. 2 (1924), 67.

vious governments has been broken."[2] The Cherokees are generally assumed to be a case study of the situation Fuller hypothesized.

Yet the Cherokees did not, as is commonly believed, break all threads of continuity with Cherokee tradition. In 1808 the tribe did draft the first written law, but this act should not be taken as evidence that all native aspects of tribal law were purged. In fact, Cherokee records suggest that traditional elements played a vital role in the development of the Cherokee legal system.

Even to this day the Oklahoma court system, which replaced the Cherokee tribal courts, is viewed by many Cherokees as being within the scope of their more traditional Indian world view. As late as 1971, Cherokee magical powers were called upon by a Cherokee to resolve a dispute with me over the use of materials supplied by an informant, even though the dispute would have been, within traditional Anglo-American law, a copyright controversy. To that considerable number of Cherokees who keep alive the old ways, the supernatural powers of the spirit, of tobacco, and of the magic are not forgotten. Such powers are often seen as more direct and certain than an order by a state-court judge.

The official records and papers of the Cherokee Nation are the primary sources upon which this book is based. They are supplemented by original accounts of observers in the Cherokee country and official federal Indian records. The focus is upon the Cherokees who, after enacting the early laws in Georgia, were removed to Indian Territory, now Oklahoma, in 1838 and 1839. The Eastern Cherokees, presently situated in North Carolina, were originally a part of this main body, but have broken away in their development and are, after 1838, beyond the scope of this book. More than seventy-five years have passed since the federal government legislatively abolished the Cherokee tribal courts. For this reason the work could not be designed primarily as a field study. The time clearly has passed for such field research into nineteenth-century Cherokee legal institutions, although I have tried to explore many of these legal questions in my field work.

The study of the emergence of a legal system has long fascinated legal historians and philosophers. With the appearance of nineteenth-century works, such as Sir Henry Maine's *Ancient Law*, the contribution of the systematic and comparative study of law in the history

[2] Lon Fuller, "Positivism and Fidelity to Law—A Reply to Professor Hart," *Harvard Law Review*, Vol. 71 (1958), 642.

of other cultures became clear. When Llewellyn and Hoebel merged the strengths of scientific anthropology and American legal realism in *The Cheyenne Way*, the classic study of jurisprudence on the American plains, North American Indian culture as a laboratory for the study of legal institutions emerged. An Indian tribe undertaking development of a new legal system offers an even greater opportunity for study. The unfolding process provides a test tube in which to view the evolution of a legal system.

Thomas Jefferson considered the Cherokee experiment something of a test case for all tribes and expressed the hope that this example would stimulate others to emulate "Cherokee progress." In the summer of 1812, Jefferson, concerned with British intrigue among the southern Indian tribes, wrote to John Adams expressing a theory often used by twentieth-century statesmen to justify foreign assistance. "On those tribes who have made any progress English seduction will have no effect," Jefferson noted, "but the backward will yield."[3] The parallel is striking between what President John F. Kennedy described as "newly emerging nations of Asia and Africa" attempting to telescope "centuries of pioneering . . . and growth . . . into decades and even years"[4] and Jefferson's picture of Indian tribes "anxious . . . to engage in . . . industrious pursuits."[5]

Since the days of Jefferson the world may have become more complex, swept by "a tidal wave of national independence" and "the industrial and scientific revolution,"[6] but the experience of the southern Indian tribes who propelled themselves from witchcraft and clan revenge into a constitutional court system shows that our efforts in promoting economic and social developments among emerging tribesmen are not uniquely modern. There is probably no better documented case study of cultural adaptation of a traditional legal system than that of the Cherokee Indians.

The Cherokees were, in reality, a laboratory for the "civilization" dreams of nineteenth-century policymakers. The advocates of this

[3] Letter, Thomas Jefferson to John Adams, June 11, 1812, *The Writings of Thomas Jefferson*, XIII, 160.

[4] John F. Kennedy, "Special Message to the Congress on Free World Defense and Assistance Program," April 2, 1963, *Public Papers of the Presidents: John F. Kennedy, 1963*, Item 118 (cited hereafter as Kennedy, *Public Papers of the Presidents*).

[5] Speech, Thomas Jefferson to "Deputies of the Cherokee Upper Towns," January 9, 1809, *The Writings of Thomas Jefferson*, XVI, 456–58. See Appendix 4, where address is set forth.

[6] Kennedy, *Public Papers of the Presidents*, Item 118.

most ethnocentric of all policies believed that by transforming Indian institutions into copies of white institutions, the Indian problem, if not the Indian, would disappear.

The Cherokee legal experience illustrates that it was, in fact, possible to create Indian versions of white ways. The result, however, was not what "civilizers" had expected. Instead of a weak carbon copy, an anemic shadow people, the Cherokees emerged as worthy adversaries who demanded that their institutions be respected. They had been schooled in the ways of the white man and demanded that they be extended the rights to which they were entitled by law. In the end, the monster, the Indian tribal state, the red man in powdered wig, had to be destroyed. He had learned his lesson too well.

The Cherokee experience demonstrates that law is more—much more—than powdered wigs, black robes, leather-bound statutes, silver stars, and blinded ladies with balanced scales. Law is also a Cherokee priest listening to the spirit world while holding the sacred wampums in hand and the Cheyenne soldier-society warrior draped in the skin of a wolf. In fact, a command from the spirit world can have greater force as law than the most elaborate code devised by the most learned of men. For law is organic. Law is part of a time and a place, the product of a specific time and an actual place.

The Cherokee experience demonstrates that law cannot be separated from the environment in which it matured. Just as we cannot transplant law into another time or another place, so we cannot judge the laws of a people by the standards of the people of another time and another place. To do so does violence to the very nature of the concept of law as a living institution. Law itself is dynamic, a vital force, organic in all respects. Thus law was to the traditional Cherokee a part of his larger world view, a command from his spirit world. And it is as such that we must view the law of the early Cherokees. For law can no more be projected into another time than it can be isolated from the cultural milieu of its own time.

To acknowledge all the debts owed for any book is an impossible task, but my obligations for this one are so great that I want to attempt to render thanks to a few of them. The American Bar Foundation through their Fellowship in Legal History sustained a full summer of research, and for that I am especially grateful. Additional research financing has been provided by the University of Tulsa, the

University of Arkansas, the University of Virginia, the University of West Florida, and St. Mary's University.

I am especially indebted to law-school faculties and deans with whom I have worked over the past ten or twelve years. These include Deans F. D. G. Ribble, Hardy Dillard, and Monrad Paulsen, of the University of Virginia; the "dean of deans," America's longest-serving law-school dean, Ernest A. Raba, of St. Mary's; and Tulsa's Edgar Wilson, Joseph Morris, and Frank Read. Several members of the Virginia Law School faculty, John Norton Moore, Calvin Woodard, Carl McFarland, Charles M. Davison, Jr., and Neill H. Alford, Jr., read earlier versions of the manuscript and provided a number of insights. For their assistance I also must thank Garrick Bailey, Ralph Eubanks, Earl Boyd Pierce, Lewis Meyer, Anna G. Kilpatrick, Cecil Dick, Frances Farmer, Thomas G. Young III, Guy Logsdon, Wilma Thrash, Marty Hagerstrand, Anne and Wayne Morgan, Jack Baker, Joan Hill, Paul Rogers, and George Washington.

Significant library and archival resources were required for this book. Foremost among these centers were the Thomas Gilcrease Institute of American History and Art in Tulsa and the Oklahoma Historical Society. My debts to Marie Keene and Pat Edwards, of the Gilcrease Institute, and to Rella Looney and Manon Adkins, of the Oklahoma Historical Society, continue to grow. I also wish to thank the staff members of all the libraries listed in the bibliography of manuscript materials and especially my friends at the Five Civilized Tribes Museum and in the Cherokee National Archives.

The dedication reflects my continuing obligation to my mother and father and to Jack and Mary Gregory.

One cannot study the Cherokees without coming to love them. One cannot know the Cherokee story without experiencing a sense of the tragedy that forced them to go from clan to court and without wondering what might have been. For the Cherokee spirit I feel a sense of wonder and admiration.

RENNARD STRICKLAND

Tulsa, Oklahoma

Contents

Illustrations

Maps

Fire and the Spirits

The Cherokees: People of the Fire

I

Toward the close of the third decade of the nineteenth century, when the Cherokee Nation began to publish a newspaper, the name *Phoenix* was selected for the masthead. It was an appropriate choice. The power of that ancient mythical bird who was consumed by fire and arose from his own ashes seems to be inborn in the soul of the Cherokee people. There is an eternal flame of the Cherokees—a fire so carefully guarded that it has continued to burn for them through forcible removal, civil war, and tribal dissolution. According to the ancient legend, as long as that fire burns, the Cherokees will survive.

The Cherokees are indeed a remarkable people, having survived in the face of overwhelming odds.[1] The Cherokee accomplishment is eloquent testimony to what William Faulkner described as the enduring spirit of man. The Cherokee story is proof that humanity will not only endure but triumph.

The struggle of the Cherokees has been long and mighty. In a migration fragment predating even the famous Delaware account, the journey of these people is said to have begun in the far north, and they are pictured as fighting the freezing rains and winds to arrive in their beloved southern homelands.

[1] For a more detailed general history of the Cherokees the reader should consult the following: David H. Corkran, *The Cherokee Frontier: Conflict and Survival, 1740–62*; Jack Gregory and Rennard Strickland (eds.), *Starr's History of the Cherokees*; Henry Thompson Malone, *Cherokees of the Old South: A People in Transition*; James Mooney, *Myths of the Cherokees*; Charles C. Royce, *The Cherokee Nation of Indians*; Marion L. Starkey, *The Cherokee Nation*; Thurman Wilkins, *Cherokee Tragedy: The Story of the Ridge Family and the Decimation of a People*; and Grace Steele Woodward, *The Cherokees*. A brief overview of tribal history is presented in Earl Boyd Pierce and Rennard Strickland, *The Cherokee People*.

The prehistoric origin of the Cherokee people is shrouded in mystery. In historic times the Cherokees were the largest of the Indian tribes on the southern frontier of English America. By the eighteenth century the tribe numbered over ten thousand and lived in sixty or more scattered villages. Through a series of treaties the Cherokee land holdings were reduced until the 1820's, when the major body of the tribe (approximately sixteen thousand) was concentrated primarily in Georgia and Tennessee. When the Cherokees were removed to Indian Territory in 1838, they joined another six thousand Western Cherokees who had voluntarily migrated to the land that became part of the state of Oklahoma.

The life of the ancient Cherokee was guided by a deep faith in supernatural forces that linked human beings to all other living things. This belief was a common bond among all Cherokees. Yet no national unity or federation existed among the early, separate Cherokee villages. Each operated as an autonomous unit, although they joined together for ceremonials and large wars and were informally grouped by settlements.

Most of the Cherokee villages were situated along small streams in scattered areas throughout the Appalachian Mountains. Villages were laid out around a large town or council house with small individual dwellings surrounding these centers. The Cherokees owned very little in the way of personal property. Hunting and warfare were central to the life of the aboriginal Cherokees, but the tribe had embraced limited agriculture and planted fields which supplemented the hunt. The Cherokee males were the hunters; women were charged with gardening, cooking, making pottery, and rearing children.

The general history of the Cherokees as a people can be divided into seven post-contact periods.[2] Each of these separate phases of development reflects a general attitude and policy shift. The issues which the Cherokee legal system faced varied considerably from period to period. The seven periods of history are:

1. Frontier contact, 1540 to 1785
2. White ascendancy, 1786 to 1828
3. Tribal dislocation, 1829 to 1846
4. Struggle for self-government, 1847 to 1860

[2] For a historical overview see the Cherokee Legal History Chronology, 1540–1907, page 193.

4

5. American Civil War and Reconstruction, 1860 to 1866
6. Establishment of the Cherokee Nation, 1867 to 1887
7. Termination and Statehood, 1887 to 1906

1. *Frontier contact (1540 to 1785)*. The period of the Cherokee frontier traces from initial white contact with De Soto in 1540 through the first treaty with the American government, signed at Hopewell in 1785. The central problem faced by the Cherokee people during this period was resistance to white advancement through merging into a national state from highly individualized Indian towns under separate and often extremely jealous village leaders. The colonial rivalry of Spain, France, and England (later among the individual American colonies) was a compelling factor which had to be faced. Furthermore, adaptation to gun, horse, and fur-trade-dominated economy was complicated by the expansion of white settlements.

2. *White Ascendancy (1786 to 1828)*. The central issue, that of adapting Indian culture to meet the demands of white civilization, was set forth in the provisions of the Treaty of Hopewell. During this period the Cherokees addressed themselves to the question of how the white legal system could be adapted to Cherokee needs and which elements would best serve Cherokee tribal goals. The means of assuring tribal acceptance and such questions as the role of the white missionary, treatment of mixed-blood and intermarried citizens, and the creation of courts to enforce the laws were being explored when the Georgia legislature attempted to end the Cherokee Republic.

3. *Tribal Dislocation (1829 to 1846)*. The election of Andrew Jackson to the presidency, passage of the Indian Removal Bill, and extension of Georgia law over the Cherokee Nation climaxed the Cherokee crisis. The ramifications of these three events dominated the life of the Cherokee Nation until 1846. From 1829 to 1838 the Cherokee Nation fought both in a series of United States Supreme Court cases and through the political pressures of Congress to retain tribal lands in their ancestral mountains. This was an all-consuming struggle which postponed consideration of other questions. Following the removal treaty signed at New Echota, the forcible eviction of fifteen thousand Cherokees and their transportation over what has come to be known as the "Trail of Tears," the Nation faced the task of rebuilding the transplanted institutions of their infant republic. This task was complicated by the wounds of the removal struggle

and the necessity of uniting the Treaty Cherokees with the "Old Settler" Cherokees already in the area. Political leadership was unable to resolve the conflicts, and open civil war followed until 1846, when the federal government forced the Cherokee factions to sign the Treaty of Washington.

4. *Struggle for Self-Government (1847 to 1860).* Following the Treaty of Washington of 1846, the Cherokee Nation began to struggle with the daily tasks of operating its government. The period was stable and was considered by some to be the "golden age of Cherokee civilization" with the establishment of the National Seminaries, or high schools, and the ascendancy of the slaveholding mixed-blood aristocracy. Yet in many respects the period was one of excesses. The Cherokees chose to borrow many institutions of white society before an adequate base to sustain the institutions had been built. The issues of sustaining a sound government were reaching a crisis stage at the beginning of the American Civil War.

5. *American Civil War and Reconstruction (1861 to 1867).* After a short period of neutrality the Cherokees formally joined the Confederacy in the spring of 1861. For more than four years the lands of the Cherokees were the center of border skirmishes and guerrilla activity. The land was made desolate by the war. The primary task of Cherokee government during this period was to feed and protect its citizens. The defeat of the Confederacy and the terms of the enforced peace, which opened the Cherokee lands to railroads, ultimately spelled the death of the Cherokee Nation. In the Treaty of Fort Smith of 1866 were the seeds of tribal dissolution.

6. *Establishing the Cherokee Nation (1867 to 1892).* After returning from the Conference of 1866, the Cherokees began the grim task of rebuilding and establishing a Cherokee Nation under federal policies which abrogated previous agreements, and forced the Cherokees to grant tribal citizenship to several thousand former slaves, transfer their tribal lands to other Indians, dispose of the Cherokee Outlet, grant permission for railroads to build across their nation, and prepare for ultimate distribution of tribal lands. The major tasks of this period were to (1) provide an economically sound and firmly based operational system of government, (2) establish a form of citizenship, control, and regulation for the freed slaves, (3) enact a system of regulation of expanding railroad activities, (4) control the increasing pressures of white population looking to settle on Chero-

kee land, and (5) establish a system of education and welfare for the Cherokee people.

7. *Termination (1893 to 1907).* The passage of the Curtis Act and the establishment of the Dawes Commission for distribution of Indian lands marked the beginning of the formal federal program terminating Cherokee lands. During this period the Cherokee legal system was faced with the task of retaining support for tribal judicial and administrative functions while coordinating the enrollment and registration of all Cherokee citizens, regulating white admissions to the nation, and preparing the way for final termination of the Cherokee Nation and distribution of tribal lands. In the midst of this struggle the Cherokee court system ceased to function under an act of Congress in January of 1898.

The Cherokee story is truly astounding. Students of Indian history are familiar with the tale of how disorganized bands of Cherokees forged themselves into a political state, created their own native alphabet, adopted a written constitution, and ultimately provided political, social, and economic leadership for a new state. What is not as well known is that these Cherokees were not an anemic people given only to simple domestic pursuits but were a tribe of Indian warriors and hunters whose conquests had given them military dominion over the heartland of the southern mountain ranges.

That the Cherokees were eventually to be known as one of the Five Civilized Tribes is testimony to their ingenuity. The Cherokees saw, paradoxically, that in change was their only hope of survival as an Indian people. Historical proof of the significance of this attitude is found in the testimony of Charles Hicks, a Cherokee chief and one of the earliest advocates of Cherokee acculturation. Hicks wrote to the Cherokee missionary Daniel Sabin Buttrick that abandonment of the old Indian way represented "the conviction that their very existence as a people depends upon it."[3]

The failure to survive as a political state was not a failure upon the part of the Cherokees. Again and again, as tribal accomplishment laid a foundation which would have preserved the Cherokees as a people, the white man stepped in and destroyed the Cherokees' accomplishment and beat them down. The triumph of the Chero-

---

[3] Charles Hicks, Typescripts of Cherokee Papers, Indian Heritage Association, Muskogee, Okla.

kees is that they have been able to survive, coming back fiercely determined that they will not only survive but prosper.

At the beginning of the nineteenth century the Cherokees cast their fate into the mainstream of the American legal process. The Cherokees kept faith with the American dream. In their great struggle to retain their ancestral homes in Georgia in the 1830's, they turned not to the bow but to the book and the law which it contained. As the Cherokees awaited John Marshall and the Supreme Court's decision in their case, Elias Boudinot wrote the following in an editorial in the *Cherokee Phoenix*:

> The Cherokees are for justice and they are trying to obtain it in a peaceable manner by a regular course of law. If the last and legitimate tribunal decides against them, as honest men they will submit and "the agony will be over." Will Georgia be as honest and submit to her own (U.S.) courts?[4]

The John Marshall court in the famous *Worcester* v. *Georgia* supported the Cherokees' cause and reaffirmed their belief in the legal process. Then Jackson is purported to have issued his famous challenge to the judiciary—"Marshall has made his law, let him enforce it."[5] Marshall had the law; Jackson had the troops. Whites turned away from the book and took up the bow as fifteen thousand Cherokees were driven by General Winfield Scott and his troops from their beloved southern mountains. Only eleven thousand finished the journey; four thousand died along the trek, which came to be known among the Indians as the Trail of Tears.

This incident is germane to our history because it vividly illustrates the dilemma of the Cherokees. As soon as the Cherokees adapted their culture so that they could survive as a people, whites stepped in and, through force of arms or legislation, destroyed what the Cherokees had accomplished. The pattern was repeated again and again.

At the close of the nineteenth century the Cherokees and their brother tribes, the Creeks, Chickasaws, Choctaws, and Oklahoma Seminoles, stood ready to accept admission to the Union as an Indian

---

[4] *Cherokee Phoenix*, March 5, 1831.

[5] Anton-Hermann Chroust, "Did President Jackson Actually Threaten the Supreme Court of the United States with Nonenforcement of Its Injunction Against the State of Georgia?" *American Journal of Legal History*, Vol. 5 (1960), 76–78; Joseph G. Burke, "The Cherokee Cases: A Study in Law, Politics, and Morality," *Stanford Law Review*, Vol. 21 (1969), 500–31.

state. The Cherokees had truly moved from clan revenge to court process and waited for the long-promised Indian state which would culminate their historic compromise. Instead, the United States Congress and the instrument of its creation, the Dawes Commission, divided tribal lands, abolished Indian courts, and ended forever the governing powers of the Cherokee Nation. The Cherokees and the other Civilized Tribes were forced to abandon their Indian state of Sequoyah and merged into the state of Oklahoma.

Yet the accomplishment of the Cherokees in making that remarkable transformation remains a tribute to the Indian people. There is a Cherokee legend which says that in the beginning the Indian was given both the book and the bow but did not use the book and so was left only the bow. After the white men came, the Cherokees, faced with the question of survival as an Indian people, turned to the book and learned to use it. If the white man had only believed in the book and not broken faith with the Indian, we might all be the richer.

There is a justifiable temptation to glory in the Cherokee transformation from clan to court. It is truly a remarkable achievement. Yet one must fight the Whig theory of history—the belief that what is later is always better, the feeling that progress is its own reward. As John Crowe Ransom has reminded us, progress as a God figure has no end and exerts no ethical judgment. The thoughtful man must ponder the question "which Cherokee society . . . was superior."[6]

Ironically, there may be a final victory for the traditional Cherokee philosophy of man's relationship with nature. The Cherokee who borrowed from the white in order to survive may, in turn, with his Indian brothers contribute an element to the survival of civilization. More and more the Indian is becoming a source of inspiration for those seeking a new philosophy, a new ethic of the earth. D. H. Lawrence is reported to have said that the Indian will again rule America—or, rather, his ghost will. As William Brandon prophesied, "The business of the Indian . . . may turn out to be the illumination of the dark side of the soul."[7]

[6] Yasuhide Kawashima, "Review of A Law of Blood," American Journal of Legal History, Vol. 15 (1971), 157–59.
[7] See Rennard Strickland, "Idea of Ecology and the Ideal of the Indian," Journal of American Indian Education, Vol. 9 (1970).

Traditional Law Ways
and the Spirit World*

II

LIEUTENANT Henry Timberlake, a British officer assigned to the Cherokee country in the mid-eighteenth century, wrote that "their government, if I may call it government . . . has neither laws nor power to support it." An early traveler, William Fyffe, reported that Cherokee "government is not supported by laws and punishments as among us." Similarly, Captain Raymond Demere, commander of Fort Loudon in Tennessee, wrote to Charles Town in 1757 that "there is no law nor subjection amongst them."[1]

Timberlake and his contemporaries were limited by the short-sightedness which afflicted most early observers of the Cherokee legal system. Englishmen were looking for native versions of British courts and, when they saw no red chief justices or Indian barristers, concluded, in a supreme gesture of ethnocentrism, that the Cherokees had no system of law.

In truth, the Cherokee conception of law was simply different from the more traditional Western idea of law. To the Cherokees

---

* Portions of this chapter appeared, in different form, in the *American Indian Law Review*, Vol. I, No. 1 (Winter, 1973).

[1] Henry Timberlake, *The Memoirs of Lieut. Henry Timberlake* (ed. by Samuel Cole Williams), 93. William Fyffe, Letter to Brother John, February 1, 1761, Thomas Gilcrease Institute, Tulsa, Okla. Captain Raymond Demere, Letter to Charles Town 1757, Cherokee Documents Collection, Indian Heritage Association, Muskogee, Okla. Students interested in specific legal institutions of the traditional Cherokees should read John Phillip Reid's excellent study of early tribal law, *A Law of Blood: The Primitive Law of the Cherokee Nation* (cited hereafter as *Law of Blood*). The major point of distinction between our interpretations of early law centers around the role of the religious complex in the Cherokee legal system.

law was the earthly representation of a divine spirit order. They did not think of law as a set of civil or secular rules limiting or requiring actions on their part. Public consensus and harmony rather than confrontation and dispute, as essential elements of the Cherokee world view, were reflected in the ancient concepts of the law.

The ongoing social process could not, in the Cherokee way, be manipulated by law to achieve policy goals. There was no question of man being able to create law because to the Cherokee the norms of behavior were a sovereign command from the Spirit World. Man might apply the divinely ordained rules, but no earthly authority was empowered to formulate rules of tribal conduct.

The Cherokee law was centered in the priestly complex of the native tribal religion. The recitation of the law was a high religious ceremony. Among the ancient Cherokees there was an office of tribal orator, a priest who was sometimes called the "beloved man." The orator's duties included, among others, the delivery of the laws of the Cherokees at the annual busk, or first-fruit celebration. Dressed in the orator's costume and wearing the wings of a raven in his hair, the lawgiver must have been an impressive and important figure. John Haywood, in *Natural and Aboriginal History of Tennessee,* reported observations of the recitation of the law:

> The great beloved man or high priest addresses the warriors and women giving all the particular and positive injunctions, and negative precepts they yet retain of the ancient law. He uses very sharp language to the women. He then addresses the whole multitude. He enumerates the crimes they have committed, great and small, and bids them look at the holy fire, which has forgiven them. He presses on his audience by the great motives of temporal good, and the fear of temporal evil, the necessity of a careful observance of the ancient laws.[2]

When the orator spoke the law, he was reading the meaning of history and tradition contained in the tribal wampum. He held the ancient and sacred wampum belts in his hand. At the earliest periods the laws were interpreted from divining crystals, whose surface might picture the events of the forthcoming year. In later times wampum beads of varying shades were strung together to symbolize events and customs of the Cherokees. Even today the Kee-too-wah Cherokees

---

[2] John Haywood, *The Natural and Aboriginal History of Tennessee,* 243 (cited hereafter as *History of Tennessee*).

are said to continue to read their ancient laws from many of the same belts used by the beloved men in Haywood's time.[3]

The law was read but once a year. The law was simple, and the people knew the law. The reading was more symbolic than informative but served, no doubt, as a reminder that the Cherokees were a people governed by the laws of the Spirits. Each year among the Cherokees there was a "great festival of the expiation of sins," at which all crimes except murder were forgiven after the expiration of a year. The Cherokees felt that "the heart cannot be weighed down with all the sorrows of past years," and thus the new year feast was a time of absolution at which "the divine fire is appeased for past crimes."[4]

The fire itself and the smoke of the fire are agents and act to grant the pardon. No Cherokee who retains a grudge or notion of revenge can participate in the renewal festival, which is a time of "joy and gladness" when the fire has "sanctified their weighty harvest." At this feast the Cherokees "rejoice exceedingly at this appearance of the holy fire, and it is supposed to atone for all their past crimes, except murder."[5] As Haywood explains:

> Here it is that all injuries are forgiven, which have been done to one another. Vengeance and cruelty are forgotten in the sacrifice made to friendship. No one who has been guilty of unpardonable offences, can partake of this feast; and all who partake of it must be forgiven, no matter what may be the nature of the offence. This feast consigns to oblivion and extinguishes all vengeance, and forever banishes from the mind all senti-

[3] John Howard Payne Papers, Roll 6987, 350 and Roll 6985, 19, 55–60, Ayer Collection, Newberry Library, Chicago, Ill. The history of the Cherokee wampum is traced in Robert K. Thomas, "The Origin and Development of the Redbird Smith Movement," (Master's thesis, University of Arizona, 1953), 119–35. The wampum belts are shown in a picture of the Keetoowah Council of 1916 in Jack Gregory and Rennard Strickland (eds.), *Starr's History of the Cherokees*, 487, Letter, William Fyffe to Brother John. For contemporary Cherokee practices see Benny Smith, "The Keetoowah Society of the Cherokee Indians," (Master's thesis, Northwestern State College, Alva, Okla., 1967) and Nancy Beverage, "The Keetoowah Society" (seminar paper, University of Tulsa, 1969).

[4] Haywood, *History of Tennessee*, 246.

[5] John Howard Payne Papers. Jack Gregory and Rennard Strickland, *Cherokee Spirit Tales: Tribal Myths, Legends and Folklore*, 26 (cited hereafter as *Cherokee Spirit Tales*). The work of David H. Corkran is especially important in interpreting the ancient ceremonies. Corkran, "Cherokee Prehistory," *North Carolina Historical Review*, Vol. 34 (1957), 455–66; Corkran, "Cherokee Sun and Fire Observances," *Southern Indian Studies*, Vol. 7 (1955), 33–38; Corkran, "The Sacred Fire of the Cherokees," *Southern Indian Studies*, Vol. 5 (1953), 21–26.

Cherokee Lawgiver, by Cecil Dick. The ancient law was recited yearly at the busk by a priestly orator wearing raven wings in his hair. Upon these occasions the crimes that had been committed during the year were named, and the orator asked the sacred fire to forgive them. Author's Collection.

Cherokee "Kings" visit England. The traditional legal system of the Cherokees was reshaped by British conceptions of what the government ought to be, including the idea of a unified political state with a monarch. Illustration from British sheet music, ca. 1770. Courtesy Thomas Gilcrease Institute.

Punishment was often inflicted by special groups, depending upon the nature of the offense. Women played a role in punishment of captives and war prisoners and in violation of women's restrictions. Painting, *Fate of the Prisoner*, by Jimmy Anderson. Courtesy Philbrook Art Center, Tulsa, Oklahoma.

A traditional Cherokee village. The legal system of the traditional Cherokees was centered around the social and political life of the village, under control of a war government and a peace government, depending upon the events at the time in question. Painting by Alfred Johnson. Courtesy Philbrook Art Center.

Ancient Cherokee wampum belts. The very earliest accounts of Cherokee law record the reading of the ways from belts of wampum held by religious leaders. Traditional Cherokee Keetoowahs are pictured with the historic wampum of the Cherokees, ca. 1900. Courtesy Oklahoma Historical Society, Oklahoma City, Oklahoma.

LAWS

OF THE

CHEROKEE NATION,

PASSED BY THE

National Committee and Council.

PRINTED BY ORDER OF THE COMMITTEE AND COUNCIL.

KNOXVILLE, Tenn.,
PRINTED AT THE KNOXVILLE REGISTER OFFICE BY
HEISKELL & BROWN

1821.

29093

The first published laws of an American Indian tribe. This title page is from the 1821 edition of *Laws of the Cherokee Nation*, which was printed in English and predates all other published laws of native American Indians. Courtesy Oklahoma Historical Society.

Cherokee laws in the syllabary of Sequoyah. The development of the written Cherokee language was an important step in the development of the legal institutions of the Cherokees, since it allowed the tribe to publish laws in the native tongue. Cherokee laws were translated from the English into Cherokee. Author's collection.

The Cherokee Supreme Court Building, restored at New Echota, Georgia. The tribe, in 1827, prior to removal, built this court house in the newly established national capital and the early cases of the Cherokee Nation were heard here. Courtesy Department of Natural Resources, State of Georgia.

ments of displeasure which before separated them from a close and friendly intercourse with each other.[6]

The purpose of this chapter is to reconstruct, as nearly as possible, the traditional legal system of the Cherokee Indians. The aim is to picture native jurisprudence as it existed before substantial modification through the introduction of alien economic and social concepts.

In order to clarify the ancient Cherokee law ways, I follow the methods outlined by E. Adamson Hoebel in his classic *The Law of Primitive Man: A Study of Comparative Legal Dynamics*. As Hoebel explains, "In the study of a social system and its law by the specialist it is his job to abstract postulates" which reflect the "broadly generalized propositions held by the members of a society as to the nature of things."[7]

To avoid the pitfalls which Timberlake faced, one must view law as an ongoing process in a specific social context. Therefore, we must attempt to formulate the basic social postulates upon which the system rests. We should strive to find "the key basic concepts of . . . culture, without which the living law . . . of that culture is not understood."[8] We are thus looking for the general propositions held by the Cherokee Indians "as to the nature of things and as to what is qualitatively desirable and undesirable."[9]

Using Hoebel's basic methodology, I have formulated the following social postulates of the civilization of the eighteenth-century Cherokees drawn from contemporary accounts.[10] These are the postulates commonly accepted by the traditional Cherokee:

---

[6] Haywood, *History of Tennessee*, 246.

[7] E. Adamson Hoebel, *The Law of Primitive Man: A Study of Comparative Legal Dynamics*, 13 (cited hereafter as *Law of Primitive Man*). Hoebel acknowledges the "influence of Pound's sociology of law" and of Julius Stone's *The Province and Function of Law*.

[8] F. S. C. Northrop, "Jurisprudence in the Law School Curriculum," *Journal of Legal Education*, Vol. 1 (1949), 489.

[9] Hoebel, *Law of Primitive Man*, 13. Perhaps the clearest summary of this approach is found in Otis Lee, "Social Values and the Philosophy of Law," *Virginia Law Review*, Vol. 32 (1946), 811–12.

[10] The following manuscript sources were consulted in preparing these postulates and the tables: George Chicken, "Journal of the Commissioner of Indian Affairs on Journey to the Cherokees and His Proceedings There, 1725," Thomas Gilcrease Institute, Tulsa, Okla.; William Fyffe, Letter to Brother John, February 1, 1761, Thomas Gilcrease Institute, Tulsa, Okla.; Alexander Longe, "A Small Postscript to the Ways and Manners of Indians Called the Cherokees," Papers of the Society for the Propogation of the Gospel, Library of Congress, Division of Manuscripts, Washington, D.C.; John Howard Payne Papers, "Traditions of the Cherokees," Daniel S. Buttrick

1. The fire is central to life. Fire and smoke are agents of Being. Spirit Beings created the world. These Beings, who possess emotional intelligence similar to that of man control the destiny of man, who, in important aspects of life, is subordinate to the souls of the Spirit Beings. Man's social order is patterned after the system of the creating Spirits. Divine Spirit retribution is always a grave danger. Displeasure may or may not be vented immediately. The Spirits allow both supernatural and secular aspects in their divinely ordained world.

2. The matrilineal clan is the primary social unit, whose purity of blood must be safeguarded at all times.

3. War and peace are separate activities which require two distinct political organizations, as well as dual obligations for all men and women.

4. Priests, as leaders of the peace organization, have been given secrets which will guard the welfare of the tribe.

5. Popular consensus is essential to effective tribal action. Leadership depends upon popular support, which may be withheld to prevent action. Withdrawal of factions may provide the solution when agreement by consensus is impossible. Social harmony is an element of great value.

6. Society is divided into separate classes and ranks which were created by the Spirits. There is no significant stigma and only limited privilege attached to class membership. All classes, both men and women, are of great value socially and have important and useful roles in Cherokee society.

7. All natural resources are free or common goods. Food supplies and wealth items are privately owned but are to be shared. Property is to be used but not accumulated, for wealth is not a desired social

Manuscript Notes on Cherokee Customs and Antiquities, "Notes on Cherokee History," Letters to John Howard Payne from Selected Cherokee Informants, all in Ayer Collection, Newberry Library, Chicago, Ill. Papers, American Board of Foreign Missions, Harvard Library, Cambridge. Published sources from which data were drawn are James Adair, *History of the American Indians* (cited hereafter as *American Indians*); William Bartram, *Travels Through North and South Carolina* (hereafter cited as *Travels*); Benjamin Hawkins, *Letters of Benjamin Hawkins*, IX; Haywood, *History of Tennessee*; Wilbur R. Jacobs (ed.), *Indians of the Southern Colonial Frontier: The Edmond Atkin Report and Plan of 1755*; W. L. McDowell, *Colonial Records of South Carolina: Documents Relating to Indian Affairs and Journals of the Commissioners of the Indian Trade*; Thomas Nuttall, *A Journal of Travels into the Arkansas Territory*; John Stuart, *A Sketch of the Cherokee and Choctaw Indians*; Henry Timberlake, *The Memoirs of Lieut. Henry Timberlake* (cited hereafter as *Timberlake's Memoirs*); Cephas Washburn, *Reminiscences of the Indians*; Samuel Cole Williams (ed.), *Early Travels in the Tennessee Country, 1540–1800*.

goal. All people are to be honored regardless of physical and personal limitations.

8. Marriage is a temporary state and may be dissolved, at will, by either party. While marriage exists, sexual fidelity is expected.

9. There is a supernatural world to which the ghosts of all men desire to go. Actions on earth, either one's own or those of a clan brother, may prevent passage into the afterworld, or Nightland. Duties of blood and oaths are, therefore, to be highly regarded.

Legal norms existed on four levels among the ancient Cherokees. This analysis, following recent anthropological scholarship, accepts a social norm as legal "if its neglect or infraction is regularly met, in threat or in fact, by the application of physical force by an individual or group possessing the socially recognized privilege of so acting."[11] The first of the norms were those governing relationships between man and the supernatural—the Spirit Beings. Second were the norms prescribing conduct of the individual Indian toward specific public order, issues relating to the entire village or tribe. Next were the norms concerning clan rights and duties. Finally, there were a limited number of norms on individual or personal questions.[12]

The Cherokees distinguished between norms regulating public conduct and those designed to assist in preventing or curing diseases. According to ancient tradition, tribal knowledge of these two kinds of regulations came from separate prophets at different times in Cherokee history. Functions are also distinguished in the tribal mythology on the origin of death and the introduction of disease. And yet there is a connection in that violation of either norm may result in punishment by disease or death inflicted from the Spirit World.[13]

[11] Hoebel, *Law of Primitive Man*, 28. For a vigorous dissent see Kenneth S. Carlston, *Social Theory and African Tribal Organization: The Development of Socio-Legal Theory*.

[12] See Tables 1–4. These should not be confused with Gearing's "structural poses." Frederick O. Gearing, "Cherokee Political Organizations, 1730–1775," (Ph.D. dissertation, University of Chicago, 1956); *Priests and Warriors: Social Structures for Cherokee Politics in the 18th Century* (cited hereafter as *Priests and Warriors*); and "Structural Poses of the Eighteenth Century Cherokee Village," *American Anthropologist*, Vol. 60 (1958), 1148–57.

[13] John Howard Payne Papers, Roll 6985, 18–27. See "Origin of Disease and Medicine," James Mooney, "Myths of the Cherokees," *Annual Report Smithsonian Institution*, 250–52; James Mooney, *The Swimmer Manuscript: Cherokee Sacred Formulas and Medicinal Prescriptions*, 15–16, 18–39, 131–34 (cited hereafter as *The Swimmer Manuscript*); John Howard Payne Papers, Roll 6985, 18–20, 27.

Thus four kinds of deviations were recognized by traditional Cherokee law: deviations which constituted an offense against the supernatural or Spirit Beings, against the entire community, against the clan, and against an individual Cherokee. Four distinct authorities were empowered to determine deviation from these norms. Supernatural norms involving, as they did, the relationship between man and Spirits were, in the Cherokee view, automatically detected. In fact, according to reports in the John Howard Payne Papers, there was "no hiding place where the Spirits did not see."[14] Most public offenses were brought before a tribal group much like a court, composed of the seven clans. Deviations which were offenses against individual members of the clan were resolved in accordance with a pre-established duty based upon particular relationships between the clan member and the offense or offender. Offenses against an individual involved little more than personal response. Divine judgment might be sought for deviations on any of the levels.

Again, the agent assigned the task of applying sanctions for any deviation was clearly delineated along one of the four lines. Divine retribution for violation of Spirit norms might be immediate or prolonged, against either the individual or the entire village. Public punishment of an established nature followed conviction for a public offense. Clan violations were avenged by individual members of the offended clan, for individual retribution was achieved by the person offended. Divine assistance might be sought for punishment of non-spiritual norm deviations.

Each Cherokee village had two distinct governmental structures, a white, or peace, government and a red, or war, government. The white government was supreme in all respects except the making of war. During times of peace the white government controlled all tribal affairs. In times of war the red government was in control of all tribal affairs. The two governmental structures were never in operation at the same time. The white government was essentially a stable theocracy composed of the older and wiser men of the tribe, who constituted a tribal gerontocracy. The red organization was, on the other hand, flexible, responsive to changing conditions and controlled by the younger warriors.[15]

14 John Howard Payne Papers, Roll 6985, 3–7.
15 See the John Howard Payne Papers for the most nearly complete primary data. See also William H. Gilbert, *The Eastern Cherokees*, 313–72; Gearing, *Priests and Warriors*, 13–75; William Shedrick Willis, "Colonial Conflict and the Cherokee Indians, 1710–1760" (Ph.D. dissertation, Columbia University, 1955), 219–77.

The Seven Counselors Court was a peace organization composed of selected officials from the white government. The officers operating the peace society were (1) the chief of the tribe or the high priest, (2) the chief's right-hand man, (3) seven prime counselors representing the seven clans, (4) the council of elders, (5) the chief speaker, (6) messengers, and (7) a number of officers for specialized ceremonial functions. Evidence indicates that all the officers above the level of messenger sat at the white court. The organizational structure was repeated in each of the tribal villages of any size large enough to be represented by each of the clans.[16]

Deviations from established norms which offended community expectations were tried in the courts of the villages. A Cherokee trial was essentially a matter of oath saying. The accused was brought before the assembled officers. The offenses against him were presented by a court prosecutor, who was generally the chief's right-hand man. The court was free to question in any manner desired. No "attorney" was allowed to represent the individual on trial. There were no juries, and the counselors and court did not act in that capacity but rather placed the accused upon a sacred oath which required him to state his own innocence or guilt. Violation of the oath would prevent the ghost from passing to the Nightland, and, therefore, the punishment for the offense with which the accused was charged would, in the view of the traditional Cherokee, be less grave than having one's ghost remain forever wandering as a result of violation of the oath. The oath taking process was described by James Adair:

The Cheeroke [sic] method of adjuring a witness to declare the truth.... On small affairs, the judge, who is an elderly chieftain asks the witness, Cheeakohga "Do you lie?" To which he answers, Ansa Kai-e-koh-ga, "I do not lie." But when the judge will search into something of material consequence, and adjures the witness to speak the naked truth, concerning the point in question, he says "O E A (sko?)" "What you have now said is it true, by this strong emblem of the beloved name of the great self-existent God?" To which the witness replies, O E A, "It is true, by this strong painting symbol of YO HE WAH." When the true knowledge of the affair in dispute, seems to be of very great importance, the judge swears the witness thus: O E A—YAH (sko?) This most sacred adjuration imports, "Have you now told me the real truth by the living

16 Gearing, Priests and Warriors, 37–47; Gilbert, The Eastern Cherokees, 323; "Wolf King's Answer to a Joint Talk," April 29, 1766, Oklahoma Historical Society, Indian Archives; Bartram, Travels, 297–98.

type of the great awful name of God, which describes his necessary existence, without beginning or end, and by his self-existent literal name in which I adjure you." The witness answers, O E A—YAH, I have told you the naked truth, which I most solemnly swear, by this strong religious picture of the adorable, great, self-existent name which we are not to profane; and I likewise attest it, by his other beloved, unspeakable, sacred, essential name.[17]

The red organization was composed of the following officers: (1) Great Red War Chief, (2) Great War Chief's Second, (3) Seven War Counselors to order war, (4) Beloved, Pretty, or War Women, (5) Chief War Speaker, and (6) Messengers, ceremonial officers, and war scouts or titled men. The Chief, Second Chief, and War Counselors served as the red court. The War Women served in a similar capacity to judge the fate of captives and other prisoners of the war.[18]

Clan investigation was never formalized into an actual court procedure but represented an investigation by clan members most immediately concerned with deviations. It was a corporate reaction, but it was never institutionalized into a court procedure as in community sanction enforcement. The offended members of the clan reacted, often immediately, as in the case of the individual who might seek revenge or retaliation for the offenses against his person.[19]

Women constituted a special class within the operation of Cherokee laws. They might serve as a court designed to punish offenses which were affronts to them and the tribe growing from the regulations of women. The lawgiver recited a "female lecture," when tribal laws were given and was reported to be "sharp and prolix" as "he urges them with much earnestness to an honest observance of the marriage-law." To violate the rules of female cleanliness was "at the risque of their lives." Women were themselves granted the right to enforce these regulations, especially those relating to the obligations of widowhood and adultery.[20]

17 Adair, *American Indians*, 48–49.

18 Haywood, *History of Tennessee*, 260; "Journal of Antoine Bonnefoy," in Samuel Cole Williams (ed.), *Early Travels in the Tennessee Country, 1750–1800*, 149–50; Nathaniel Knowles, *The Torture of Captives by Indians of Eastern North America*, 151; Adair called the Cherokees "a petticoat government." Adair, *American Indians*, 145.

19 A statement of A-Kee-la-nee-ga shows the survival of this feeling. *Cherokee Messenger*, December, 1844, 29. John Howard Payne Papers, Roll 6987, 524.

20 Timberlake, *Timberlake's Memoirs*, 93; Adair, *American Indians*, 107, 123–24, 186–87, 190; Haywood, *History of Tennessee*, 243, 260; John Howard Payne Papers, Roll 6987, 401.

It was apparently possible for an individual to seek some form of supernatural adjudication from the Spirit World without the use of the priest as an intermediary. The process in the case of adultery is explained in considerable detail in the Daniel S. Buttrick notes. A Cherokee took "two white beads, and blackened one of them." The white bead became the symbol of innocence and the black of guilt. "The white bead . . . was then placed between the thumb and finger of his right hand [and] the black bead between the thumb and finger of his left hand." The inquirer would ask certain questions in ritualistic form and asked whether a certain member of a certain clan was guilty. Finally, "If the black bead vacillated between his left thumb and finger, at the mention of any particular clan, he was certain of his wife's guilt, and watched till he personally detected with whom."[21]

The most thoroughly documented study of Cherokee norm deviations center around the clan blood regulation of homicide. The clan was, without doubt, the major institution exercising legal powers. The survival of important sources of information on murder regulation was assured for two reasons. Control of murder was no doubt an ancient and major public-order question among the Cherokees and had become fully institutionalized. A second factor which accounts for our detailed knowledge of the regulation of murder is the fascination which this crime held for white travelers who noted the cases with considerable detail. The following statements represent the general Cherokee attitudes toward control of murder:

1. Homicide was an offense against the blood of the clan.
2. The ghost of the murdered clansman could not pass from the earth until the blood had been revenged.
3. Revenge for the murder rested with members of the clan of the victim and was a sacred duty.
4. Blood revenge required the death of a member of the clan of the murderer.
5. Clans were corporate units for revenge purposes, all being brothers.
6. It was desirable to kill the murderer himself, but if he was not available, then a member of his clan, especially a close relative of the murderer, might be avenged.
7. Revenge was a duty and fell to the oldest male relative of the

21 John Howard Payne Papers; Mooney, *The Swimmer Manuscript*, 132.

victim's generation, generally his oldest brother. To fail to avenge was to be held up to public ridicule.

8. There were no degrees of murder. The necessity of revenge to free the ghost was the same whether the death was accidental or deliberate.

9. There was no need for a public trial, witnesses, or hearings. The clan member with the duty of revenge would determine guilt. If assistance was needed, he could call upon other members of his clan.

10. The members of the clan of the murderer might serve a self-policing or protecting purpose by executing the member of their own clan and thus eliminate the risk that innocent clansmen might be made to suffer the blood revenge.

11. An individual who had innocently or by accident taken the life of another might flee to one of four "free cities," or "sacred cities of refuge," where the murderer would be safe. A priest might offer the same protection on sacred ground in any town.

12. Compensation was occasionally possible, but only with the replacement of a member of the clan through capture of a prisoner or delivery of the scalp of an enemy in blood revenge. No fixed monetary compensation appears to have existed in the primitive system.

13. Execution in blood revenge could be carried out by any means selected by the clansmen designated to make the revenge.

14. The clans served as public executioner but this often increased the chances of public disorder with the danger of blood feud. However, generally the sanction was so strongly supported that the clan which suffered the blood revenge considered the execution justified.[22]

One of the most serious blood-regulation threats to the Cherokee community stemmed from the presence of a witch who could cause sickness and death.[23] The Reverend Cephas Washburn noted that

[22] John Reid, *Law of Blood*, 73–112; Letter, I. P. Evans to John Howard Payne, John Howard Payne Papers, Roll 6986, 4–5.

[23] John Stuart, *A Sketch of Cherokee and Choctaw Indians*, 46; Mooney, *The Swimmer Manuscript*, 29–33; Cephas Washburn, *Reminiscences of the Indians*, 107–12 (cited hereafter as *Reminiscences*); Adair, *American Indians*, 36; Haywood, *History of Tennessee*, 251. The Cherokees are said to have feared the morning star because "long ago a very wicked conjurer killed people by witchcraft . . . but on hearing of a resolution formed by the other Indians to kill him, he took all his shining instruments of witchcraft, and flew away . . . and appeared as a bright star. [T]hose Indians who wish to kill others [by] witchcraft pray to him." John Howard Payne Papers, Roll 6987, 569.

"it should be considered not only lawful, but even a duty [for a Cherokee] to put to death every one who could exercise this malignant power."[24] Witchcraft was considered a capital crime—more dangerous than homicide. Some witch cases might be tried by the Seven Counselors Court, but generally there were no trials, no witnesses; the dangers were too great. All that was required to ensure execution was "to accuse him and refer to some instance of painful disease of death."[25]

One of the most difficult tasks of law under a clan-revenge system is to prevent escalation of revenge into open clan warfare and blood feud. The buildup is easy to understand because the revenge killing is a private act with no public determination of fairness. In most instances the consensus of support for the system was so great that the retaliation produced no additional revenge, and, in fact, the revenge killing was occasionally executed by the clan of the murderer.[26] However, there is a record of "one instance [in which] a man was killed as a witch who had several brothers. These avenged his death by killing the witchkiller. His relatives avenged his death, and so it went on till seven individuals were killed."[27]

Protection of blood lines and the difficulty of freeing the ghost of the deceased were probably the major reasons for the stigma attached to suicide. Since the deceased was responsible for his own death, the ghost could not be set free by the clan brothers, since they could only accomplish this by taking the life of the murderer. Cherokees would, however, if they felt sufficiently disgraced, choose death by suicide. There are recorded cases of priests disfigured by smallpox who "cut their throats, stabbed themselves with knives, . . . with sharp-pointed canes; many threw themselves with sudden madness into the fire."[28]

The clan-blood relationship explains why there was so little social emphasis attached to male sex practice in the matrilineal structure of the society. Clan membership, inheritance, and social status depended upon the mother and her family. Sexual activity constituted little threat to society unless there was a violation of clan-intermar-

[24] Washburn, *Reminiscences*, 108. Nustawi reported that "witches were always killed." John Howard Payne Papers, Roll 6987, 527.
[25] Washburn, *Reminiscences*, 108; Emmet Starr, *Cherokees "West,"* 1794–1839, 53 (cited hereafter as *Cherokees "West"*).
[26] *Cherokee Phoenix*, Feb. 18, 1829.
[27] Washburn, *Reminiscences*, 111; Starr, *Cherokees "West,"* 56.
[28] Adair, *American Indians*, 233–34.

riage restrictions. As Chief Blanket, an informant for Cephas Washburn, explained, "Every mother knows who are her children, but fathers have not such knowledge. My wife was a singing bird [and] had four [children] while she lived with me, and she said I was their father."[29]

Public punishment was rare and was inflicted by officers chosen for the purpose. Tribal humiliation was common and was administered by the entire tribe. An effort was made to select individuals related to the offense in cases of assaults, arson, or witchcraft. If the punishment involved death, a member of each clan constituted the execution group to prevent the danger of revenge. Apparently there was no institutionalized post of public executioner. In the instance when an acknowledged witch was put to death, "These executions were accomplished by a company designated by the headmen of some village, within whose jurisdiction the witch resided."[30] Priests might provide the more common punishments, such as scratching the legs of young warriors who violated prescribed codes of military conduct. Scratching of the young was often the duty of the mother's brother.

The temptation to abuse individual or clan punishments was great. There are recorded instances of abuses in the punishment of witches. Any enemy found it simple to suggest crop failures or unexplained deaths were the result of witchcraft by an old enemy or a bitter rival. The case of Whirlwind, an informant for Cephas Washburn, who inspired a young orphan to kill the elderly chief who had befriended him, is typical.[31]

The Journal of Dwight Mission provides an excellent example of abuse of the traditional powers regulating death for witchcraft. "A man," the journal notes, was "murdered in a most shocking manner by his nephew":

The mother of the nephew died some months since of a very singular disease, and several other relatives were affected in the same way, all efforts to effect a cure proved entirely unavailing. A man, who had inimical feelings towards the uncle, told the young man that his mother & other relatives were bewitched by the uncle, & that if he was killed the surviving relatives would recover. Accordingly the nephew called upon his uncle & as they were walking together, the young man discharged his rifle & shot

29 Washburn, *Reminiscences*, 167–68; Starr, *Cherokees "West,"* 94–95.
30 Washburn, 108; Starr, *Cherokees "West,"* 53–54.
31 Washburn, 109–11; Starr, *Cherokees "West,"* 54–56.

his uncle through the body. He then shot again as soon as possible. Stabbed him in many places, & finally fractured his skull by beating him with a large stone. Notwithstanding all these wounds, the old man survived several hours & intreated, but in vain, to be informed for what he was put to death. This is the second instance of murder committed within a few days by this benighted people.[32]

Spirit or supernatural punishments might be invoked in response to violations of the norms of society. The Spirit World was often called upon to atone for deviations affecting the community, the clan, and the individual. These divine punishments were not, however, automatic and must be requested by the offended Cherokee. Most often such assistance would be sought when supernatural forces were needed to determine guilt for the offense. Divining crystals were regularly used to determine the location of stolen property and the name of the thief. The clearest instance of this practice is found in an individual retaliation against an adulteress by her husband. In this instance:

When the priest was consulted on such occasions, he would set his crystal and pray for information. In the event of innocence, it never changed; but in that of guilty, two persons would be discovered in it. The priest would next take some flies which he had previously killed for the purpose. He then solemnly pronounced evil which would befall the woman, if guilty. He declared that if, on opening his hand, one of the flies came to life again, it would fly to her in the instant, and with bitter tortures, in seven days she would feel it gnawing into her heart, and die. Accordingly, the woman invariably died on the seventh day; but whether the fly received any assistance from the husband or the priest is not reported.[33]

Among certain early traders there was a belief that "the Cherokee are an exception, in having no laws against adultery."[34] Adair blamed this situation on "petticoat government," which gave "women full liberty to plant their brows with horns as often as they pleased without fear of punishment."[35] But Adair failed to comprehend that, with divorce as easy as "splitting the blanket," adultery was consid-

---

[32] Journal of Dwight Mission, Papers, American Board of Foreign Missions, Harvard University Library, Cambridge.

[33] Journals, John Howard Payne Papers.

[34] Adair, American Indian, 145–46; Letter, William Fyffe to Brother John. Interestingly, the Cherokees never enacted a law against adultery. In re Mayfield, 141 U.S. 107 (1890).

[35] Adair, American Indians, 145.

ered a direct affront to the warrior's ego. Punishment might be death, but was not invoked often since the option of enforcement rested with the offended husband. Adair himself recorded one of the most unusual punishments for adultery:

Once in my time a number of warriors, belonging to the family of the husband of the adulteress, avenged the injury committed by her, in her own way; for they said, as she loved a great many men, instead of a husband, justice told them to gratify her longing desire—wherefore, by the information of their spies, they followed her into the woods a little way from the town, (as decency required) and then stretched her on the ground, with her hands tied to a stake, and her feet also extended, where upwards of fifty of them lay with her, having a blanket for covering.[36]

A great pride was involved in acceptance of justified punishment. The Cherokee was resentful of one who did not accept his punishment. The practice of scratching the young was more often a ritual related to powers rather than punishment. War leaders are said to have scratched harder and deeper when warriors flinched when being scratched as punishment for violation of a battle order. The case of Crane-Eater (reported by an early Indian informant) illustrated the extreme personal pain which a Cherokee was willing to endure to accept the sanctioned justice:

Some few years ago, a man in his village by the name of Crane-Eater had stolen a horse. He was tried and found guilty, and was sentenced to receive a hundred lashes on his bare back. When tied to the tree for the purpose of receiving the penalty of the law before the first blow was struck, he fainted from mere terror of the dreadful punishment. . . . At this juncture, a brother of Crane-Eater's came forward and thus addressed the executioner of the law. "This person," said he, "is my brother. I am ashamed of him. He thought he was a man, and he dared to steal a horse; but now when called to meet the consequences of his act, he finds he is a woman. I pity him. Untie him and let him go. I will take his place. I am a man, and though I have stolen no horse, I can bear the punishment which is due him. And . . . so they untied Crane-Eater and whipped his brother.[37]

Violation of established order might result in punishment of the entire tribe. It was believed by the Cherokees that the severe smallpox epidemic of 1738, which is said to have reduced population by one-half, was "brought on by their unlawful copulation in the night

---

[36] *Ibid.*, 146.
[37] Washburn, *Reminiscences*, 175; Starr, *Cherokees "West,"* 100.

dews."[38] The violation of the Divine Spirit order was considered the cause. The dangers of women violating "their lunar retreats" illustrate individual violations being vested upon the entire tribe.[39] Adair notes that, "Should they be known to violate that ancient law, they must answer for every misfortune that befalls any of the people, as a certain effect of the divine fire."[40]

Within this universe of divinely ordered laws the Cherokees faced the question introduced by the arrival of the white man—the question of adapting their laws to new or changing circumstances. Adaptation was begun with a form of supernatural fiction found among many primitive people and probably used by the ancient Cherokees. This procedure is recorded by an early traveler in the Cherokee country:

The principal chief pretends that he has been *inspired* that a spirit has come to him and delivered a bit of wampum, whispering in his ear, and again returned to his invisible abodes. The fiction is not discountenanced, because the good of the nation requires secrecy and the chief is responsible only for the truth and importance of the subject, which a supernatural communication often gives to the most trivial affair.[41]

[38] Adair, *American Indians*, 232.
[39] John Howard Payne Papers. Photostats in author's collection.
[40] Adair, *American Indians*, 124.
[41] Haywood, *History of Tennessee*, 258.

Tables 1 through 4 list the spirit, community, clan, and individual deviations from Cherokee law, the authority determining the deviation, the agent enforcing the punishment, and the punishment itself.

Table 1. *Spirit Deviation*

Deviation	Authority expected to determine deviation	Agent enforcing sanction for deviation	Sanction
Unauthorized person learning religious secrets	Either Spirits or white priest who calls Spirits	Demons sent from Spirit world	Death before next day
Theft of sacred religious relics	Spirits or white priest who calls Spirits	Spirits themselves	Immediate death
Assault on Priest, i.e., touching his beard; assault or entering sacred religious areas	Spirits or white priest who calls Spirits	Spirits themselves	Death, but uncertain date or manner
Widespread deviation from general norms of conduct so frequent as to offend Spirits, i.e., adultery	Priest must call upon Spirits	Spirits through agents of disease	Sickness, suffering, smallpox, plague
Women's taboos	Spirits, white priests, or other women	Spirits themselves; agents of disease; demons sent from Spirit world	Death, sickness; entire village will suffer
Failure to follow rituals such as bathing, singing songs, eating corn; drunkenness at festivals	Spirits or white priest who calls Spirits	Agents of Spirits	Sickness, bad luck Entire village may suffer

Table 2. Community Deviation

Deviation	Authority expected to determine deviation	Agent enforcing sanction for deviation	Sanction
Arson—frequent burning of individual or public property	Council of Seven Clans (White Courts)	Appointed by Seven Clans Council; select group which should be composed of individuals whose property was burned if possible	Death (throwing from cliff or high place)
Assault—frequent and aggressive attacks upon the person of others	Council of Seven Clans (White Courts)	Group appointed by Council, should be those assaulted if possible	Whipping or infliction of similar assault
Food and field regulations, refusal to work, contribute share of work and crops	Council of Seven Clans (White Courts)	Select group or elder members of individual's clan	Whipping, insult, possible expulsion (outlawry)
Hunting regulations	Council of Seven Clans	Select group or elder clan members	Whipping, insult, and possible outlawry; scratching legs
Misrepresentation, wearing fraudulent insignia, using wrong war name, etc.	Either Council of Seven Clans for peace offense or Military Court of Red Organization for war offense	Public Executioner	Whipping, name calling, public disgrace

Treason—deliberate violation of community interest which benefits recognized enemy of group	Either Council of Seven Clans or Military Red Court	Select group of significant leaders, one from each clan	Death
War regulations, order of fire, command, restrictions on attack	Military or Red Court	Enemy in battle or tribal executioner	Place violator in battle position where certain to be killed, death by tribal executioner, scratching legs
Women's taboos, separation, childbirth, etc.	Council of Beloved Women of the Seven Clans; informal groups of women	Select women of community	Stoning, mutilating, whipping, death
Widower or widow remarriage or mourning requirements	Council of Beloved Women of the Seven Clans; informal group of women	Select women of community	Death, stoning, mutilation, whipping
Witchcraft (see also individual)	Council of Seven Clans (White Courts)	Enforcement Company appointed from each of the Seven Clans	Death

Table 3. Clan Deviation

Deviation	Authority expected to determine deviation	Agent enforcing sanction for deviation	Sanction
Intermarriage within clan	Clan members especially immediate family of violators	Clan members selected by family	Death for the couple
Homicide	Clan members of immediate family of deceased	Oldest male relative (generally brother) of the deceased clansman; but a member of murderer's clan might execute punishment	Death for the murderer or a member of his clan
Incest	Informal clan consensus	Clan representative	Death
Infanticide Mother	No stigma for mother	No penalty or enforcement	None
Father	Informal clan decision	Wife's relatives as clan revenge	Death
Sex crimes—bigamy, prostitution, incest, only to extent violate clan blood customs; see Intermarriage within clan			
Suicide	Clan offense but death prevents earthly retribution so punishment left to spirits	Spirits; clan should cleanse blood but cannot punish the suicide	Ghost must always remain in this land; cannot pass to Nightland
Theft from dead or graves of dead	Members of clan of the deceased	Bone bearer assisted by clan	Death

Table 4. *Individual Deviation*

Deviation	Authority expected to determine deviation	Agent enforcing sanction for deviation	Sanction
Arson (see also community)	Individual immediately injured	Injured individual	Death (?)
Adultery (see also Spirit)	Husband or husband might ask divine assistance to locate guilty	Injured husband or divine intervention	Punish wife with whipping, mutilation, death; death by divine intervention
Assault (see also Spirit)	Injured individual	Injured individual	Return in kind, related to nature of assault
Rape	Husband of rape victim; the victim apparently had no authority	Husband	Death
Theft (see also Spirit, clan)	Individual from whom item was stolen; divine assistance from priest to locate thief	Individual injured, no divine recovery of goods	Recovery of goods in question and public humiliation of thief
Witchcraft	Threat is so great that any individual can determine; no community standards or tests to determine who is a witch	Any person who feels in danger from a witch	Death to the witch

Changing Cherokee Conditions

III

IN EARLY colonial times the southern mountains had shielded the ancient Cherokees from the Christianizing Spaniard and slowed the ubiquitous development of French and English settlement and trade. Essentially the life ways of the traditional Cherokees remained unchanged as late as the year 1710, which has been marked as the beginning of "expansion of Cherokee trade with Charles Town."[1] Thus white influence came slowly into the Cherokee country; but when it came, it was swift and startling.

The one hundred years which followed the expansion of British trade were years of dynamic change for the Cherokee people. The magnitude of the change can be seen by comparing the economic condition of the earlier Cherokee hunters with the property-owning tribe pictured by the first official Cherokee national census in 1810. This census showed that individual Cherokees owned "113 negro slaves; cattle, 19,500; horses, 6,100; hogs, 19,600; sheep, 1,037; several grist and saw mills; three saltpeter works; and one powder mill; 30 wagons; 480 plows; 1,600 spinning wheels; and 467 looms."[2]

The contrast is even greater if made with the year 1826, when Elias Boudinot reported that "upwards of 1000 volumes of good

[1] The date 1710 was selected because of intensification of trade but should not be taken as the beginning of trade. William S. Willis, "Colonial Conflict and the Cherokee Indians, 1710–1768," (Ph.D. dissertation, Columbia University, 1955), 23. Verner Crane concluded that "progress of the Charles Town traders . . . produced among the Indians an economic and social revolution." Crane, *The Southern Frontier, 1670–1732*, 116.

[2] Cherokee Census, 1810, Cherokee Documents, Indian Heritage Association, Pensacola, Florida; reproduced in part *Cherokee Advocate*, July 11, 1874.

books and 11 different papers" were found in one Cherokee district. The property census for that year showed "22,000 cattle; 7,600 horses; 46,000 swine; 2,500 sheep; 2,488 spinning wheels; 172 wagons; 2,943 ploughs; 31 grist-mills; 62 blacksmith shops; and 18 schools and ferries."[3]

In the face of change modern man may occasionally feel not unlike the old Cherokee warrior of this era who lamented, "I was born in another world."[4] We can feel the pathos in the words of Skiagusta, the head warrior of the Lower Towns of the Cherokees. "My people," the Indian pleaded, "cannot live independent of the English. . . . The clothes we wear we cannot make ourselves. They are made for us. We use their ammunition with which to kill deer. We cannot make our guns. Every necessary of life we must have from the white people."[5]

What prepared the way for these changes? How did the simple hunter become the slaveholder? How was it possible to make such a shift? What produced the abandonment of traditional blood revenge of the clan and the adaptation of an Anglo-American court system?

A number of significant influences can be isolated as factors in this movement from clan to court. Among these are (1) a changing economic base, (2) a breakdown of the traditional religious complex combined with increased missionary pressures, (3) discredit of conservative war leadership and withdrawal of traditional factions, (4) emergence of a substantial class of mixed-breed Cherokees, and (5) government policy combined with increased pressures for lands and tribal dissolution.

The economic life of the early Cherokees was a simple one, described by anthropologists as the way of the hunter and gatherer modified by early rudimentary agriculture. Max Gluckman described this stage of development in his seminal analysis *Politics, Law and Ritual in Tribal Society*. Early village society, Gluckman noted, "[have] primary goods, only, and no luxuries . . . practically all their goods [have] to be consumed at once."[6] In such a state accumulation

---

[3] Elias Boudinot, *An Address to the Whites Delivered in the First Presbyterian Church on the 26th of May, 1826*, 8 (cited hereafter as *An Address to the Whites*).

[4] Talk, Head Warrior of Tunissee, 1725, Cherokee Documents, Indian Heritage Association, Muskogee, Okla.

[5] "Indian Books of South Carolina," III, 321–23, cited in David H. Corkran, *The Cherokee Frontier: Conflict and Survival, 1740–62*, 14 (cited hereafter as *The Cherokee Frontier*).

[6] Max Gluckman, *Politics, Law, and Ritual in Tribal Society*, 13.

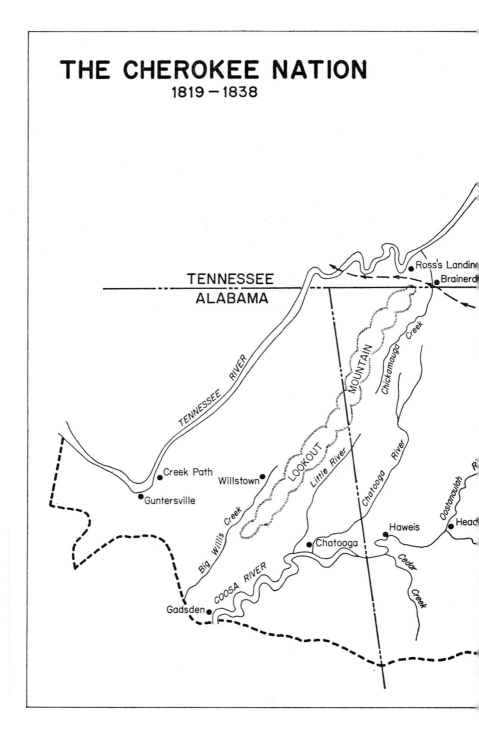

THE CHEROKEE NATION
1819 – 1838

TENNESSEE
ALABAMA

Ross's Landing
Brainerd

TENNESSEE RIVER

MOUNTAIN

Chickamauga Creek

LOOKOUT

Little River

Chatooga River

Oostanaulah R

Creek Path
Willstown
Guntersville

Big Willis Creek

Haweis

Head

Chatooga

Cedar Creek

COOSA RIVER

Gadsden

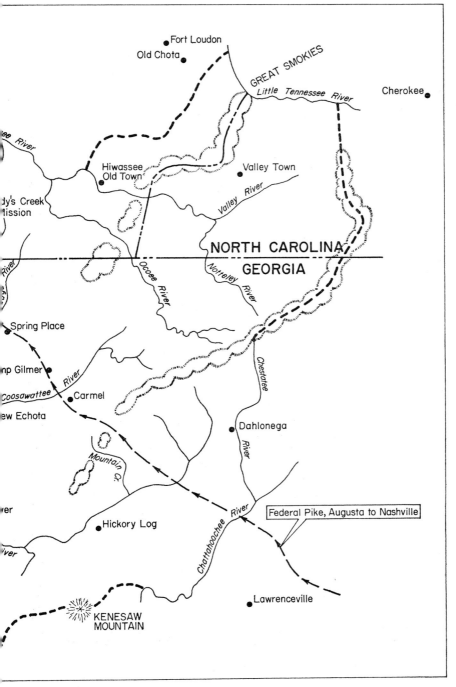

The Cherokee Nation, 1819–38.

of wealth was almost impossible. The life of the wealthiest was almost, in material terms, indistinguishable from the poorest.

In ancient times the occupation of the Cherokee male was hunting, while the Cherokee female was equally occupied with the tasks of tending the garden, gathering the wild foods, and nurturing the new generation. Personal property was either utilitarian or ceremonial, and, despite the importance of the Cherokee religious complex, even the priests lived a life which was, in terms of economic and material resources, almost identical with the life of all other Cherokees.

The expansion of the Carolina trade changed all of this. The values of the old life were significantly altered by shifts in the tribal economic base. There is an element of oversimplification in saying that the fur trade revolutionized occupational roles, and yet it can be argued that the Cherokee male became an employee of the trading companies for the purpose of hunting and selling the deerskin. There is no doubt about the changes this new source of wealth introduced. A class of individuals was created which was beyond the traditional warrior roles.[7]

The tribe began to acquire goods that were not immediately consumable. Emphasis shifted from tribal to individual achievement. Soon enterprising Cherokees were serving as agents for trading companies. Furthermore, a chronic shortage of trade goods developed. The Indians gradually came to rely upon English traders to supply guns and munitions which were necessary to hunt deer. This dependency, plus the unscrupulous conduct of Indian traders and the Indians' developing taste for rum and gambling, created a chronic commercial insolvency for the Cherokees. Another important economic shift—one which has received little attention—was the development of a form of commercial agriculture among numbers of Indian women, in which produce was sold to the trader and the military both in the Nation and at more distant points. Thus there was created an additional wealth possessing class.[8]

[7] And yet no great wealth class was produced at this date. Profits were relatively small and belonged to white traders. The most complete picture of the life of a long time white resident is Adair's *American Indians*. Another view is found in Gregory and Strickland (eds.), *Starr's History of the Cherokees*, 20, 305, 466–67.

[8] Willis, "Colonial Conflict and the Cherokee Indians, 1710–1768," (Ph.D. dissertation, Columbia University, 1955), 127, 259–61. This can be seen from the numerous requests to the government at Charles Town for weapons. William L. McDowell, Jr., (ed.), *Colonial Records of South Carolina: Documents Relating to Indian Affairs, May 21, 1750–August 7, 1754*, 51, 62, 69, 75, 119, 174, 194, 247, 253, 259, 356, 488, 519 (cited hereafter as *South Carolina Indian Documents*). See Letter,

Ancient life—economic, political, and social—had been centered in the religious cult. Therefore shifts in tribal values were directly reflected in the religious-ceremonial complex. The emerging values of Cherokee society were secular—those associated with trade, hunting, warfare, diplomacy, and commercialization.

The priestly class could have fought a mighty battle with the agents of commercialism for continued control of the Cherokee people—except for one fact. The priests were the first to worship at the altar of Mammon. As the most influential class and the only obvious leadership group, the cultheads were looked to by the colonial governments as the primary diplomats. The rewards of secular diplomacy were great, and the priests, no doubt, enjoyed the gifts presented by the colonial governors and local traders. Unfortunately for the priests, the new role identified their religious function with a secular task which, in the nature of things, could not be profitable for the Indian people. In the struggle for power with the Charles Town government the Cherokees were not equipped to be effective advocates. Any hope that reaction against the new economic life might produce a revival of the ancient religion was undermined by the close identification of the ancient priestly class with the new commercialism.[9]

A significant factor in the ultimate decline of the governing and lawmaking role of the priests stemmed from the priests' failure as public healers. Ancient medicines could not cope with that chronic scourge of tribal peoples—the dreaded smallpox. Many of the priests, according to Adair, blamed violation of the ancient laws for the major smallpox epidemics. The people turned to their religious leaders, who were the doctors. The cures proved ineffective. In fact, the priests ordered the fevered patients immersed in cold water, a treatment which hastened death.[10]

The priests, in turn, lost faith in themselves and in their ability

Lud. Grant to Governor Glen, March 4, 1752, *South Carolina Indian Documents,* 222–24; Affidavit of David Downey, May 25, 1751, *South Carolina Indian Documents,* 57–58; Ordinance For Regulating the Cherokee Trade, *South Carolina Indian Documents,* 198–200; Talk of Governor Glen to the Cherokees Concerning Their Treaty, *South Carolina Indian Documents,* 191.

[9] See generally Wilbur R. Jacobs, *Diplomacy and Indian Gifts* and for specific Cherokee data note *South Carolina Indian Documents,* 61, 88, 89, 153, 160–62, 195–98, 258, 259, 453–54, 485, 527.

[10] Adair, *American Indians,* 232–234. The French, in turn, blamed the English traders and officers. William Thomas Corlett, *The Medicine Man of the American Indian and His Cultural Background,* 149.

to heal. With the failure of the priestly theology in a time of crisis, the significance of native ceremonial rituals began to decrease. Widespread suicide among the religious leaders served to speed the end of the full complex. Adair has recorded that

[all] the magi [*sic*] and prophetic tribe broke their old consecrated physicpots, and threw away all the other pretended holy things they had for physical use, imagining they had lost their divine power by being polluted; and shared the common fate of their country. A great many killed themselves; seeing themselves disfigured . . . some shot themselves, others cut their throats, some stabbed themselves with knives, and others with sharp-pointed canes; many threw themselves with sudden madness into the fire, and slowly expired, as if they had been utterly divested of the native power of feeling pain.[11]

So swift was the decline in influence of this class that one student of Cherokee history, basing his research upon Carolina trade documents, has concluded that "there never was any Cherokee religion more sophisticated or more organized than professional conjuring."[12]

Thus the significant religious sanctions which had motivated the ancient law ways were reduced in power among the leaders of the Cherokee tribe. It was then possible for the Christian missionary to move among the tribesmen offering a different version of divine spiritual help. However, the vast majority of the Cherokee people were slow in substituting Christian concepts for the ancient and, while, the power of the priestly class decreased, the strength of the Spirit Being and the desire to move into the Nightland somehow persisted.[13]

Nonetheless, the Christian missionary spoke with great force to revolutionize the law ways of the Cherokees. To the missionary the connection between God's order and the "civilized law" was as strong as the ancient Cherokee merger of spirit ways and law ways. "The period has at last arrived on which I have long fixed my eager eye," wrote the Reverend Gideon Blackburn, a young Presbyterian min-

---

[11] Adair, *American Indians*, 233.

[12] Reid, *A Law of Blood*, 22. The author feels that the survival of elements from the ancient complex when read in connection with the contemporary accounts suggest a very elaborate religious system.

[13] For nineteenth and twentieth century survival of these religious doctrines see Mooney, *The Swimmer Manuscript*, 142–43 and Jack Frederick Kilpatrick and Anna Gritts Kilpatrick, *Run Toward the Nightland: Magic of the Oklahoma Cherokees*, 101–12, 113–31, 157–64 (cited hereafter as *Run Toward the Nightland*).

ister, when he heard of the adoption of the Cherokee written laws. "Toward this," he continued, "my exertions have been unremittingly directed since the commencement of my mission to them."[14]

The demands of tribal leadership could not be met by the individual who had risen to power in the duality of the old Red-White Cherokee government. The prime qualification for leadership in the new Carolina-dominated Cherokee world became the possession of commercial connections and an understanding of and ability to manipulate trade and colonial aspirations. The colonies themselves first turned to the priestly class to fill the vacuum. When it became apparent that priestly support was waning, a new class of "Indian Kings" was created by the South Carolina government. These were drawn from the old Red portion of the tribal government.[15]

The British, incapable of or unwilling to understand that the Cherokees were a disorganized village society, attempted to superimpose their monarchical concepts in diplomatic relations. As early as 1730 the English sent a group of "Cherokee Emperors" to the Court of Saint James to meet "the father, the white king."[16] Soon it became clear that authority no longer rested solely in the village but extended to Charles Town and even to London. Recognition of this change coincided with a general tribal idealization of the warrior as hunter and soldier. The war chief soon came to dominate tribal affairs.[17]

Administrations of the war chiefs lacked stability and were destined to fail. First, there was intense rivalry among the chiefs of the individual village settlements and the so-called four main tribal settlements.[18] Second, younger aspiring warriors were ready to chal-

---

[14] "An Account of the Origin and Progress of the Mission to the Cherokee Indians; in a series of Letters from the Rev. Gideon Blackburn, to Rev. Dr. Morse," *Panopolist*, (December, 1808), 325.

[15] This process is best seen in the detailed examination of tribal politics in the years 1740–1762 as drawn from extensive study of primary colonial documents. Such an overview is found in Corkran's remarkable book *The Cherokee Frontier*.

[16] The contemporary newspaper accounts of the Cherokee visit provide the basis for Carolyn Thomas Foreman's entertaining monograph *Indians Abroad*. Several prints and paintings of the visiting Cherokees are reproduced in Thomas Gilcrease Art Staff, "Three Cherokees . . . to see 'The King their Father,'" *American Scene Magazine*, Vol. II (1963), 6.

[17] For a short summary of developments during this period see Gregory and Strickland (eds.), *Starr's History of the Cherokees*, 24–34.

[18] These were the Lower, Overhill, Upper, and Valley settlements. Sometimes known as Lower, Middle, Valley, and Overhill. At one time these represented significant regional blocs with distinct language dialects. Gearing, *Priests and Warriors*, 1.

lenge the chiefs as their personal prowess in war declined.[19] Further-more, increased tribal mobility and the tendency to centralize tribal control, fostered by British monarchical concepts, intensified tribal intrigue.[20] But in the final analysis the old war leadership collapsed because of the same uncontrollable events which undermined priestly power. The Cherokees, because of their location, were subject to attack from enemy tribes, both southern and northern, and yet they were not sufficiently close to the French-English rivalry to bargain effectively for arms as the Creeks were able to do.[21] Dissatisfaction with the state of affairs was naturally transferred to general dissatisfaction with the tribal leadership of the warriors.

The disastrous losses by the Cherokees in a long series of wars, plus the failure of Charles Town adequately to support the war leaders identified with the colonial government, discredited the basis of power for the red leadership.[22] Finally a renegade group sought alliance with France but received even less support, which demonstrated the futility of Indian-colonial military alliances.[23] The devastating blow to the trading and political complex of the war leaders came in the Anglo-Cherokee War of the 1760's and in the Cherokee-British alliance during the Revolutionary War.[24]

An important factor paving the way toward modification of the legal system was the voluntary exile of the most conservative remnants of the war leadership. Following the American Revolution the most aggressive branch of the tribe, under the leadership of Dragging Canoe, withdrew into Tennessee, where they became known as the "Chickamaugas" and ultimately provided the nucleus for the con-

---

[19] Willis, "Colonial Conflict and the Cherokee Indians, 1710–1760," (Ph.D. dissertation, Columbia University, 1955), 241–45.

[20] The rivalry of AttaKullaKulla (Little Carpenter) and Ostenaco (Judd's friend) is the most notable instance of such intrigue. Lieutenant Henry Timberlake records "there is often great animosity, and the two leaders oppose one another in every measure taken." *Timberlake's Memoirs*, 95–96.

[21] This becomes strikingly apparent if Corkran's Cherokee volume is compared with his Creek study of approximately the same period. David H. Corkran, *The Creek Frontier, 1540–1783*. Willis, "Colonial Conflict and the Cherokee Indians, 1710–1760," (Ph.D. dissertation, Columbia University, 1955), 279–81.

[22] William T. Hagan notes that the "Cherooks took up the hatchet . . . only to be soundly defeated" and "the Cherokee losses includ[ed] half of their warriors." Hagan, *American Indians*, 23.

[23] These Indians may be traced directly from the French alliance to the Chickamaugas to the Arkansas, or Western Cherokees, and into the mainstream of tribal society in the 1840's.

[24] Howard H. Peckham, *The Colonial Wars, 1689–1762*, 201–205.

servative Arkansas and Western Cherokees.[25] In addition, another conservative and highly religious portion of the tribe was concentrated in the upper settlements, away from the increased political activity.[26]

The shift from priestly to warrior leadership occurred gradually in the period between 1710 and 1770. In fact, there was continued influence from both classes during these years, with interchange and succession frequently crossing back and forth between the red and white organizations. However, the final discrediting of the warrior aristocracy had occurred by the end of the American Revolution, and full-blood leadership was almost bankrupt.

Into this vacuum gravitated the mixed-blood element of the Cherokee tribe. The Cherokees, more than any other native tribe in American history, intermarried with the whites. The first white groups to make a permanent home in the Cherokee Nation were the early Scotch and English traders, who were followed by a substantial number of itinerant German artisans, adventurers, and some escaped criminals.[27] The matrilineal nature of Cherokee society made absorption of the children of these assignations simple. The early traders, travelers, and adventurers were joined in the Cherokee country by colonial officials and military officers, some of whom stayed and others who visited only temporarily. An important supplement of white men came during the American Revolution, when Tories fled into the country of the Cherokees, who were a British ally.[28]

Thus there came to be a large class of citizens who were half white and half Cherokee. Although the first of these children were born at the beginning of the eighteenth century, only an occasional reference was made to mixed-blood leadership before 1770, and no pattern of political power emerged until the last three decades of the century.[29] Only when the warrior leadership had been discredited

[25] Malone, *Cherokees of the Old South*, 38–45; Gregory and Strickland, *Starr's History of the Cherokees*, 35–38.

[26] Many of these remained in the East and today form the basis of the Eastern Cherokees.

[27] Gregory and Strickland, *Starr's History of the Cherokees*, 21–34, 466–75.

[28] See for an example Samuel C. Williams, "The Father of Sequoyah: Nathaniel Gist," *Chronicles of Oklahoma*, Vol. 15 (1937), 200. Following the war the Cherokees were required, by treaty, to give up all British officers who had sought sanctuary with the tribe but were allowed to exempt those who had married Cherokees or had been adopted into the tribe.

[29] Willis, "Colonial Conflict and the Cherokee Indians, 1710–1760," (Ph.D. dissertation, Columbia University, 1955), 259–62.

and the assets of the bicultural individual became apparent did the mixed blood emerge as a leader, and only then after the English trade companies were dispersed following the Revolution.[30]

The role of the Cherokee mother in family life and the "traders' inattention of their children" combined to produce a mixed-blood class which was strongly identified with tribal culture.[31] However, the bicultural individual differed significantly in economic terms and in appreciation and understanding of the white culture. Nonetheless, the mixed blood considered himself a Cherokee and came eventually to be respected by the tribe for the valuable skills he possessed. Not only was the mixed blood a recognized leader, but the Cherokees evidenced considerable respect for the immigrant white man, especially the Tories who arrived just as the British trade complex was being shattered by the American Revolution.[32] During this period the simple act of intermarriage became sufficient to confer tribal rights upon the white man.

The ascendancy of mixed-blood leadership was assured when many recalcitrant Cherokees followed Dragging Canoe to the west and the goals of the remaining full-blood leadership became merged with those of the intermarried citizens.[33] Thereafter, economic resources were concentrated in the hands of the mixed blood, the white man's interest in his children undermined the matriarchy at this level, and the "white-Indians" soon united with the Christianizing missionaries. As second and third generation mixed bloods intermarried, a true class of white-Cherokees emerged, and by the 1810 Cherokee national census there were more than 450 whites and

---

[30] Note the McDonald and Ross families which produced the most important and powerful leader of the full-blood Cherokees John Ross. Rachel Caroline Eaton, *John Ross and the Cherokee Indians*, 1–6.

[31] Benjamin Hawkins, *Letters of Benjamin Hawkins, 1796–1806*, 57.

[32] An excellent example of this tribal acceptance is Captain John "Hell-Fire-Jack" Rogers, a wealthy Scotch trader who had been a Tory Captain in the American Revolution and later directed Cherokee emigration to Arkansas. Jessie Dawson Blackwell, *Families of Samuel Dawson and Polly Ann Rogers*, 16–19; Gregory and Strickland, *Starr's History of the Cherokees*, 305–307, 466–76, notes A1, A5, A6, A7, A41; Narcissa Owen, *Memoirs of Narcissa Owen, 1831–1907*, 100–101.

[33] The influence of the full-blood support in social change is symbolized by the appearance of the name of the last nonmixed-blood Cherokee Chief Path Killer on the early written laws. An interesting picture of the changing Cherokee society is given by the missionary Ard Hoyt on his visit to the Cherokee council in 1818. Brainerd Mission Journal, October 30, 1818, *Panopolist*, Vol. 15 (1818–1819), 42–43.

whites with Indian wives in an Indian nation with a population of about 12,000.[34]

Both full-blood and mixed-blood Cherokees stood united in opposition to pressures to surrender tribal lands. The history of the emergence of the Cherokee legal system might well be written as a futile effort to block the series of treaties and acts which surrendered more and more of the ancient tribal dominion and ultimately led to the abolition of the Cherokee Nation.

The British had encouraged the formation of a national state from the disorganized and scattered Cherokee settlements. The colonial officials had created the idea of corporate responsibility by holding the entire tribe responsible for the acts of individual villages and by dealing with the chiefs whom South Carolina viewed as speaking for the entire Cherokee tribe. And surprisingly, the fiction created in Charles Town almost became a fact as a spirit of nationalism and a recognition of mutual dependence arose.[35]

The United States took an even more positive attitude toward the formulation of a "United Cherokee Nation" which was to be "civilized" with the help of the United States and its Indian agents. The Treaty of Holston, one of the first documents signed with the new American republic, contained provisions for United States assistance in this civilization.[36]

Both Presidents Washington and Jefferson exerted considerable pressure to encourage the Cherokees to adopt a new legal system.[37] Jefferson advocated a "simple . . . plan for advancing by degrees to a maturity for receiving our laws," since the Cherokees' success would "have a powerful effect towards stimulating the other tribes in the same progression." This plan was outlined by Jefferson in a speech, "To the Deputies of the Cherokee Upper Towns," delivered in

---

[34] Cherokee Census, 1810, Cherokee Documents, Indian Heritage Association. Grant Foreman estimated that the number of mixed bloods at this time was more than 1,000.

[35] See generally Fred O. Gearing, "The Rise of the Cherokee State as an Instance in a Class: The 'Mesopatamian' Career to Statehood," in William N. Fenton and John Gullick (eds.), *Symposium on Cherokee and Iroquois Culture*, 127–31.

[36] Archibald Henderson, "The Treaty of Long Island of Holston, July, 1777," *North Carolina Historical Review*, Vol. 8 (1931), 55–116.

[37] *Cherokee Phoenix*, May 21, 1828; Dec. 3, 1831; March 17, 1832; James D. Richardson (comp.), *A Compilation of the Messages and Papers of the Presidents, 1789–1897*, I, 80; Thomas Jefferson, *The Writings of Thomas Jefferson*, XVI, 455–58.

Washington on January 9, 1809. The essence of his advice was "to adopt from ours . . . for the present [only such laws] as suit your present condition; chiefly . . . those for the punishment of crimes, and the protection of property." The President offered the assistance of "our beloved man . . . Colonel Return Jonathan Meigs . . . to inform them . . . of our methods of doing business . . . so as to preserve order" and concluded, "I sincerely wish you may succeed in your laudable endeavor to save the remains of your nation by adopting industrious occupation and a government of regular laws."[38]

The Cherokees sincerely believed, as Jefferson suggested, that they might save their nation with the adoption of a new system of laws patterned after those of the white man. Probably the most important factor in the transition from clan to court was the identification of the adoption and enforcement of a new legal system with the goal of preservation of tribal lands. Even the religious, traditionally conservative full bloods came to believe in the necessity of convincing white society of tribal progress in adopting new laws as *the* means to prevent removal from the native lands. Failure to observe the emerging tribal laws came to be considered as treason in the context of the fight for tribal lands. Ultimately the removal controversy with Georgia not only solidified the Cherokees behind new laws but also stimulated the social changes important to the new system, including advancement in farming methods and interest in learning to read and write. No doubt the geographic change from Georgia to Oklahoma also contributed to these changes.

[38] Thomas Jefferson to James Pemberton, Letter, June 21, 1808, *The Writings of Thomas Jefferson*, XII, 74–75.

Stages in Development

IV

E. Adamson Hoebel, in his admirable essay "Law and Anthropology," rejects the "mere static comparison . . . of civilized rules of law with examples from sundry primitive tribes . . . served up for exhibition as an ethnological curiosa."[1] Rather, Hoebel argues, the student of the history of laws must deal with more than "static juridical tidbits" by examining the movements of laws. As Jefferson warned the Cherokees, laws develop slowly.

The Cherokees were, in fact, so much impressed by Jefferson's advice that a *Cherokee Phoenix* editorial reprinted the statement that "their system of government was drawn by the same pen that drafted [the] Declaration of Independence."[2] Yet the Cherokees, to borrow Hoebel's concept, had taken "steps" toward a new government long before the Sage of Monticello expressed interest in their legal development.

The Cherokee legal system, emerging from clan to court, went through many stages. These developments beyond the traditional system might be divided into steps, as follows: the secularization of tribal government (1710 to 1789), emergence of Tribal Council (1780 to 1808), council and regulating parties (1808 to 1817), Chiefs and Warriors in National Assembly with Standing Committee (1817 to 1820), reorganized government (1820 to 1827), constitutional Cherokee government (1827 to 1838), and Cherokee Nation united (1839 to 1906).

[1] E. A. Hoebel, "Laws and Anthropology," *Virginia Law Review*, Vol. 32 (1946), 835.

[2] *Cherokee Phoenix*, March 17, 1832.

In the traditional Cherokee legal system the law was an earthly representation of a divine or Spirit way. As faith in Spirit Beings and the priestly leadership began to sway, those laws with a clear connection with the traditional Cherokee religion began to change. Secularization was the dominant theme of Cherokee legal evolution during the eighteenth century.

The secularization process might best be illustrated by the regulation of homicide. Blood revenge was the control pattern of the ancient Cherokee society. One of the reasons for blood regulation was that the soul of the deceased could not pass into the Nightland until avenged. Living relatives simply did not want to be haunted by a ghost unable to cross to the Spirit World. For this reason compensation or payment of money for damages was not a part of the traditional Cherokee murder regulation. Likewise, it was impossible to provide adjustment for the accidental or non-intentional homicide.[3] However, with the lessening of power of the religious complex, came the rise of compensation for murder with payment of cash or goods in lieu of the life of the deceased. A case which ultimately appeared before the Cherokee Supreme Court illustrates the manner in which the old blood-revenge system was replaced. A white trader had mistreated his wife, causing her death. Rather than risk the blood revenge of her clan, he undertook an exchange procedure. The affidavit of a witness at the Supreme Court proceedings declared:

A white man and an Indian trader who had a Cherokee woman for his wife but who, by his usage of her in beating and otherwise mistreating of her when in a state of pregnancy, died. The clan or tribe to whom she belonged determined to kill the said white man by name of Sam Dent who to appease them and satisfy said tribe or clan went off to Augusta in Georgia and did then purchase a female slave by name of Molly and brought female unto the Cherokee Nation and did offer her to the clans renumeration for the wrongs he had done, a Town Council and Talk was then had at Chota Old Town on Tennessee River and the said female was then and there received by D Clan and by the authorities agreeable to the Indian law and usage in the place of the murdered wife of said Sam Dent.[4]

---

[3] *Ibid.*, Jan. 28, 1829; Feb. 18, 1829; April 1, 1829; Thomas Nuttall, *Journal of Travels into the Arkansas Territory*, 189; George Wilson Pierson, *Tocqueville in America*, 388–89.

[4] "Record Book of the Supreme Court of the Cherokee Nation, 1823–1835," Tennessee State Archives, Nashville. For another similar incident in which a trader "had wiped off all their tears with various presents" see Adair, *American Indians*, 159.

James Adair reported the following incident in which the ancient spiritual institution of "the town of refuge, which is a sure asylum to protect a manslayer" was abandoned when the continued use of this religious practice might have provoked colonial reprisals:

Formerly, when one of the Cherokee murdered an English trader he immediately ran off for the town of refuge; but as soon as he got in view of it, the inhabitants discovered him by the close pursuit of the shrill war whoops; and for fear of irritating the English, they instantly answered the war cry, ran to arms, intercepted, and drove him off into Tennessee River (where he escaped, though mortally wounded).[5]

Another instance of secularization was identified by Lieutenant Henry Timberlake, who noted that in antiquity "the dead having commonly their guns, tomahawkes, powder, lead, silver ware, wampum, and a little tobacco buried with them."[6] As Adair amplified, "The Cherokees of late years, by the reiterated persuasion of the traders, have entirely left off the custom of burying effects with the dead body."[7] Furthermore, the ceremonial and religious office of bone gatherer and the spiritual rites of purification passed with the abandonment of the practice of burial of individual property with the deceased.[8]

We have seen that in traditional Cherokee communities the form of government of the individual Cherokee village was a town council. It was only natural that when the pressures for national action became strong the local system should be duplicated on a tribal or national level. As early as 1721 the royal governor of South Carolina required the tribe to select one spokesman or chief for all towns, and Wrosetastow was chosen.[9] The Treaty of Dover, signed in 1730, reflected an early action of "head warriors," but this group was neither representative nor organized.[10] The colonial records of both Virginia and South Carolina are filled with agreements and negotiations by small and independent assemblies of Cherokee chiefs.[11]

---

[5] Adair, *American Indians*, 158–59.
[6] Timberlake, *Timberlake's Memoirs*, 90–91.
[7] Adair, *American Indians*, 178, 180.
[8] John Howard Payne Papers; Adair, *American Indians*, 180.
[9] Chapman J. Milling, *Red Carolinians*, 273.
[10] When the treaty was affirmed in the palace at Whitehall these Cherokees confirmed their words by presenting the King with a "crown of five eagle-tails and four scalps." Mooney, *Myths of the Cherokees*, 35–36. For provisions check Charles C. Royce, *The Cherokee Nation of Indians*, 144–45.
[11] Such negotiation with small branches or villages of a tribe is responsible for

Clearly in Cherokee prehistory there was no national government, no national council. Christian Priber's Kingdom of Paradise provided such an early agency.[12] By 1757 the Cherokees had undertaken a rudimentary form of national assembly which, according to Edmond Atkins, the first British superintendent for southern Indian affairs, required agreement not by representatives of a majority of the Cherokees but by the majority itself assembled at one council.[13] Such a procedure was obviously awkward and rarely utilized. Some evidence suggests that the Green Corn Ceremony and the National Ball Play provided the setting for these national councils.[14] However, Governor James Glen of South Carolina is known to have called such a council to consider construction of a proposed fort.[15]

The procedure of government by council had been institutionalized by the end of the American Revolution, for, when the United States commissioners met at Hopewell to negotiate a treaty in 1785, the agreement was signed with the "headmen and Warriors of all the Cherokees."[16] By the end of the eighteenth century the council had evolved from a group occasionally assembled to assent to a treaty or declare war into a deliberative council.

Benjamin Hawkins, United States agent to the southern Indians, reported on a council of the Cherokees which he attended in April,

---

much of the appearance of Indian duplicity since the signatory unit might abide by the agreement but the treaty would be in no way binding on the entire body.

12 For a much fuller discussion of this mysterious fellow see Rennard Strickland, "Christian Gotelieb Priber: Utopian Precursor of the Cherokee Government," *Chronicles of Oklahoma*, Vol. 48 (1970), 264–75.

13 Edmond Atkin Papers, Photostats, Indian Heritage Association, Pensacola, Florida.

14 The papers of Tennessee Cherokee Agent Return J. Meigs clearly show the significance of the Green Corn in tribal government. See especially Meigs, Letters of April 7, 1802 and Sept. 21, 1802. Cherokee Microfilm, Series 208, Roll 1, National Archives. John Howard Payne Papers. Raymond David Fogelson, "The Cherokee Ball Game: A Study in Southeastern Ethnology," (Ph.D., dissertation, University of Pennsylvania, 1962); James Mooney, "The Cherokee Ball Play," *American Anthropologist*, Vol. 3 (1890), 105–32; John Howard Payne, "The Green-Corn Dance," *Chronicles of Oklahoma*, Vol. 20 (1932), 170–95; Preston Skarritt, "The Green-Corn Ceremonies of the Cherokees," *National Intelligencer*, April 4, 1829; J. Wittloft, "The Cherokee Green Corn Medicine and the Green Corn Festival," *Journal of the Washington Academy of Science*, Vol. 36 (1946), 213–19.

15 James Glenn, A *Description of South Carolina*, in *Historical Collections of South Carolina*, II, 243.

16 "Treaty Concluded November 28, 1785," in Royce, *Cherokee Nation of Indians*, 133–34.

1797, at which time the tribe took formal steps toward establishing tribal law enforcement officers:

> The Cherokees are giving proofs of their approximation to the customs of well regulated societies; they did, in full council, in my presence, pronounce, after solemn deliberation, as law, that any person who should kill another accidently should not suffer for it, but be acquited; that to constitute a crime, there should be malice and an intention to kill.

> They at the same time gave up, of their own motion, the names of the great rogues in the nation, as well as those in their neighbourhood, and appointed some warriors expressly to assist the chiefs in preventing horse stealing, and in carrying their stipulations with us into effect.[17]

Return Jonathan Meigs, long-time Cherokee agent, made extensive use of the early Cherokee Council of Headwarriors when he undertook the "maintenance of peace and order," which has been called the first duty of the Indian agent. Beginning in 1801, Meigs dealt on an informal basis with this council.[18] The agency records compiled during the early years of the nineteenth century show an ever-increasing volume of letters from "the Cherokee Council," "the Headmen and Warriors Assembled," and the "National Council."[19]

Cherokee government during the final stages of the council has been described in an essay by one of the most important and informed figures in the early Indian Administration of the United States. Thomas L. McKenney reported:

> The government of the Cherokee nation was, at that time, vested in a council, composed of the principal chief, the second principal chief, and the leading men of the several villages, who made treaties and laws, filled the vacancies in their own body, increased its number at will, and in short, exercised all the functions of sovereignty. The executive and more active duties were performed chiefly by the junior members, a requisite number of whom were admitted for that purpose. The powers of the mind are but little exercised in an Indian council, especially in a season of peace, when there is nothing to provoke discussion, and these assemblages are convened rather in obedience to custom than for the actual discharge of business.[20]

---

[17] Hawkins, *Letters of Benjamin Hawkins, 1796–1806*, 136.

[18] "Journal of Occurrences in Cherokee Nation, 1801–1804," Manuscript Division, Library of Congress. Henry Thompson Malone, "Return J. Meigs: Indian Agent Extraordinary," *East Tennessee Historical Society's Publications*, No. 28, 1956.

[19] Letters of Return J. Meigs, Bureau of Indian Affairs Microfilm Records, Cherokee Agency, 1801–1807, Series 208, Numbers 1–7, National Archives.

[20] Thomas McKenney and James Hall, *The Indian Tribes of North America*, 376–77 (cited hereafter as *Indian Tribes*).

At Brooms Town on September 11, 1808, the Chiefs and War-riors in National Council Assembled enacted the first written law of the Cherokees. The law formalized and expanded the institution which Benjamin Hawkins, United States Commissioner, recorded in 1797 and which had been functioning since that date. The first written law of the Cherokee Indians provided as follows:

Resolved by the Chiefs and Warriors in a National Council assembled, That it shall be, and is hereby authorized, for the regulating parties to be organized to consist of six men in each company; one Captain, one Lieutenant and four privates, to continue in service for the term of one year, whose duties it shall be to suppress horse stealing and robbery of other property within their respective bounds, who shall be paid out of the National annuity, at the rates of fifty dollars to each Captain, forty to the Lieutenant, and thirty dollars to each of the privates; and to give their protection to children as heirs to their father's property, and to the widow's share whom he may have had children by or cohabited with, as his wife, at the time of his decease, and in case a father shall leave or will any property to a child at the time of his decease, which he may have had by another woman, then, his present wife shall be entitled to receive any such property as may be left by him or them, when substantiated by two or one [*sic*] disinterested witnesses.

Be it resolved by the Council aforesaid, When any person or persons which may or shall be charged with stealing a horse, and upon conviction by one or two witnesses, he, she, or they, shall be punished with one hundred stripes on the bare back, and the punishment to be in proportion for stealing property of less value; and should the accused person or persons raise up with arms in his or their hands, as guns, axes, spears and knives, in opposition to the regulating company, or should they kill him, or them, the blood of him or them shall not be required of any of the persons belonging to the regulators from the clan the person so killed belong to.

Accepted.—BLACK FOX, Principal Chief,
PATH KILLER, Sec'd.
TOOCHALAR.

CHAS. HICKS, Sec'y to Council.
Brooms Town, 11th Sept. 1808[21]

The act established "regulating parties to be organized to con-sist of six men in each company" whose duties were (1) to supervise and protect children and widows as heirs, (2) to investigate and locate criminals, (3) to try criminals upon statements of witnesses, and (4) to decide upon and administer punishment. The criteria for punishment were set forth in the act. Probably the most important provision was the section declaring "the blood of him or them shall not be required of any of the persons belonging to the regulators from the clan the person killed belong to."[22]

White Path, in his early history of the Cherokees prepared in his last years for the *Cherokee Advocate*, recalled that the regulators acted with great flexibility and adapted punishment and procedure to the equities of the case.[23] Another contemporary report noted the work of Major Ridge in establishing the early law:

To enforce the laws among a barbarous people required a vigorous administration, and this office was assigned to twelve horsemen, persons of courage and intelligence who were the judges, jurors, and executors of justice. Major Ridge was placed at the head of this corps, whose duty it was to ride through the nation, to decide all controversies between individuals. In the unsettled state of the community, the want of forms, and the absence of precedent, much was left to their discretion; and after all, these decisions were enforced rather by the number, energy, and physical power of the judges, than through any respect paid to the law itself.[24]

Still there is no doubt that the regulators became an important "grass-roots" law enforcement agency. The recollection of one of these light-horsemen has survived. The officer, U-li-sga-sti, addressed a meeting of the Cherokee Temperance Society on June 7, 1844. The editor of the *Cherokee Messenger* recorded the talk:

He observed [that] he himself served as an officer, a number of years, in his younger days. In the discharge of his duty, he was never loaded down with pistols and bowie knives. All he carried with him was a little switch, to hurry his horse along, to the place where he had to perform his duty as an officer. We had no written laws then. They were given to us verbally. But he did not stop to enquire whether the laws were constitutional or not, all he wanted to know was how to discharge the duties required of him by the Chiefs of the Nation. He would now say no more, for he was weak and old, and his strength would not permit.[25]

The council continued to meet in public session, presided over by a speaker of the council and secretary and assisted by a chief and

[21] Laws of the Cherokee Nation (1852), 3–4 (cited hereafter as LCN).
[22] LCN 3–4.
[23] *Cherokee Advocate*, Jan. 9, 1895; Dec. 9, 1876.
[24] McKenney, *Indian Tribes*, 382. For amplification see the study of Thurman Wilkins, *Cherokee Tragedy: The Story of the Ridge Family and the Decimation of a People*, especially Chapter Two, "Young Chief," pages 25–50.
[25] *Cherokee Messenger*, August 1844.

principal chief. We are given a remarkable picture of the acculturation process by the study of the Abrogation of Clan Revenge, the second written law of the Cherokees—a law considered by many to be the most significant enacted by the council. The law was adopted as follows:

Be it known, That this day, the various clans or tribes which compose the Cherokee Nation, have unanimously passed an act of oblivion for all lives for which they may have been indebted, one to the other, and have mutually agreed that after this evening the aforesaid act shall become binding upon every clan or tribe; and the aforesaid clans or tribes, have also agreed that if, in future, any life should be lost without malice intended, the innocent aggressor shall not be accounted guilty.

Be it known, also, That should it happen that a brother, forgetting his natural affection, should raise his hand in anger and kill his brother, he shall be accounted guilty of murder and suffer accordingly, and if a man has a horse stolen, and overtakes the thief, and should his anger be so great as to cause him to kill him, let his blood remain on his own conscience, but no satisfaction, shall be demanded for his life from his relatives or the clan he may belong to.

By order of the seven clans.

TURTLE AT HOME, Speaker of Council
Approved.—BLACK FOX, Principal Chief,
PATH KILLER, Sec'd
TOOCHALER.

CHAS. HICKS, Sec'y to the Council.
Oostanallah, April 10, 1810.[26]

One commentator on the life of Major Ridge reported the process of adoption and early enforcement of this law. Ridge is reported to have suggested the provision "in an able speech [which] exposed the injustice of that part of [the ancient blood revenge] law which substituted a relative for a fugitive murderer" and to have "successfully advocated its repeal." Ridge then undertook "the more difficult task which involved the breaking up of an ancient usage." The account continues:

Ridge having proposed the measure, was required to carry it into effect, and readily assumed upon himself that responsibility; taking the precaution, however, to exact from every chief, a promise that he would advocate the principle of the new law, and stand prepared to punish its infringe-

[26] LCN 4.

ment. It was not long before an opportunity occurred to test the sincerity of these pledges. A man who had killed another fled. The relations of the deceased were numerous, fearless, and vindictive, prompt to take offence, and eager to imbue their hands in blood upon the slightests provocation. They determined to revenge the injury by killing the brother of the offender. The friends of the latter dispatched a messenger to Ridge, to advise him of the intended violation of the new law, and implore his protection; and he, with creditable promptitude, sent word to the persons who proposed to revenge themselves, that he would take upon himself the office of killing the individual who should put such a purpose into execution. This threat had the desired effect, not only in that instance, but in causing the practice of substituting a relative in the place of an escaped homicide to be abandoned.[27]

Although a discussion of the specific administration and enforcement of the new laws is not pertinent to this book, one story illustrates the flexibility with which these early Cherokee laws operated. The story—possibly apocryphal—passed on by word of mouth, concerns the speedy nature of the new Cherokee justice:

In the early days, at a dance . . . a man was knocked in the head by another. The dance was stopped, the oldest man in the crowd was called out for judge, the evidence taken and sentence passed, the offender was to be killed by a brother of the slain man. The weapon was to be a club. The penalty was carried out, the bodies of the two slain men dragged aside and the dance went on.[28]

Fifty-four Cherokee towns and villages assembled in May, 1817, at the tribal village of Amoah to enact a resolution undertaking the revision of tribal government. The purpose of the meeting was clearly set forth: "We . . . have convened in order to deliberate and consider on the situation of our Nation, in the disposition of our common property of lands, without the unanimous consent of the members of Council."[29] The full body of Chiefs and Warriors in National Council Assembled had proved to be too bulky and slow to negotiate with the federal government. The Cherokee Nation was faced with tremendous pressures to sell tribal lands in the East and, in fact, a sizable portion of the tribe signed the Treaty of 1817, where-

[27] McKenney, *Indian Tribes,* 379.
[28] Joe Lynch, quoted in Eula E. Fullerton, "Social Life of the Cherokees, 1820–1906," (Master's thesis, University of Oklahoma, 1931), 44–45, n. 10.
[29] LCN 4–5.

by lands in the old nation were exchanged for lands west of the Mississippi.[30]

The act establishing the Standing Committee is sometimes erroneously known as the Constitution of 1817 because it provided for the creation of a special committee appointed by the Chiefs and Warriors in National Council Assembled. The committee was to consist of thirteen members each serving two-year terms with the vacancies filled by the chief. The resolution further provided that "affairs of the Nation shall be committed to the care of the standing committee . . . but acts of this body shall not be binding in our common property on the Nation without unanimous consent of the members and Chiefs of the Council." Among the duties delegated to the Standing Committee was to "settle with the Agency for our annual stipend and report the proceedings to the members and Chiefs in Council."[31] The chiefs and warriors unanimously pledged themselves to observe the limitations, especially those on common property as contained in the 1817 resolution. The Standing Committee was "required to be governed by the . . . articles," which could be amended only "at our electional time."[32]

The Standing Committee operated as an executive, legislative, and judicial body of government from 1817 to 1820. Complaints submitted to the full council were generally shifted to the committee, as in the cases of a controversy over ownership of a turnpike company and of the responsibility of an owner for acts of a runaway slave. The decision in the slave case was probably typical of the committee's work:

New Town, Cherokee Nation, November 1st, 1819.

In Committee.

The National Committee have taken up the case submitted to them by the Council relating to the exchange of horses between Otter Lifter and a runaway negro man, belonging to Wm. Thompson. The horse delivered to Otter Lifter by said negro man was proven away from him, and the question submitted to the Committee was, whether or not, the master of the negro man, Wm. Thompson, should be accountable to the Otter

---

[30] John P. Brown, *Old Frontiers: The Story of the Cherokee Indians from Earliest Times to the Date of their Removal to the West*, 463–77; Charles Kappler (ed.), *Indian Affairs, Laws and Treaties*, II, 140–44; Cherokee Nation, *Treaties Between the United States of America and the Cherokee Nation from 1785*, 41–50.

[31] LCN 4–5.

[32] *Ibid.*

Lifter for the horse so proved away from him on account of the transgression of his said negro man; the Committee therefore have decided that Wm. Thompson ought not to be accountable for the contract entered into with his runaway negro man by any person contrary to his approbation, and, *Resolved by the Committee*, that no contract or bargain entered into with any slave or slaves, without the approbation of their masters shall be binding on them.

JNO. ROSS, Pres't N. Com.

his

PATH KILLER,

mark.

CHAS. R. HICKS

A. McCOY, Clerk.[33]

Generally the national committee and the council met jointly for the purpose of legislating. In other instances the national committee might create a rule of law growing out of a case. Typically, the enactments of the period were short, simple statements issued by both committee and council, as, for example, the following concerning emigrating Cherokees:

Resolved by the National Committee and Council, That in case any person or persons, citizens of the Nation, not enrolled for the Arkansas country, who has or may take possession of, and occupy any improvement or place where Arkansas emigrants had left before any privileged emigrants to continue in this Nation, shall retake possession of such place or places aforesaid, shall be entitled to an exclusive right of the same.

By order—JNO. ROSS, Pres't N. Com.

his

Approved—PATH X KILLER,

mark.

CHAS R. HICKS.

A. McCOY, Clerk.[34]

A resolution passed by the national committee and council in 1820 reorganized the Cherokee government through the creation of a judicial branch for the purpose of "holding councils to administer justice in all cases and complaints that may be brought forward for trial."[35] Thus the Standing Committee was to cease functioning as a

[33] *Ibid.*, 8–9.
[34] *Ibid.*, 9–10.
[35] *Ibid.*, 11–12.

court, and all cases involving interpretation of tribal laws were to be decided by the court system.

The original act creating the judiciary was revised several times before the enactment of the Constitution of 1827, but as originally conceived the Cherokees modeled the system after what they considered the Anglo-American pattern. The system consisted of four circuit courts and eight district courts with "one circuit judge, to have jurisdiction over two districts, to associate with the district judge in determining all causes agreeable to National law."[36]

In addition to the judges the offices in the original act were marshals, light-horsemen, and rangers. Eventually the light-horsemen were replaced by sheriffs, deputy sheriffs, and constables.[37] The marshals were "to execute the decisions of the Judges" in their respective districts, the light-horsemen were "to execute such punishment on thieves as the Judges shall decide agreeable to the law," and the district rangers were to supervise stray horses.

Amendments to the judiciary act during this period were frequent. The most important occurred in 1823, when the superior court was created to serve as a supreme judiciary and hear cases on appeal. The following year an act provided that "the Lighthorse in each District Court shall serve as jurors" and the judge "shall act as foreman of the jury." However, in the following year "disinterested persons" replaced the light-horsemen as jurors.[38]

Despite the creation of a court system and an act declaring a "limitation on government" and the "independent and final decision of the Judiciary,"[39] the committee and council continued to hear judicial questions. Members of the tribe looked to the popular assembly to check the courts, and the committeemen and counselors responded, as in the case of Samuel Henry:

New Town, Cherokee Nation, October 27, 1825.

The National Committee concur with the Council so far in remitting the fine imposed by the Court on Samuel Henry as the Nation is concerned, excepting the Marshal's fee and the confiscation of the brandy, the proceeds arising from the sale of the brandy to revert to the informer agreeable to his consent;

[36] *Ibid.*, 14–15, 31–32, 37, 39, 45–46, 48, 51, 60.
[37] *Ibid.*, 12, 19, 28, 51.
[38] The resolution was passed on Nov. 12, 1822, and was effective beginning in 1823. LCN 28; LCN 39; LCN 44, 46.
[39] LCN 45–46.

Provided, that the said Samuel Henry also obligates himself under bond and security, in future never to violate the laws of this Nation, by the introduction of ardent spirits into the Nation, under the penalty of making good the fine herein remitted, and also, of being dealt with as the law directs.

JNO. ROSS, Pres't Com.

MAJOR RIDGE, Speaker

his

Approved—PATH X KILLER

Mark

CH. R. HICKS[40]

The euphoria resulting from the adoption of the Cherokee Constitution of 1827 was perhaps best shown in an editorial in the *New York Observer,* which noted that "their laws . . . , if we judge from what we have seen, are superior to the wisdom of Lycurgus or Solon."[41] The adoption of a written constitution seemed the ultimate step in civilization. The Cherokee Constitution was copied in most respects from the Constitution of the United States. The preamble, for example, began: "We, the Representatives of the people of the Cherokee Nation, in Convention assembled, in order to establish justice, ensure tranquility, promote our common welfare, and secure to ourselves and our prosterity the blessings of liberty."[42]

The document created three branches of government and enumerated their powers. The dual legislative bodies of national committee and national council were retained with a provision for joint sessions. The executive power was entrusted to the principal chief, assistant principal chief, treasurer, and national marshal. A three-member council, appointed by the legislative committee and council, was to advise and meet with the chiefs. The judicial system was not significantly modified.[43]

Personal liberties and safeguards were borrowed from the United States Constitution.[44] Yet surely the most important provisions, from the standpoint of the laws of the Cherokees, were those which were not a part of the United States Constitution. Absolutely essential to the maintenance of the Cherokee Nation were the restrictions making all land the "common property of the Nation." In part, this section provided:

[40] *Ibid.,* 49.
[41] Reprinted in *Cherokee Phoenix,* Jan. 14, 1829.
[42] LCN 118.
[43] *Ibid.,* 125.
[44] *Ibid.,* 118–130.

The sovereignty and Jurisdiction of this Government shall extend over the country within the boundaries . . . described, and the lands therein are, and shall remain, the common property of this Nation; but the improvements made thereon, and in the possession of the citizens of the Nation, are the exclusive and indefeasible property of the citizens respectively.

Provided, that the citizens of the Nation, possessing exclusive and indefeasible right to their respective improvements . . . shall possess no right nor power to dispose of their improvements in any manner whatever to the United States, individual states, nor individual citizens thereof; and that whenever any such citizen or citizens shall remove with their effects out of the limits of this Nation, and become citizens of any other Government, all their rights and privileges as citizens of this Nation shall cease.[45]

The Cherokee Constitutional Convention was called by a resolution of the committee and council in October, 1826, and met in July of 1827.[46] Much fanfare attended the adoption of the new articles of government, but the constitution was, in effect, stillborn. During much of the next decade the Cherokees fought to retain the constitution while living under control of the Georgia militia and the martial law of United States Army.[47] Yet all the while the Cherokee Nation proclaimed that its constitution remained its supreme law.

The discovery of gold on Cherokee land coincided almost exactly with the Constitutional Convention.[48] While the Cherokees viewed the formation of the constitutional government as an important step in the preservation of their tribal lands, ironically it was the very success of the Cherokees in adopting a constitution and written code which convinced the "land hungry Georgians" of the necessity of Indian removal.[49] Therefore, in 1828 the Georgia legislature prevented the Cherokees, whose land was within the boundaries of the

---

[45] *Ibid.*, 119.

[46] *Ibid.*, 73–76.

[47] An excellent contemporary picture is provided by James F. Smith, *The Cherokee Land Lottery* and Winfield Scott, *Memoirs of Lieut.-General Scott, LL.D., Written by Himself,* I, 317–30. Congressional speeches are reprinted in *Speeches on the Passage of the Bill for the Removal of the Indians, Delivered in the Congress of the United States,* April and May, 1830, while other relevant materials are found in Louis Filler and Allen Guttmann (eds.), *The Removal of the Cherokee Nation: Manifest Destiny or National Dishonor?*

[48] *Cherokee Advocate,* Oct. 6, 1882; Minter Uzzell, "The Cherokee Gold Rush in Georgia: A Forgotten Chapter in Indian Removal," (Paper presented before a seminar in American history, Northeastern State College, Tahlequah, Okla., 1955); F. M. Green, "Georgia's Forgotten Industry: Gold Mining," *Georgia Historical Quarterly,* Vol. 19 (1935), 93–111, 210–28.

state of Georgia, from acting as an independent government and extended state laws into the Indian country.[50]

The struggle between the Cherokees and Georgia was climaxed in 1838 by the forcible removal of more than 16,000 Cherokees over a Trail of Tears to what became the state of Oklahoma.[51] The years between 1828 and 1838 were years of chaos in which the Cherokees fought to retain tribal land and law. John Marshall's decisions in *Cherokee Nation v. Georgia* and *Worcester v. Georgia* provided disappointment and then hope, but ultimately it became clear that Marshall might make the law but Jackson enforced the law.[52] So the Cherokees met in council in 1838 and resolved to carry their system of constitutional government with them to the Indian Territory.[53]

An interesting parallel development was taking place among the more traditional Cherokees who had begun the migration toward the west at the end of the eighteenth century. This conservative group, known as the Western Cherokees, Arkansas Cherokees, or "the Old Settlers," slowly began to enact written laws.[54] These were important to the stages of development of the main body of the tribe because of the ultimate union of the two bodies and because the Cherokees of Georgia were removed into the lands governed by the Cherokee Nation, West.

[49] The *Cherokee Phoenix* contains the most articulate presentation of the Cherokee position while the standard reference on the Georgia attitude is Governor Wilson Lumpkins, *The Removal of the Cherokee Indians from Georgia.*

[50] Thomas R. R. Cobb (ed.), *A Digest of the Statute Laws of the State of Georgia* (1851), 377–79; Arthur Foster (ed.), *A Digest of the Laws of the State of Georgia* (1831), 124–29; William A. Hitckiss (comp.), *A Codification of the Statute Law of Georgia* (1845), Art. IV, "Indians," 320–22; Oliver H. Prince (comp.), *A Digest of the Laws of the State of Georgia* (1837), 278–85; *Acts of the General Assembly of the State of Georgia* (1834), 293–94, 304–305, 337–39; *Acts of the General Assembly of the State of Georgia* (1836), 135–37. For background resolutions consult *Acts of the General Assembly of the State of Georgia* (1826), 206–208; 227–38.

[51] More than 4,000 Cherokees died on the forced march and in the stockades where the Indians were herded. The standard history of this tragedy is Grant Foreman, *Indian Removal: The Emigration of the Five Civilized Tribes of Indians*, 229–314. A popular history is Dale Van Every, *Disinherited: The Lost Birthright of the American Indian.*

[52] 30 U.S. (5 Pet.) 1 (1831) and 31 U.S. (6 Pet.) 515 (1832); Joseph C. Burke, "The Cherokee Cases: A Study in Law, Politics, and Morality," *Stanford Law Review*, Vol. 21 (1969), 500–31; Anton Hermann Chroust, "Did President Jackson Actually Threaten the Supreme Court with Nonenforcement of Its Injunction Against the State of Georgia?", *American Journal of Legal History*, Vol. 5 (1960), 76–78.

[53] Journal of Cherokee Council, John Howard Payne Papers.

[54] No general history of the Western Cherokees is available, but see Cephas Washburn, *Reminiscences* and Starr, *Cherokees "West."*

The Western Cherokees were a notoriously independent and paradoxical people who visited New Orleans, Philadelphia, and Washington to purchase the latest fashions and china but who continued blood raids and scalping against their Osage neighbors.[55] These were the Cherokees to whom Sam Houston fled when he sought exile from white civilization.[56] Slower in adjusting to white culture, they did not enact their first written law until 1820. This law was remarkably like the first law written by the Eastern Cherokees in 1808:

The first law established among the Cherokees on Arkansas, and entered by request of the old Chief, John Jolly.

Resolved, That there be and is hereby appointed a Light-Horse company whose duty shall be to preserve peace and good order among the Cherokees on Arkansas, to suppress stealing, and punish such as may be caught in such an act.

Resolved further. That the Light-Horse company shall not have anything to do with a case for stealing which had been committed previous to this date, neither shall it be lawful for any Light-Horse company hereafter appointed, or Chiefs to have any cognizance of such cases, (stealing) if committed previous to this date.

Dardenelle Rock, 1820.

JOHN JOLLY, Prin'l Chief

Walter Webber, Black Fox, Spring Frog, Too-cho-wuh, and others, Chiefs, Headmen and Warriors of the Cherokee Nation.[57]

The basic attitudes of the Western Cherokees were reflected in their governmental structure. The written laws provided not for a single chief but for three equal chiefs whose power was most clearly limited by the committee and council, which even retained power of decisions over the district courts.[58]

From 1829 to 1833 the number of tribal laws almost tripled and the nature and scope of regulation expanded.[59] One may safely conclude that the Western Cherokees made remarkable strides in understanding the power of the law. Therefore, when the Eastern Cherokees arrived in 1838, they faced a more formidable opponent than

---

[55] "Cherokee West," Foreman Vertical File, Oklahoma Historical Society.
[56] Jack Gregory and Rennard Strickland, *Sam Houston with the Cherokees, 1829–1833* (cited hereafter as *Sam Houston*).
[57] LCN 85.
[58] *Ibid.,* 89.
[59] Gregory and Strickland, *Sam Houston,* 108.

they had anticipated. A clash which developed between the two divisions of the Cherokee nation was thus cast in terms of governmental theory and representative democracy.

On September 6 of each year, the Cherokees gathered at Tahlequah, Oklahoma, to celebrate the adoption of the Cherokee Constitution by the United Eastern Western Cherokees. The document served, with minor modification, from 1839 until the ultimate termination of Cherokee government, surviving an internal Cherokee civil war and the American Civil War.[60]

The 1839 Constitution followed the form of the older Cherokee Constitution of 1827 in most respects. The revision was undertaken

[60] For the complete text see *The Constitution and Laws of the Cherokee Nation: Passed at Tahlequah, Cherokee Nation, 1839–1851,* 5–15 and Gregory and Strickland eds., *Starr's History of the Cherokees,* 121–33.

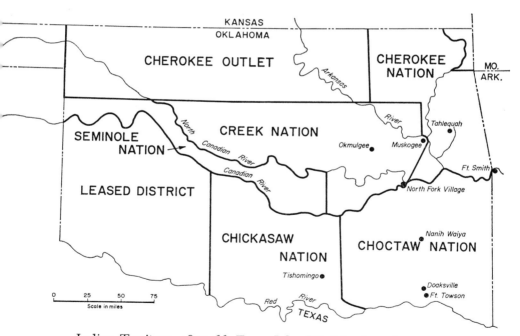

Indian Territory, 1855–66. From John W. Morris and Edwin C. McReynolds, *Historical Atlas of Oklahoma* (Norman, University of Oklahoma Press, 1965).

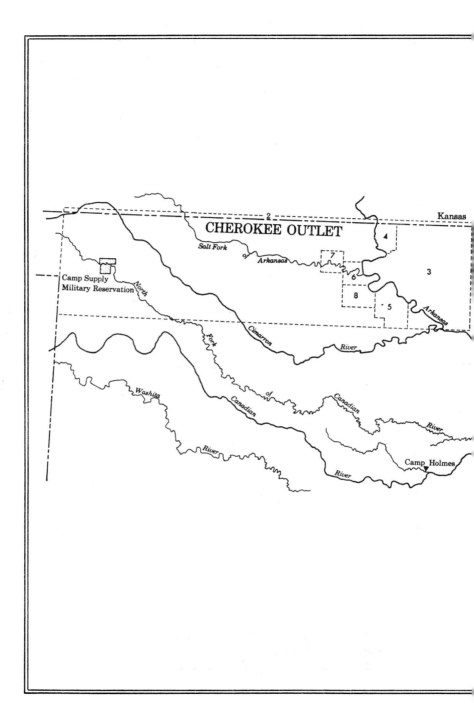

CHEROKEE OUTLET

Kansas

Salt Fork of Arkansas

Camp Supply
Military Reservation

North

Fork

Cimarron

River

Arkansas

2

4

7

6

3

8

5

Washita

Canadian

of

Canadian

River

River

River

Camp Holmes

River

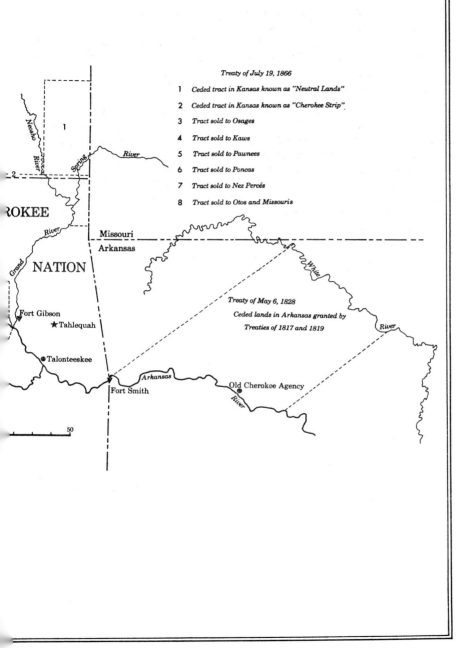

Treaty of July 19, 1866

1   Ceded tract in Kansas known as "Neutral Lands"

2   Ceded tract in Kansas known as "Cherokee Strip".

3   Tract sold to Osages

4   Tract sold to Kaws

5   Tract sold to Pawnees

6   Tract sold to Poncas

7   Tract sold to Nez Percés

8   Tract sold to Otos and Missouris

Neosho River

Spring River

River

ROKEE

River

Grand

NATION

Missouri

Arkansas

White

River

Treaty of May 6, 1828

Ceded lands in Arkansas granted by

Treaties of 1817 and 1819

Fort Gibson

★ Tahlequah

● Talonteeskee

Arkansas

Fort Smith

River

Old Cherokee Agency

50

Cherokee lands in the West. From *Historical Atlas of Oklahoma.*

by many of the same leaders who drafted the earlier work and contained much of the original wording.[61] This act has been called "a milestone in the achievement record of all earliest known people's throughout the world."[62] W. W. Keeler, principal chief of the Cherokees, evaluated the constitution in the foreword to a recent edition of the old tribal laws:

When the Cherokees arrived in their new homeland west of the Mississippi, they had their own tribal government, designed after the republican form of government complete in all three phases. Shortly after their weary and tragic march west, the Cherokees took steps to reorganize their tribal government. . . . Pursuant to [the] Act of Union between the Eastern and Western Cherokees . . . a Constitution for the new government was drafted. . . . It is interesting to note in this Constitution, written one hundred thirty years ago, that it provided for the eighteen year old vote, and established procedures for the removal and replacement of the Principal Chief in the event of disability or impeachment. Both of these issues are receiving considerable thought and discussion throughout America today.[63]

The foregoing analysis suggests that the Cherokee legal system did not spring forth as a mature instrument. The historical development of Cherokee law ways illustrates the process of gradual evolution building upon existing social institutions. That the Cherokees pursued slow and systematic adaptation is not a condemnation but rather a tribute to the wisdom of tribal leadership. For, in this way, the early and less sophisticated procedures of the tribal regulators and light-horsemen built a firm foundation for the more complex written constitution and tribal courts.

[61] *Cherokee Advocate*, Feb. 28, 1877. William Shorey Coodey was the primary architect of the Act of Union and George Lowery and John Ross again served in the drafting of the new document. Grant Foreman, *The Five Civilized Tribes*, 300, 302–303 and Rachel Caroline Eaton, *John Ross and the Cherokee Indians*, 53–59, 138–44.
[62] W. W. Keeler, "Foreword," *The Constitution and Laws of the Cherokee Nation* (1969), 5.
[63] *Ibid.*, 5–6.

Tribal Goals and Values in Cherokee Law

V

IN THE Record Book of the Supreme Court of the Cherokee Nation an Indian recorded in florid penmanship the first case, "James Griffin versus Nancy West, a Suit for Damages."[1] The title tells much. Nancy West is thought to have been a descendant of Nancy Ward, the "beloved woman" of the Cherokees, whose legendary fame includes the introduction of the domesticated milk cow into the nation, marriages to prominent white men, and warnings to foreign soldiers.[2] Nancy Ward was equally well known as a shrewd businesswoman who accumulated much property, including several Negro slaves.[3] It seems appropriate that the first case before the new court should involve the title to a farm claimed by a granddaughter of this important figure. It illustrates, as does the early record of the entire legal system, that much of the early written Cherokee law was an instrument designed to serve the needs of the small group of wealthy mixed-blood Cherokees.

The mixed bloods freely acknowledged that the system was designed and introduced by a tribal minority. The *Cherokee Advocate* of January 9, 1895, noted:

The policy of our fore-fathers in establishing our present government was largely paternal. The educated and enlightened Indians to foster and guard the interests and rights of the full blood while he was gradually being led, by precept and example into the way he should go; that is give

---

[1] "Record Book of the Supreme Court of the Cherokee Nation, 1823–1835." Tennessee State Archives, Nashville.

[2] Carolyn Thomas Foreman, *Indian Women Chiefs*, 72–83.

[3] Gregory and Strickland, eds., *Starr's History of the Cherokees*, 32, 470–71.

up the bow, the arrow, the chase, the tomahawk, the wigwam and the customs of his fore-fathers for the equipment and habits of civilized man.

A Virginian noted that the Cherokees' "civil jurisprudence has been imported among them by the white emigrants."[4]

Cherokee government was born and nurtured in Georgia, where for slightly more than twenty years (1808 to 1829) Cherokee counselors wrote laws, and, for nearly thirteen years (1823 to 1835), Cherokee justices heard cases. The almost 200 legislative resolutions[5] and the 246 cases provide a clear insight into tribal motivations.[6] If ever there was an instance of the economic and political needs of an elite class reforming a legal system, this was such a case.

Agent Return Jonathan Meigs emphasized these economic aspects of the Cherokee laws in his reports to the War Department,[7] as did Cherokees William Coodey,[8] David Brown,[9] and Elias Boudinot[10] in their correspondence. The vast majority of the new laws of the Cherokees either provided for the organization of the government itself[11] or regulated ownership of land;[12] monopoly control of roads, turnpikes, and ferries;[13] inheritance;[14] introduction of laborers and craftsmen to work within the nation;[15] regulation of slaves;[16] taxation;[17] power to borrow or contract;[18] and livestock control.[19]

4 "Reflections on the Institutions of the Cherokee Indians from Observations Made During a Recent Visit to that Tribe: In a letter from a Gentleman of Virginia, to Robert Walsh," June 1, 1817, Thomas Harrison Collection, Item 3, Oklahoma Historical Society, 42. For full-blood support of the tribal court system see *Cherokee Advocate*, Feb. 27, 1895, and June 26, 1897.

5 See summary of these laws and *Laws of the Cherokee Nation: Adopted by the Council at Various Periods* (1852).

6 The tabulations were supplied by Malone, *Cherokees of the Old South*, 83.

7 Letters of Return J. Meigs, Bureau of Indian Affairs Microfilm Records, Cherokee Agency, National Archives.

8 William S. Coodey, Letters, Grant Foreman Typescripts, Oklahoma Historical Society, Indian Archives.

9 David Brown, "Views of a Native Indian, as to the Present Condition of His People," *Missionary Herald*, Vol. 21 (1825), 354–55.

10 Boudinot, *An Address to the Whites*, 8–14.

11 LCN 3–4, 6–7, 11–12, 14–18, 20, 22, 26, 28, 29, 31–33, 37, 39, 40, 42, 44, 46, 48, 51–52, 56, 58–59, 61–62, 73–75, 77, 90, 91, 94, 97–99, 101–104, 105–107, 110, 111, 114–117, 144–145, 147.

12 LCN 4–5, 9–10, 19, 23–24, 33, 40–41, 45–46, 50, 56, 59, 62–64, 66, 80, 99–100, 113, 131–132, 136–137, 139–141, 142.

13 LCN 6–8, 13, 20, 21, 22–23, 25, 29–30, 35–36, 86–87, 94–96, 105–106, 108, 109, 138–139.

14 LCN 3–4, 10, 52–53, 57, 58, 111–113, 131–132, 142.

15 LCN 6–7, 10–11, 13–14, 30, 34, 39–40, 60, 88, 90, 99–100, 109, 110, 131–132.

The initial term of the Cherokee court was fairly typical of the docket, which was mostly civil and generally involved commerce among the mixed bloods. In 1823 the high court heard 21 cases. Thirteen were "pleas of debt," 3 were "pleas for damages," 2 were "pleas of defraud," and 1 each was for ejectment, grand larceny, hog stealing, and "plea of settlement." Of the 246 cases the court decided, 26 were debt cases, and more than 75 per cent involved economic questions.[20] Clearly much of the early legal action centered on the difficult problem of collection of debts. The process was described in considerable detail by an outside observer in the Cherokee country:

A debt which can be proved to be due, is exacted from an unwilling debtor by an application on the part of the creditor to the justices in Eyre, who are a troop of light horse called un-ut-le-ke-haw-kee (or riders of the circuit.) These seize as much of the property of the debtor as will satisfy the demand. I did not understand that they had a right to confine the person in case he had no property. In this respect, their laws are more humane than our own.[21]

Very few criminal cases reached the high court, and many of these were for offenses such as harboring a slave or illegal hiring of United States citizens. A study of the names and background of the litigants before the court confirms the fact (which one would suspect), that the litigants continued to represent mixed bloods—the Nancy Wests, John Martins, James Hugheses, and Richard Rattifs.

As late as the 1880's and 1890's the Cherokees were engaged in a prolonged debate over an economic question phrased by the *Cherokee Advocate* as "the Permit Law, Its Objects and Results."[22] The arguments in this controversy clearly establish that the Cherokees understood the use of law as an instrument of social policy. The permit issue revolved around the admission into the Cherokee Nation

[16] LCN 8–9, 24–25, 34, 37–39.
[17] LCN 6–7, 12–13, 29, 30, 42, 48, 55–56, 64–65, 83, 87–89, 93–94, 97, 100, 108, 109, 115–116, 139. In addition there are many appropriations bills.
[18] LCN 21, 49–51, 59–60, 79, 87–88, 92, 93, 95–96, 101, 113, 137–138.
[19] LCN 12, 19, 34–35, 39, 41–43, 54–55, 57–58, 80, 93.
[20] "Record Book of the Supreme Court of the Cherokee Nation, 1823–1835," see Malone, *Cherokees of the Old South*, 83.
[21] "Reflections on the Institutions of the Cherokee Indians from Observations Made During a Recent Visit to That Tribe: In a letter from a Gentleman of Virginia, to Robert Walsh," June 1, 1817, Thomas Harrison Collection, Item 3, Oklahoma Historical Society, 42.
[22] *Cherokee Advocate*, Feb. 1, 1879; March 26, 1879; April 16, 1879; May 16, 1884; Feb. 23, 1887.

of noncitizens whose Cherokee employers were issued "permits" for these workers.[23] The Nation did not have sufficient native or intermarried citizens to utilize effectively the resources of the land.[24] On the other hand, the admission of a large class of laborers into the Nation clearly disrupted the social order and opened the community to scrutiny by land speculators.[25]

Similar controversies over the use of laws focused on the cattle and stock-raising regulations,[26] limitations on carrying weapons,[27] restrictions upon timber uses,[28] and limitations upon railroad liability.[29] A frequent argument was stated simply in the terms that "we cannot achieve without proper laws."[30] The debate over the use of the legal system was not a new one. The Cherokees had long realized the relationship between their laws and the central issue of tribal politics, the retention of national land and tribal status. The legal system had been used as an instrument in preservation of tribal lands almost as long as the pressures from white men had forced the Cherokees to guard their shrinking domain.

One of the first recorded instances of a Cherokee trial is the case of Cheesto-Kaehre, or "the Old Rabbit," who served as an interpreter for the chiefs and head warriors sent to London in 1730.[31] On the night of September 7 of that year, in their rented room beneath a tavern in London, the chiefs considered "whether they should not kill him" for his favorable answer to the king's claim "not only [to] their lands, but [to] all the other unconquered countries of the neighboring nations, as his right and property." The decision was to save him and the chief who had supported him. Upon their return to the Cherokee Nation "they were tried again, by the national sanhedrin, for having betrayed the public faith and sold their country, for acknowledged value, by firm compact, as representatives of the country . . . having received a certain quantity of goods." They were again "honorably acquited" in a decision which considered the

---

[23] *Ibid.*, May 16, 1884; Feb. 27, 1895.
[24] *Ibid.*, April 30, 1879; June 11, 1879.
[25] *Ibid.*, Sept. 26, 1888; June 10, 1893; Feb. 28, 1894.
[26] *Ibid.*, Aug. 15, 1877; July 11, 1884.
[27] *Ibid.*, Nov. 9, 1881; Oct. 12, 1883; Sept. 15, 1882; Nov. 3, 1886; May 12, 1886.
[28] *Ibid.*, Sept. 29, 1882 and for similar questions on mining *Cherokee Advocate,* March 14, 1884, and June 6, 1894.
[29] *Ibid.*, July 27, 1881, and May 23, 1888.
[30] See, for example, the editorial "Practical Legislation" by W. P. Boudinot, *Cherokee Advocate,* Aug. 15, 1877.
[31] Adair, *American Indians,* 50–51.

equities of the situation that "the interpreter was bound, by . . . oath" and that "surprise, inadvertense, self-love, and the unusual glittering show of the courtiers, exorted the sacred assent."

By the beginning of the nineteenth century, however, the Cherokees were no longer willing to exert such tolerance. Doublehead, a distinguished and somewhat troublesome chief who had been noted for his conservative and warmaking disposition, signed the Treaty of 1805, which relinquished tribal claims to reserved lands.[32] The treaty contained a secret agreement. Upon discovery of the secret land grant made to Doublehead in the unpublished codicil, the chiefs and warriors of the tribe met to consider his fate. By an interesting twist the council ordered the chief's death and selected a body of executioners to be headed by Major Ridge, who carried out the tribal sentence himself.[33]

The desire to protect Ridge and the other members of his party was an important factor in the adoption of the first written law of 1808, which made blood revenge inapplicable to public regulators and in the Abrogation of Clan Revenge, enacted two years later.[34] The incident left an indelible mark upon the minds of Cherokee leaders who were called to negotiate private treaties. More than twenty-five years later Major Ridge recorded that he was signing his own execution papers when he approved the controversial Treaty of New Echota, exchanging lands in Georgia for those west of the Mississippi.[35]

Desire to retain tribal lands as a motivating force behind the adoption of new laws was never as apparent as in the Council of 1828 debate on the motion made by Choonnagkee of the Chickamauga District. The bill proposed that an old law, making death the penalty for selling land without the authority of the Nation, be committed to writing. The act was approved after a speech by the aged Womankiller of Hickory Log District. The octogenarian warrior argued, "I am told that the Government of the United States will spoil their

---

[32] Return J. Meigs conducted an investigation of Doublehead's execution with the relevant documents found in Letters Received, Bureau of Indian Affairs, Microfilm publications, Roll No. 208, National Archives.

[33] McKenney and Hall, *Indian Tribes*, 385–86.

[34] John P. Brown, "Eastern Cherokee Chiefs," *Chronicles of Oklahoma*, Vol. 16 (1938), 30.

[35] John Ridge, son of Major Ridge, and a party to the document told J. F. Schermerhorn that "I may yet die by the hand of some poor infatuated Indian. . . . I am resigned to my fate, whatever it may be." *Arkansas Gazette*, Oct. 2, 1839.

treaties with us and sink our National Council under their feet,—It may be so, but it shall not be with our consent, or by the misconduct of our people."[36]

The "rhetoric of reform" which the Cherokees formulated during the transformation of their legal system uniformly identified adoption of white-based laws with resistance of removal from ancient tribal lands. Supreme faith was placed in the operation of courts of justice. George Gilmer, governor of Georgia, wrote to Andrew Jackson on June 20, 1831:

Meetings of the Indian people have been called at most of their towns, at which their chiefs have used these [Supreme Court] opinions to convince them that their rights of self-government and soil were independent of the United States and Georgia, and would be secured to them through the Supreme Court, and the change (which they represent to be certain) in the administration of the General Government.[37]

The inability of the United States Supreme Court to uphold that faith shook the very basis of the Cherokees' belief in law.[38] At the height of the Georgia-Cherokee removal controversy, when tribal unity appeared certain to shatter, the Cherokees brought forward the primitive institution of tribal outlawry. The provision was added as a second clause to the act making cession of land a capital offense. The section provided that any persons who "enter into a treaty . . . to sell . . . National Lands are declared to be outlaws, and any person . . . may kill him . . . within the limits of [Cherokee] Nation, and shall not be held accountable to the laws."[39]

While retention of tribal lands was clearly a national goal, on some issues there were wide discrepancies between the statutes en-

36 *Cherokee Phoenix*, Oct. 28, 1829.

37 Reprinted in *Cherokee Advocate*, Oct. 22, 1831.

38 The author has always contended that the failure to enforce the Supreme Court Decision in *Worcester v. Georgia*, 21 U.S. (6 Pet.) 515 (1832) was the ultimate factor in the development of Treaty Party position on removal. Elias Boudinot expressed the Cherokee attitude in an editorial in the *Cherokee Phoenix*, July 3, 1830. "We are glad to find that the determination of the Cherokees to bring their case before the Supreme Court meets with [approval]. We will merely say that if the highest judicial tribunal in the land will not sustain our rights and treaties we will give up and quit our murmurrings." See also *Cherokee Phoenix* editorials and reports on the Supreme Court litigation in the following issues: July 17, 1830; July 31, 1830; Oct. 1, 1830; April 9, 1831; Jan. 21, 1832; May 12, 1832; May 19, 1832; Sept. 8, 1832; Sept. 22, 1832; Oct. 27, 1832; March 2, 1834.

39 LCN 136–137. John Ridge, one of the ultimate victims of this act, was purported to be the author. Morris L. Wardell, *A Political History of the Cherokee Nation, 1838–1907*, 18 (cited hereafter as *A Political History*).

acted by the committee and council and the policy followed by the nation as a whole. Such instances illustrated the situation in which tribal values were not adequately reflected in the statutes passed by the legislative branch. There was no better example of this than the series of regulations concerning the conduct of Negro slaves owned by the Cherokee Indians.

Slavery as an institution came early to the Cherokees. Colonial records have shown the Indian country as a haven for escaped black men and that the first Negro slaves owned by the Cherokees were brought to the tribe before 1700; South Carolina officials were presented slaves as "presents" from Cherokee chiefs as early as the 1730's.[40] By 1820 the official census of the Nation listed 1,277 Negro slaves owned by the Cherokee people.[41] The number is thought to have reached 4,000 by the time of the Civil War.[42] As a tribe the Cherokees did not possess an institution for use of captive Indian slaves.[43]

Despite the early establishment of the institution, the initial regulation of slave conduct remained highly informal. Yet certain norms of conduct did emerge in the eighteenth century. If anything, the native regulation resembled more closely tenant farmers or hired servants whose control involved very little restriction on private life but retained a clear separation between the red and black races. There was apparently little intermarriage between the Cherokees and the Negroes. The rules controlling the behavior of slaves which were ultimately established did not reflect native experience but were borrowed from the southern states surrounding the Cherokee tribes.

[40] The most authentic and complete picture of the Indian as slaveholder is Annie H. Abel, *The American Indian as Slaveholder and Secessionist* especially Volume I. This section draws upon the excellent analysis found in Michael D. Roethler, "Negro Slavery Among the Cherokee Indians, 1540–1866," (Ph.D. dissertation, Fordham University, 1964). A clear and concise summary is found in J. B. Davis, "Slavery in the Cherokee Nation," *Chronicles of Oklahoma*, Vol. 9 (1933), 1056–1072.

[41] Census, Cherokee Documents, Indian Heritage Association, Pensacola, Florida.

[42] Commissioner of Indian Affairs, *Annual Report*, 1859, 173. The 4,000 total represented all Negroes, free and slave, but the number of freedmen in the Cherokee Nation before 1865 was small since it was illegal for free Negroes to reside in the Nation. *The Constitution and Laws of the Cherokee Nation*, 71, (cited hereafter as CLCN). As a matter of fact, the council of the Northern Cherokees endorsed the Emancipation Proclamation almost immediately after Lincoln issued the document. "Council of Cow Skin Prarie," November 14, 1863, Oklahoma Historical Society.

[43] See especially Nathaniel Knowles, *The Torture of Captives by Indians of Eastern North America*. Timberlake records "the white prisoners . . . becoming slaves." Timberlake, *Timberlake's Memoirs*, 111.

Lewis Ross and a group of slaveholding Indians are reported to have declared in 1845 that the Cherokees inherited "the evil of slavery from the people of the United States and whenever it shall be abolished in the states it shall be likewise abolished in the Cherokee Nation."[44]

As a pattern of plantation agriculture began to emerge, the role of the slave began to conform more closely to that of blacks in the southern cotton kingdoms.[45] The Removal Claims Book shows that in 1835 Joseph Vann owned 110 slaves. Chief John Ross is reported to have kept more than 100 slaves to tend his Rose Cottage in Oklahoma and cultivate those fields. The Lynch family, including all cousins, are said to have supervised more than 400 Negroes. Probably the largest single slaveholder was quarter-blood Joseph Martin, who owned three plantations, one of which was located as far south as Pensacola, Florida.[46]

However, most of the Cherokees were never part of the tribal plantation aristocracy. This group was clearly a minority of mixed bloods, who more closely resembled the white planter than the Indian farmer. While the few Cherokee planters owned large numbers of slaves, most of the slaves remained in the hands of the small farmer, who most likely owned only one or two Negroes, who assisted him with his chores and crops, often on a share basis.

Many Cherokee families, even the poor ones, had slaves. As for the nature of Cherokee slavery, one missionary reported that the "institution was derived from the whites" and had "all the general characteristics of Negro slavery in the Southern portion of our Union." He added, however, that "there must of necessity be some modification of the system."[47]

Just as the institution was borrowed from the southern white,

---

[44] Michael D. Roethler, "Negro Slavery Among the Cherokee Indians, 1540–1866," (Ph.D. dissertation, Fordham University, 1964), 118–19. The southern Indians ultimately paid a high price for this slavery, being forced to share their resources, including land and land-claim payments with their former slaves and the descendants of these freedmen. Worcester to Green, Jan. 17, 1845, Mission Papers of the American Board of Commissioners for Foreign Missions, Harvard University Library, Cambridge.

[45] Henry Rowe Schoolcraft, *Information Respecting the History, Conditions, and Prospects of the Indian Tribes*, I, 339.

[46] Removal Papers, Phillips Collection, University of Oklahoma; Albert D. Richardson, *Beyond the Mississippi, 1857–1867*; Indian-Pioneer Papers, Oklahoma Historical Society.

[47] Mission Papers of the American Board of Commissioners for Foreign Missions, Andover Library, Harvard University.

the means of lawful regulation was also borrowed. Many of the acts designed to restrict Negro conduct were copied from the laws of Alabama and Georgia.[48] While a large number of regulations were adopted and the details of these were modified from time to time, the restrictions were essentially as follows: (1) as a protection for Negro slaves the legislature provided that "any person [who] shall willfully or maliciously . . . kill or mistreat any negro or mulatto slave . . . shall be deemed guilty of murder . . . and shall suffer death by hanging";[49] (2) "no contract or bargain entered into with any slave or slaves, without the approbation of their masters, shall be binding on them";[50] (3) no slave may "sell or purchase spiritous liquors";[51] (4) intermarriage between Negro slaves and Indians or whites was prohibited;[52] (5) no person could purchase goods from a slave without permission of the slave's owner;[53] (6) Negro slaves were prohibited from "possessing property in horses, cattle or hogs";[54] (7) "no person who is of negro or mulatto parentage . . . shall be eligible to hold any office";[55] (8) no Negro could own or carry weapons;[56] (9) Negroes "aiding, abetting, or decoying any slave to leave his or their owner or employer . . . shall receive 100 lashes";[57] and (10) it was unlawful "to teach any negroes . . . to read or write."[58]

Evidence clearly demonstrates that most of these restrictions were ignored. Samuel Worcester wrote the American Board of Foreign Missions that "public sentiment nearly nullifies [the] law."[59] After emancipation former Cherokee slaves recalled that care of the family guns was often "entrusted to a slave who kept them in shape

---

[48] In substance but not form. The Cherokee laws are found in several of their statute books including LCN (1852), CLCN (1852), and LCN (1853) and (1860).
[49] LCN (1853), II, 212.
[50] LCN (1853), I, 9.
[51] LCN (1853), I, 24–25.
[52] *Ibid.*
[53] *Ibid.*
[54] LCN 39–40.
[55] LCN 120.
[56] LCN (1853), II, 44.
[57] LCN (1853), II, 63.
[58] LCN, II, 55–56. In 1855 the Nation enacted legislation making it "unlawful for the Superintendent of Schools to employ any person as teacher suspected of entertaining sentiments favorable to abolitionism." LCN (1860), 23. Those interested in following through Negro education among the Cherokees are referred to T. L. Ballenger, "The Colored High School of the Cherokee Nation," *Chronicles of Oklahoma*, Vol. 30 (1952–1953), 454–62.
[59] Mission Papers of the American Board of Commissioners for Foreign Missions, Andover Library, Harvard University.

and made shots for them."[60] There are many references to use of guns in hunting and fighting by Negroes.[61] The "law prohibiting inter-marriages," while generally followed, the American Board was informed, "is not enforced."[62] Furthermore, the missionary papers note that "it is not uncommon for negroes to possess horses, cattle and swine and no one interfered with their claim or possession."[63]

An illustration of enforcement of a Cherokee law regulating slaves was given by Daniel Buttrick in a letter written to discourage the American Board of Missions from undertaking abolitionist activities among the Cherokees. Buttrick wrote the Board:

In 1841 or 1842, a law was enacted prohibiting the instruction of slaves in reading, writing, etc. I have since instructed a black boy . . . without difficulty. They have sometimes sent their black children to school [and] I have uniformly favored them with the privilege of attending meetings, sabbath schools, etc. so that many of their slaves can read very well the Bible.[64]

The slave laws were not well adapted to the peculiar conditions of the Cherokee people. The enactment of laws lifted from the context of planter society did not fit the slave in an Indian society. The relationship between the Cherokee slaveowner and his slave was more likely to be a personal business relationship in a one-to-one setting. The vast majority of Cherokees never developed any fear of general slave uprisings and were, in fact, quite willing to leave the slaves unregulated as long as they provided a minimum of assistance.[65]

The slave had played a peculiar role in the emerging Indian civilization, for many Cherokees had historically depended upon the Negro as a bridge to white society, especially the full-blood slaveowners who relied upon the Negroes to be English interpreters and

---

[60] Foreman, "Indian and Pioneer Papers," Grant Foreman Collection, Indian Archives Division, Oklahoma Historical Society.

[61] *Ibid.*

[62] D. S. Buttrick to David Greene, Jan. 1, 1845, Photocopy, Indian Heritage Association, Pensacola, Florida.

[63] Mission Papers of the American Board of Commissioners of Foreign Missions, Harvard University Library, Cambridge.

[64] Buttrick to Greene, Indian Heritage Association, Pensacola, Florida, Jan. 1, 1845.

[65] Michael D. Roethler, "Negro Slavery Among the Cherokee Indians, 1540–1866," (Ph.D. dissertation, Fordham University, 1964), 172–73. The immediate impetus to the acts, however, came from the large-scale holders such as the Vanns, whose slaves had been involved in an attempted escape. Wardell, *A Political History,* 119.

translators. An extreme statement of this attitude is found in a report written on the eve of the Civil War by a member of the southern oriented Indian Department. He concluded:

I am clearly of the opinion that the rapid advancement of the Cherokees is owing in part to the fact of their being slaveholders, which has operated as an incentive to all industrial pursuits, and I believe, if every family of the wild roving tribes were to own a negro man and woman, who would teach them to cultivate the soil . . . it would tend more to civilize them than any other plan that could be adopted.[66]

While the regulations were designed for the slave conditions of the Cherokee planters such as Principal Chief John Ross, they did not fulfill the needs or expectations of most Cherokee slaveowners.[67] The rules were enacted by the large-scale Cherokee planters. Buttrick tells us that the restrictions on education "received the sanction of Andrew Vann," who was one of the richest farmers with more than one-hundred slaves.[68] Similarly, the reason for prohibiting slaves from keeping livestock was that their "horses, cattle, hogs, etc. . . . became a nuisance to the master, and a temptation to the slave to steal corn, fodder, etc."[69] Yet the Negro ownership of cattle would not be a nuisance to the slaveowner who relied upon sharing crops with his single Negro tenant.

The needs of the Cherokees responsible for the enactment of legislation were at such variance with the needs and the expectations of the majority of the tribe that the laws were widely ignored. A factor which added to this reluctant enforcement was the nature of the criminal prosecution. Grand juries and tribal prosecution by an official solicitor were not introduced into the Cherokee legal system until after the Civil War. Until that time criminal indictment was essentially a private procedure instituted by a wronged individual, especially in the period following the abolition of the light-horse troops. Therefore, the large-scale planter might enforce the regulation upon his own slaves but was not likely to be concerned whether or not the single slave of a Cherokee full blood kept cattle, purchased goods, or was taught to read or write.[70]

[66] Commissioner of Indian Affairs, *Annual Report*, 1859, 172, 540.
[67] Recent historical research by Gary Moulton indicates that Ross may not have owned as many slaves as is suggested by some of the pre-war accounts.
[68] Buttrick to Greene, Indian Heritage Association, Pensacola, Florida, Jan. 1, 1845.
[69] *Ibid.*
[70] See *An Act Authorizing Appointment of Solicitors or Attorneys*, CLCN 52–53.

Although there was a minor slave rebellion, the system was never faced with the task of regulating hostile slaves because of the generally liberal treatment of the slaves by all Cherokees, especially the plantation owners, and the geographic isolation of the Cherokee country.[71]

In considering the question of transmission of wealth, the Cherokees faced an entirely new problem. This was an area in which little traditional tribal law existed. The Cherokees as a tribe did not begin to accumulate property which could devolve until the mid-eighteenth century to early nineteenth century. Therefore, the problem was not to adapt an existing tribal control into a more civilized form but to create or adopt a system for distribution of wealth where one never existed. The Cherokees were thus free to select a pattern which would reinforce the tribal goals.

The Cherokees, like the later-day framers of the laws for the newly created state of Israel, were making a new start and could adopt a system which reflected "important political, cultural, social and economic" needs of the Nation. In adopting the code for Israel three sources were considered: Jewish law, foreign law, and the law in force in Israel.[72] The Cherokees "copied what suited them in the laws of the whites, rejected what did not suit them, changed and modified and added to them until they obtained a system adapted to their conditions."[73]

My purpose is not to detail the system of distribution of decedent's estates which was established in the Cherokee Nation. Whether one or two witnesses were required to make a valid will is only of antiquarian value. I am attempting to consider the broader implications of the use of "dead hand control" as a device of implementing the Cherokee social policy. Since the Cherokees never developed a concept of trusts or future interests, the analysis presented is what Lewis M. Simes called "the dead hand controlling *at death*,"[74] or social policy dictating to whom property may or may not be devised.

[71] Wardell, *A Political History*, 119. For specific legislation connected with the rebellion see CLCN (1852), 62–63.

[72] Uri Yadin, "The Proposed Law of Succession for Israel," *American Journal of Comparative Law*, Vol. 2 (1953), 143.

[73] William P. Ross, "An Address at a May Celebration, to the Students of the Male and Female Seminaries, of the Opening of Their Schools Fifty Years Ago," in *The Life and Times of Hon. William P. Ross*, Ed. by Mrs. William P. Ross, 228–29 (cited hereafter as *Life and Times*).

[74] Lewis M. Simes, *Public Policy and the Dead Hand*, The Thomas M. Cooley Lectures, Sixth Series, 3.

The Cherokee Indian Council, 1843. One of the very few contemporary paintings of an early gathering of the Cherokee people in Indian Territory is by the famous frontier artist John Mix Stanley. Painted on March 20, 1843, this work portrays the Cherokees with United States agents and representatives of other tribes. Courtesy Oklahoma Historical Society.

ᏣᎳᎩ ᏧᎴᎯᏌᏅᎯ.

CHEROKEE PHŒNIX, AND INDIANS' ADVOCAT

PRINTED UNDER THE PATRONAGE, AND FOR THE BENEFIT OF THE CHEROKEE NATION, AND DEVOTED TO THE CAUSE OF INDIANS.—E. BOUDINOTT, EDITOR.

VOL. II. NEW ECHOTA, WEDNESDAY NOVEMBER 11, 1829. NO. 31.

PRINTED WEEKLY BY
JOHN F. WHEELER,

At $2 50 if paid in advance, $3 in six months, or $3 50 if paid at the end of the year.

To subscribers who can read only the Cherokee language the price will be $2,00 in advance, or $2,50 to be paid within the year.

Every subscription will be considered as continued unless subscribers give notice to the contrary before the commencement of a new year, and all arrearages paid.

Any person procuring six subscribers, and becoming responsible for the payment, shall receive a seventh gratis.

Advertisements will be inserted at seventy-five cents per square for the first insertion, and thirty-seven and a half cents for each continuance; longer ones in proportion.

☞All letters addressed to the Editor, post paid, will receive due attention.

[illegible]

AGENTS FOR THE CHEROKEE PHŒNIX.

The following persons are authorized to receive subscriptions and payments for the Cherokee Phœnix.

Messrs. Peirce & Williams, No. 20 Market St. Boston, Mass.
George M. Tracy, Agent of the A. B. C. F. M. New York.
Rev. A. D. Eddy, Canandaigua, N. Y.
Thomas Hastings, Utica, N. Y.
Pollard & Converse, Richmond, Va.
Rev. James Campbell, Beaufort, S. C.
William Moultrie Reid, Charleston, S. C.
Col. George Smith, Statesville, W. T.
William M. Combs, Nashville, Ten.
Rev. Benney Roberts, Powal, Me.
Mr. Thos. R. Gold, (an itinerant Gentleman.)
Jeremiah Austill, Mobile, Ala.
Rev. Cyrus Kingsbury, Mayhew, Choctaw Nation.
Capt. William Robertson, Augusta, Georgia.
Col. James Turk, Bellefonte, Ala.

INDAINS.

DOCUMENTS

RELATING TO THE BOUNDARY LINE BETWEEN THE CHEROKEES AND CREEKS.

In Executive Council.

New Echota, Cherokee Nation, October 26th, 1829.

Col. H. Montgomery, U. S. Agent,

Sir—Your letter of the 7th of September last enclosing a copy of a letter from the Honorable Secretary of War to yourself could not well have been replied to sooner, for the want of documents containing facts necessary to be referred to in relation to the boundary line between the Cherokee, and Creek Nations. I have taken extracts from sundry official documents which have come to my notice, and I transmit them herewith, for the information and consideration of the War Department.

Document A. No 1, shows that the United States and the Creek Nation by the Treaty entered into at Fort Jackson, on the 9th day of August 1814, have acknowledged, and declared that the south boundary line of the Cherokee nation *crosses* the *Coosa river*; and by refering to No. 2, it will be clearly seen that the United States in treaty with the Cherokee nation made at Washington City, on the 22d day of March 1816, have recognized and definitely established the point of crossing Coosa river as designated by the treaty of Fort Jackson, *to be at the lower end of the Ten Islands on the Coosa river.* No. 3 shews, that the Cherokee nation ceded to the United States, by treaty made at the Cherokee Agency on the 8th day of July 1817, lands east of the Chattahoochee river, "Beginning at the high shoals of the Appalachie river, and running thence, along the boundary line between the Creek, and Cherokee nations, westwardly to the Chatahoochee river, thence up the Chatahoochee river," &c. Thus it will seen that so far as the United States become an interested party in the boundary line between the Cherokee and Creek nations, east of the Chattahoochee, and west of the Coosa rivers, they have fully acknowledged and clearly established it by the treaties herein refered to, and it only remains then, for the Cherokee and Creek nations to define, establish and run out the line between the two nations from the Chatahoochee river to the Coosa rivers; & No. 4 shews, that the United States Government through Jno C. Calhoun, then Secretary of War, in his instructions to the United States commissioners who were appointed to negotiate a treaty with the Creek Nation, dated 8th August, 1820, recognized the lands south of the Etowah and Coosa rivers, to a certain imaginary line, to be the property of the Cherokee Nation.

Document B. No. 5, exhibits a treaty of boundary entered into between the Cherokee and Creek nations, definitively establishing, running, and marking out the boundary line between the two nations, dated 11th December 1822.

Document C. No. 6, shews that the United States through their commissioners on the 25th day of October, 1823, recognized the boundary as established between the two nations and proposed to treat with the Cherokee nation for all their lands lying within the chartered limits of Georgia north of that boundary line, and south of the Etowah and Coosa rivers. No. 7. shews that Jno. C. Calhoun, Secretary of War, in his report on the 24th day of October, 1824, again admits that the Government in 1819, and previous to the running out the boundary line between the two nations, recognized the lands south of the Etowah and Coosa rivers as the property of the Cherokee nation.

Document D No 8, exhibits the exposition of the United States' commissioners who negotiated the treaty of the Indian Springs with McIntosh and his party, shewing that they have fully recognized the boundary line between the two nations as run and marked out, from the Chatahoochee river at Buzzard Roost, near Sand Town, and that the lands claimed, occupied and ceded by the Creeks in that treaty, lay south of and is bounded by said line; and by the treaty entered into between the United States and the Creek nation at Washington city, in the year 1826, the treaty of Indian Springs is declared to be null and void to all intents and purposes, and by this treaty the boundary line established between the Cherokee and Creek nations is especially, and fully recognized and acknowledged—"Beginning at the Buzzard roost on the Chatahoochee river," &c. &c. No. 9, exhibits a letter from Col. H. Montgomery, United States Agent for the Cherokee nation, to Charles R. Hicks, Principal Chief of said nation, under the direction of Governor Troup of Georgia, notifying the nation to appoint commissioners on their part to attend the United States commissioners and surveyor in *retracing* the Cherokee boundary line with the Creeks agreeably to the aforesaid treaty, and Mr. Hicks' reply thereto annexed.

Document E. exhibits a letter of instructions to the Commissioners appointed by Charles R. Hicks on the part of the Cherokee nation, agreeably to the notification received through Col. Montgomery, for the purpose of acting, and attending with the United States commissioners, in retracing the boundary line between the Cherokee and Creek nations, according to the treaty made between the United States and the Creek nation.

Document F. contains the report of the Cherokee commissioners of their proceedings, together with a plot of the survey made by the United States surveyor.

I presume that the United States commissioner, Mr. Bright of Tennessee, who was instructed to survey this boundary, has also made a report to the General Government of his proceedings accordingly.

It is believed that upon examination letter will be found in your office from the late Charles Hicks, Principal Chief, to Return J. Meigs then United States Agent for this nation, enclosing a copy of the treaty of boundary between the Cherokee and Creek nations, requesting that it be transmitted and reported to the War Department; and also a copy of a letter from Col. Meigs to the Secretary of War in compliance with the request, —these facts together with all others on the subject in your office and possession, I trust you have already collected, and communicated to the Hon. Secretary of War in compliance with his instructions to you. It is an incontrovertible fact, that the lands now claimed by Georgia as having been purchased from the Creeks have *always* been in the *peaceful possession* of the Cherokees as *their soil*—and that the Creeks have never occupied nor owned them, nor have they ever ceded them to the United States in any of their treaties—and that no other boundary line has ever been run and marked out between the two nations, previous to the one established from the Buzzard roost on the Chatahoochee river to the Coosa river, thence down the same to the lower end of the Ten Islands,—and that previous to the definitive establishment of this boundary line, the Cherokee nation claimed lands south of said line, and that the boundary as established has been agreed to on the part of the Cherokee nation as a concession from motives of reconciliation, as well as from an anxious desire to have the subject definitively closed.

The claim set up by the state of Georgia, within the new line run under her authority, is altogether *presumed*, and without a shadow of documentary evidence; on the contrary, ours is established by the most sacred of all obligations, our treaties, &c. with the General Government at different periods. It is the established doctrine of all nations, that whenever a difficulty arises in relation to boundaries or otherwise, the question is settled before the occupancy of the territory in dispute—the contrary is the course adopted in the present case; possession is allowed indirectly to be taken by the citizens of Georgia, and the right determined at an after period. We strongly remonstrate against this course of adjusting our difference, inasmuch as it is calculated to encourage the base and lawless border-citizens to intrude upon our rights to the soil, &c. The Secretary of War's late instructions to you is calculated to encourage a further intrusion of the whites, and unless *prompt* and *energetic* measures be not immediately adopted, there is not the least doubt but several hundred families will remove over, and take possession of the territory of the Cherokees before many months.

You will please to advise me for the information of the General Council whether you have reported to the Government, and also the import of the same, likewise if you have received any further instructions from the Secretary of War respecting removing the intruders.

There is another class of intruders removing in possession of the improvements abandoned by the emigrants, under the pretext of obtaining permission of the emigrants,—you will please to state distinctly whether these facts are known to you, and if they are approbated by you, and the grounds upon which they are allowed to do so. if sanctioned. For the information of the General Council you will please furnish a list of the names of all those persons who have enrolled themselves as emigrants for Arkansas. It is hoped that you will not consider this application as unreasonable, when you reflect that it concerns the deep interest of the nation; and the only motive in view is to detect any fraud, or imposition that may be attempted to be palmed on the General Government as well as the nation, by persons enrolling themselves who are not entitled to the rights of citizenship in this nation.

I am sir, very respectfully, your obedient servant,

JNO. ROSS.

[A. No. 1.]

Extract from the 1st Article of the treaty entered into between Major Gen. Andrew Jackson, and the Chiefs deputies and Warriors of the Creek nation, at Fort Jackson, on the 9th day of August, 1814, respecting the cession therein made—to wit:

"Beginning at a point on the eastern bank of the Coosa river, where the south boundary line of the Cherokee nation crosses the same; running from thence down the said Coosa river," &c.

[No. 2.]

The 1st article of a treaty between the Cherokee nation and the United States, entered into at Washington City on the 22d day of March, 1816—to wit:

"Whereas doubts have existed in relation to the northern boundary of that part of the Creek lands lying west of the Coosa river, and which were ceded to the United States by the treaty held at Fort Jackson, on the ninth day of August. One thousand eight hundred and fourteen; and whereas, by the third article of the treaty, dated the seventh of January, one thousand eight hundred and six, between the United States and the Cherokee nation, the United States have recognized a claim on the part of the Cherokee nation to the lands south of the Big Bend on the Tennessee river, and extending as far west as a place on the waters of Bear creek, (a branch of the Tennessee river,) known by the name of Flat Rock, or Stone; it is therefore, now declared and agreed, that a line shall be run from a point on the west bank of the Coosa river, opposite to the lower end of the Ten Islands in said river, and above Fort Strother, directly to the Flat Rock or Stone, on Bear creek, (a branch of the Tennessee river;) which line shall be established as the boundary of the lands ceded by the Creek nation to the United States by the treaty held at Fort Jackson, on the ninth day of August, one thousand eight hundred and fourteen, and of the lands claimed by the Cherokee nation lying west of the Coosa and south of the Tennessee rivers."

[No. 3.]

Extract of the 1st article of a treaty between the Cherokee nation and the United States, entered into at the Cherokee Agency, on the 8th day of July, 1817, respecting a cession therein made—to wit:

"Beginning at the high shoals of the Appalatchy river, and running thence, along the boundary line between the Creek and Cherokee nations, westwardly to the Chatahochy river; thence up the Chatahochy river," &c.

[No. 4.]

Extract of the instructions given by the Hon. John C. Calhoun, Secretary of War, to the Commissioners who negotiated the treaty of the Indian Springs, on the 8th day of January, 1821, dated August 8th 1820—to wit:

"On consulting with the members from Georgia, I am of the impression that a cession from the Creeks of the northern position of their territory, so as to admit of a white population between them and the Cherokees, would be prefered, which you will accordingly first propose and urge on them. In the event of their agreeing to such proposition, it may be proper to observe that there is some uncertainty as to the true line between the Creeks and the Cherokees; and that after investigating the subject two years, in the presence of a delegation from both nations, it is believed that the claims of the Creeks do not justly extend north of a line drawn due west from the high shoal of the Appalachee."

[B. No. 5.]

Creek nation, at Gen. William McIntosh's, in council between the Creeks and Cherokees have this day made a Treaty about their boundary line, viz:

Art. 1st. A line we do hereby acknowledge, shall be run from the Buzzard Roost, on the Chattahoochee river, a direct line so as to strike the Coosa river, opposite the mouth of Will's creek, thence down the bank of said river opposite to Fort Strother, on said river; all north of said line is the Cherokee lands, all south of said line is the Creek lands.

Art. 2d. We, the Commissioners, do further agree that all the Creeks that are north of the said line above mentioned, shall become subjects to the Cherokee nation.

Art. 3d. All Cherokees that are south of the said line shall become subjects of the Creek nation.

Art. 4th. If any chief or chiefs of the Cherokees, should fall within the Creek nation, such chief shall be continued as chief of said nation.

Art. 5th. If any chief or chiefs of the Creeks, should fall within the Cherokees, that is, north of said line, they shall be continued as a chief of said nation.

Art. 6th If any subject of the Cherokee nation, should commit murder and run into the Creek nation, the Cherokees will make application to the Creeks to have the murderer killed, and when done, the Cherokee nation will give the man who killed the murderer, $200.

Art. 7th. If any subject of the Creek nation, should commit murder and run to the Cherokees, the Creeks will make application to the Cherokees to have the murderer killed, and when done the Creek nation will give the man who killed the murderer $200.

Art. 8th. If any Cherokees, should come over the line and commit murder or theft on the Creeks, the Creeks will make a demand of the Cherokees for satisfaction.

Art. 9th. If any Creeks should come over the line and commit murder or theft on the Cherokees, the Cherokees will make a demand of the Creeks for satisfaction.

Art. 10th. All claims of theft from the time of the meeting held at Hickory ground, Coosa river, near Fort Jackson, with the Four Nations, at the time Bools was taken up to this date, it is agreed by the commissioners of both nations that they shall be foreclosed by this treaty.

Art. 11th. All individual debts, the creditors will look to their debtors.

Art. 12th. The Commissioners of both nations do agree the lines described in the foregoing treaty, shall be ratified, when the heads of both nations sign the treaty.

We the Commissioners, do hereby set our hands and seals this eleventh day of December, 1821.

The above treaty of boundary run by Gen. Wm. McIntosh and Samuel Hawkins, commissioners duly authorised by their nation, and Thomas Pettit and John Beamer, authorised commissioners of the Cherokee nation, is forever hereafter acknowledged by both nations to be permanent.

CHEROKEE NAMES.

Chuliod, (Seal)
Old Turkey (Seal)
Ta,car,sut,tah, (Seal)

[See 4th page.]

The newspapers *Cherokee Phoenix* and later *Cherokee Advocate* served the Cherokees by making laws, treaties, and other material generally available to them. Many of the editors were also lawyers who used legal items so often that the Cherokee newspapers were like lawyers' advanced sheets and law reviews.

Original act of the Cherokee National Council. Cherokee laws were first recorded by hand in manuscript copies, which were collected in the official tribal papers. This particular enactment provides for the establishment of the Park Hill Press in 1835. Courtesy Thomas Gilcrease Institute.

Old Cherokee Home, ca. 1850, by Paul Rogers. As the Cherokees began to acquire property and build permanent homes, a need arose for laws regulating inheritance and use of economic resources. New tribal laws were responsive to new social conditions. Courtesy Philbrook Art Center.

William Shorey Coodey was regarded as the principal author of the Cherokee Constitution and is credited with writing the major provisions of the Act of Union of 1839. Courtesy Oklahoma Historical Society.

Jesse Bushyhead. The Cherokees depended upon Bushyhead as a leader in almost every field of endeavor. He was noted as a lawyer and was one of the most distinguished of the Cherokee judges. Courtesy Oklahoma Historical Society.

verend Stephen Foreman. The transi-
n from clan to court was eased by men
e Foreman who served as lawyers and
lges in the newly emerging legal system.
number of these men, including Jesse
shyhead, were also ministers.

Judge John Thompson Adair. A steady
hand and moderating influence in the
Cherokee judicial system was provided by
such men as Adair. Courtesy Thomas Gilcrease Institute.

Judge John Thompson Adair.

A full-blood Cherokee judge. One of t
major reasons for the success of the Che
kee legal system was the participation
both mixed- and full-blood members
the tribe. This full-blood district judge
shown wearing a traditional hunting jack
over his suit. Courtesy Oklahoma Histo
cal Society.

Even after the hunters and trappers had come to the Cherokee Nation, very little personal property was owned by the average Cherokee. A gun, a tomahawk, and perhaps a few horses were the only property of a Cherokee warrior.[75] Women had separate property but even fewer objects. The lands were owned in common by the tribe. Corn was grown on a "common plantation," and a part of each harvest was contributed to the council, who granted it to needy tribesmen.[76] What little property that existed was generally in the hands of the white traders who had married the Cherokees.[77]

The Cherokees feared death and evil spirits connected with death, and as late as 1760 it was reported that "they seldom bury their dead, but throw them into the river."[78] The dead, despite the rare instances described in Timberlake's assertion, were most often buried in a ceremony of considerable religious significance. A Cherokee burial ceremony and the concepts connected with the ceremony were reported by a young military officer who noted that the corpses, "having commonly their guns, tomahawkes, powder, lead, silver ware, wampum, and a little tobacco, buried with them . . . nothing belonging to the dead is . . . kept, but every thing at his decease destroyed." He believed that the custom had been introduced to prevent avarice and "by preventing hereditary acquisitions, [to] make merit the sole means of acquiring power, honour, and riches."[79]

In 1880 the Cherokee informant to anthropologist James Mooney reported that "in former times it was customary to bury with the deceased some of the property belonging to him and to burn the house in which he lived." Mooney noted that, even after the tribe was "drawing an annual pension of $50 in gold from the government," this practice continued.[80] He observed that, "Once a girl died

---

[75] The extent of Cherokee property ownership in the eighteenth century has never been fully considered. However, the best picture can be obtained from a listing of the goods which the English and French brought into the country for trade. An excellent account of this trade is given in John Richard Alden, *John Stuart and the Southern Colonial Frontier: A Study of Indian Relations, War, Trade, and Land Problems in the Southern Wilderness, 1754–1775*, 16–18; also note Jacobs, ed., *Indians of the Southern Colonial Frontier: The Edmond Atkin Report and Plan of 1756*, 11–15.

[76] William Bartram, *Travels*, 512–13.

[77] The best picture of the property of a Cherokee trader who had married into the tribe is found in Eaton, *John Ross and His Nation*, especially Chapter 2, "Andrew Ross Establishes A Cherokee Empire," 48–67.

[78] Samuel Cole Williams, (ed.), *The Memoirs of Lieut. Henry Timberlake*, 90.

[79] *Ibid.*, 90–91.

[80] Mooney, *The Swimmer Manuscript*, 134–35.

and it happened that her annual pension arrived the same day [and so] her mother insisted that the golden coins be buried with her in the coffin."[81]

This "savage" disrespect for property attracted the attention of early missionaries who were eager to introduce the Cherokees to "the advantages of a civilized life." One who visited the tribe in 1760 observed that they had acquired little property and concluded with disgust that "the sole occupation of an Indian life, are hunting, and warring abroad, and lazying at home. Want is said to be the mother of industry, but their wants are supplied at an easier rate."[82]

Those interested in promoting Cherokee progress encouraged acquisition of property through the pursuit of agriculture and industry. Treaties with the United States provided funds and equipment "for the advances of civilization."[83] The Cherokee council began to demand that the government promote economic advances. An indication of this interest is shown by the demands which the Cherokees submitted to their agent in 1803. Their demands included "50 Brass Kettles, 100 Tin Kettles, 200 pairs of Cotton Card, 1000 Blankets, . . . and 1 Gross of Scizzars."[84]

Thus the Cherokees gradually became a people of property. The official census of the Cherokee Nation taken in 1824 and published in the *Cherokee Phoenix* in 1828 revealed that the Cherokee Indians possessed considerable wealth, including slaves, livestock, wheels, and looms, as well as 120 gins, 10 ferries, 9 stores, a turnpike, 6 public roads, and a threshing machine. Elias Boudinot, editor of the *Phoenix*, estimated the aggregate value of this property at $2,200,000.[85]

The exact nature of the ownership of property varied according to the nature of the property. The general concepts of ownership were summarized in the Constitution of 1827, which provided that "the land . . . shall remain, the common property of the Nation . . . but the improvements thereon, and in the possession of the citizens of the Nation, are the exclusive and indefeasible property of the citizens

---

81 *Ibid.*

82 Notes from a Moravian Mission Book transcribed by Grant Foreman. These are found in the Oklahoma Foreman Notebooks, Book 9, Section 3, page 12. Dr. Foreman says "the author of these lines is unknown" but was one of a large group which went into the Cherokee country in 1760.

83 Treaty of Hopewell, in Cherokee Nation, *Treaties* (1852), 14.

84 Letters Received by the Office of Indian Affairs, Cherokee Agency, 1803, National Archives Microcopy.

85 *Cherokee Phoenix*, May 14 and June 11, 1828.

respectively who made . . . or may be rightfully in possession of them."
These requirements were most clearly stated in a petition prepared by
the Cherokee Nation and submitted to Congress when the Dawes
Committee was considering a bill to compel Indian tribes to divide
their land holdings among their individual members. Improvements
could be sold, but land could not. The report concluded that "occupancy and possession are indispensable to holding [land in the
Cherokee Nation], and its abandonment for two years make it
revert to the public domain."[86]

The land was the common property of the nation but could be
used by the individual citizen.[87] Items such as livestock, plows, guns,
and spinning wheels were the sole property of the Cherokee who had
legally "earned" them.[88] Slaves were individually owned and regulated by special laws.[89] Certain properties, such as valuable minerals,
tollroads, turnpikes, and ferries, were operated under lease arrangements and special statutes for the benefit of the entire nation.[90]
Although women had the same rights of ownership as men, certain
classes such as slaves and white noncitizens were forbidden ownership
of property.[91]

It appears that by the beginning of the nineteenth century the
Cherokees had begun to acquire the two essential prerequisites for
the devolution of property after death.[92] They had (1) a permanent
group association and (2) a concept of private property. The groups
of mixed-blood Cherokees who had arrived at this stage, almost fifty
years before the remainder of the tribe, had generally distributed
wealth outside the tribal system.[93]

As early as 1806, when speaking to a group of Cherokees, Thomas
Jefferson predicted the Cherokees' need for laws of inheritance.
Jefferson noted that "when a man has enclosed and improved his

---

[86] *Congressional Record*, 46 Cong., 3rd sess., 781.
[87] LCN 119.
[88] *Ibid.*, 119–120.
[89] *Ibid.*, 8–9, 24–25, 37, 39, 107.
[90] *Ibid.*, 13, 29, 50.
[91] *Ibid.*, 38–39, 143.
[92] Joseph Dainow, "Testamentary Freedom in England," *Cornell Law Quarterly*,
Vol. 14 (1940), 339. The historic rise of control of property by the dead is considered
in the following articles: Austin Wakeman Scott, "Control of Property by the Dead,"
University of Pennsylvania Law Review, Vol. 85 (1936), 139; and Lewis M. Simes,
"Protecting the Surviving Spouse by Restraints on the Dead Hand," *University of
Cincinnati Law Review*, Vol. 26 (1957), 1–16.
[93] Eaton, *John Ross and His Nation*, 48–67.

farm, builds a good house on it and raised plentiful stocks of animals, he will wish when he dies that those things shall go to his wife and children."[94] This question was faced two years later when the Cherokees adopted their first written law. While we have seen that this law established light-horsemen, or Cherokee police, who possessed a very broad power to prevent robbery and "horse stealing," they were also instructed "to give their protection to children as heirs to their father's property, and to the widow's share."[95]

Despite the early statute, as late as 1817 questions of inheritance were yet unsettled. A "Virginia gentleman" reported that "there is no established order of inheritance." He concluded:

After the death of the parents, the relations of the father or mother take away from the children whatever they wish . . . law only binds parents to support their children so long as they live. It is difficult to perceive why they are not under an equal obligation to secure as far as they have power, the means of subsistence to their infants after their death. . . . It is unimaginable that any system of succession, however arbitrary, could be so bad as none at all: and the fact of there being none among the Cherokees, is a great hindrance to the progress of their improvement.[96]

From a crudely written and unenforced statement of broad policy, the Cherokees progressed to a detailed statute regulating such matters as the appointment of administrators, accountings, and publication of notice to the decedent's creditors. By the time of removal from Georgia an elaborate system had been established.

That the Cherokee inheritance laws reflected a uniquely national goal is suggested by the fact that these laws were not directly copied from any state legal system. Traces and even specific wording of the Statute of Frauds is present in the later and more sophisticated codes, but even these represent a distinctly Cherokee approach adapted to meet the needs of the Indian society.[97]

94 Speech, Thomas Jefferson to "Children . . . of the Cherokee Nation," January 10, 1806, The Writings of Thomas Jefferson, XIX, 146.
95 LCN 1.
96 "Reflections on the Institutions of the Cherokee Indians from Observations Made During a Recent Visit to That Tribe: In a letter from a Gentleman of Virginia, to Robert Walsh," June 1, 1817, Thomas Harrison Collection, Item 3, Oklahoma Historical Society, 43–44.
97 The author was certain that these laws were copied in a very literal fashion from those of some other state. However, a detailed examination of the statutes of other states at the time of the adoption of the Cherokee legal system has indicated that this was not an instance of exact adoption. The following were examined and compared with Cherokee law: Acts of Alabama, (1825), (1826), and (1827) especially Title

At least five major social policies or goals of Cherokee society are reflected in the inheritance laws. Perhaps the most obvious of these is the policy of strengthening the family social unit. Another equally clear policy is the prevention of tribal lands from passing into the control of noncitizens. A third is preventing marriage between Cherokees and Negro slaves. The idea of equality of women is also reflected in these inheritance laws. Finally, the announced resistance to Cherokee migration to the Cherokee Nation West motivated these laws.

The problems associated with inheritance reflect a much deeper struggle going on within the Cherokee social body. The shift from a clan-oriented structure, with relationships growing from clan ties, to a nuclear family-oriented system was not easy. Members of the tribe had to restructure their kinship thinking. Priorities had to be reassigned. In essence the matrilineal social structure was supplanted. The new system built upon the strong parent-child relationship. Cherokee attachment to family is legend. The relationship between parent and child was so strong that the National Council, in response to the demands of missionaries, was forced to place a fine on parents who withdrew their children from school during the term.[98]

It was natural that the love of family and desire to strengthen the family social unit should be reflected in the laws of property. The laws of intestate succession clearly provided that "where a person possessing property . . . dies intestate . . . the property shall be divided equally among his lawful acknowledge[d] children, allowing the widow an equal share with the children."[99] But these requirements have also been applied when a valid will disposed of property in a different manner.

James Vann, a wealthy mixed blood, died in 1809 leaving an estate including a large house, slaves, livestock, and a ferry on the

---

IV and Title V; *The Public Statutes of Connecticut, 1824*, Title 31; *Laws of Delaware* (1829), Chapter CCVIII; *Kentucky Laws*, (1821), Chapter CCCXXXVIII; *Laws of the State of Maine*, (1821), Chapter XXXVIII; *Maryland Code* (1829), Chapter XCII; *The Laws of the Commonwealth of Massachusetts From 1780 to 1807*. "An Act directing the settlement of the Estates of Persons Deceased, and for the Conveyance of Real Estate in Certain Cases;" *Laws of the State of New Hampshire, 1828*, Chapter XXV. The author had always suspected that these laws were copied from those of Georgia and was especially disappointed when *A Digest of the Laws of the State of Georgia*, published in 1822, showed that this was not, in fact, the case. See "Statute of Frauds, 29th Charles II" in *Digest of the Laws of the State of Georgia* (Milledgeville: Grantland & Orme, 1822).

98 LCN 14.
99 LCN 53.

Chattahoochee River. He was survived by his second wife, Margaret (known as Peggy), and six sons and daughters. Vann's will, dated May 8, 1808, disposed of his possessions in the following manner:

1st. I hereby give & bequeath unto my beloved wife, Peggy . . . all my household furniture.

2nd. All the rest residue of my property which I shall or may die possessed of by that whatsoever it may or wheresoever it may I give and bequeath to my natural son, Joseph to have and hold forever.

In the name of God amen.

s/ James Vann
Witness: s/ John Ross
s/ A. McCoy[100]

The Cherokee council met and considered the will under the first written law of 1808, which authorized regulating companies "to give protection to children as heirs to their father's property." The council concluded "that all the children are of one father who ought to receive some share of the property & also the widow ought to share alike with the other children & to remain in the House as long as she pleases." The final decree set aside the original will and ordered that "the executor shall allow the greatest share to Joseph Vann & after which you are to allow to the other children & widow such share of the property as you judge right."[101]

Thus the Cherokee council established the rule that an individual must provide for his wife and children. We see an inheritance system along the father's bloodlines which protects children of the same father equally by contrast with the older matrilineal structure. This idea of fairness toward all children is reflected in the law, which included, as citizens with all rights, those children of mixed blood.[102] The same policy of family unity can be seen in the law which precludes sale for debts of "houses, farms and other improvements; household and kitchen furniture, farming utensils; and also, one cow and calf, one sow and pig, and one gun."[103] These inheritance provisions also sought to strengthen the family by excluding from the

---

[100] Grant Foreman Typescripts, Southern Indian Records, Oklahoma Historical Society.
[101] Ibid.
[102] LCN 57.
[103] Ibid., 84.

right to inherit those who were not legally married or those who had abandoned their Cherokee husband or wife.[104]

The second tribal policy which was furthered by the laws of succession was described by John Ross as "limitation of the . . . use of Cherokee property to Cherokee citizens."[105] This policy was shown by a Cherokee National Resolution declaring an intention to resist white maintenance or use of the lands and improvements of the Cherokee Nation.[106] No person other than a citizen of the Cherokee Nation could qualify to inherit property from a Cherokee citizen.[107] The restriction was so strong that a white man could not receive property even from a deceased Cherokee wife unless the couple had living children.[108] This limitation was broader than the inheritance laws, as shown by a general restriction which prohibited a noncitizen from owning any improvements within the limits of the Cherokee Nation.[109]

The intention to preserve "tribal blood" by limiting intermarriage with the Negro is herein reflected. Illegal Negro-Indian marriages prevented inheritance by children of such unions, since property could only descend to "lawful children." Negroes were considered property and were generally prohibited from inheritance of other property.

References to the administration of a Cherokee estate, found in the *Cherokee Phoenix* for November 11, 1829, and June 12, 1830, illustrated the problems of enforcing the policy against inheritance by Negroes. The Cherokee chief Shoe Boots had married a white woman, by whom he had two children. This wife deserted him and took the children with her into Georgia. Shoe Boots then married his favorite Negro slave, who was known as "Lucy" or "Lilcy." The two children born of this marriage were not citizens in the Cherokee Nation. Shoe Boots, one of the most powerful Cherokees, made a special petition to the National Committee and Council requesting that the two black-red children be granted a free status and admitted to tribal membership. The children were given a free status but were not granted tribal membership. The will which Shoe Boots prepared left his entire estate to these two children. However, the chief was

---

[104] *Ibid.,* 10.
[105] Speech, John Ross, October 14, 1826, Broadside, author's private collection.
[106] LCN 10–11.
[107] *Ibid.,* 10.
[108] *Ibid.,* 131–132.
[109] *Ibid.,* 10–11.

induced by a white man to set his mark on a piece of paper as a gesture of friendship. This paper was a will bequeathing his children to the white man.

The National Committee and Council refused to recognize the second will, which had been induced by fraud. In interpreting the first will, the council did not make a clear decision. The status of the free Negro children was recognized. The council decided that the wife and two children in Georgia could not receive the property. Apparently the council did not honor the will and transferred the property to the two Negro children, since, it declared, they were not granted status as "Cherokee citizens."[110]

In the mid-eighteenth century James Adair in his *History of the American Indian* called the Cherokees a "petticoat society" because women were given a position of equality.[111] Others noted that by the beginning of the eighteenth century women had begun to assume a less important role in Cherokee life.[112] However, the inheritance laws of the Cherokees indicated that equality of women was still a basic social goal. Cherokee women were free to own, manage, sell, and devise property in the same manner as Cherokee men. In fact, Cherokee women had complete control of their property, and this property could not be managed by their husbands without consent. A resolution of the National Committee and Council provided "that the property of Cherokee women after their marriage cannot be disposed of by their husband, or levied upon by an officer to satisfy a debt of the husband's contracted contrary to her will and consent."[113] The law was even more strict toward intermarried white men in the Cherokee nation. They were required to forfeit all property to their wives if the couple should part.[114]

The law of inheritance made special provisions for the administration of the estate of a woman. "A woman claiming and having exclusive right to property who dies and leaving a husband and children, her property shall revert to her children and husband."[115]

---

110 *Cherokee Phoenix*, Nov. 11, 1829, and June 12, 1830. This is reported by Starkey who notes that the John Howard Payne Papers contain the "full story" but he reports what is found in the *Phoenix*. Starkey, *The Cherokee Nation*, 18–19.

111 Adair, *American Indians*, 418.

112 Robert Tambory, *Visits in the American Wilderness*.

113 LCN 142–143.

114 *Ibid.*, 10.

115 *Ibid.*, 111–113.

These same rights and duties were extended to white women who had become Cherokee citizens by marriage to Cherokee men.[116]

The provisions of Cherokee law that no Indian "shall possess . . . right nor power to dispose of their improvements in any manner whatever to the United States, individual states, nor individual citizens" was intended to exclude Cherokees who had migrated to Arkansas from ownership of property in the "old nation" in Georgia.[117] The policy of discouraging migration became so strong that the National Committee and Council enacted a bill providing that "if any citizen of this Nation, shall bind themselves by enrollment or otherwise as emigrants to Arkansas [he] shall forfeit . . . all rights and privileges . . . as citizens of this Nation."[118] The social purpose of this act is demonstrated by a decision of the Cherokee Supreme Court in 1830. An old Cherokee named Dark Horse who had four sons provided that each should have a part of the large estate that he had accumulated during his lifetime. However, the court refused to honor the will, which provided for equal distribution of land and divided the property between two sons who remained in the eastern Cherokee lands.[119] The court reflected the attitude of Elias Boudinot in a *Cherokee Phoenix* editorial explaining the relationship with the Western, or Arkansas, Cherokees: "They are our brothers. But they have left us [and] have rights in their own country. They are citizens of another Nation."[120]

Compare these restrictive laws, aimed at preventing movement to the Western Cherokee Nation, with those of the Cherokees in the West. Those already located in Arkansas were eager to encourage their brothers to join them. There were no restrictions upon inheritance rights of the Cherokees in the Nation in Georgia. In fact, inheritance of property was a device which often brought Cherokees to Arkansas.

The ancient Cherokee Indians had developed a primitive institution to limit greed by a religious ceremony of burying property with the deceased. The same use of the laws of inheritance as a social control institution was achieved by the tribe when they adopted many of the elements of the Anglo-American legal system. The

[116] This is suggested by Cherokee Law. LCN 57.

[117] LCN 119, also consider LCN 139–140.

[118] LCN 139–140.

[119] *Cherokee Phoenix*, March 14, 1830.

[120] *Ibid.*, March 18, 1829.

deceased warrior was limited in his choice of heirs by a number of clearly defined tribal goals. These goals are shown by an examination of the early provisions for the transmission of wealth from one generation to the next.

Even if no record of the Cherokee Indians survived except a copy of their laws of succession to property, a fairly accurate picture of the tribal values could be reconstructed. At least five clearly defined social goals would be reflected. These laws show (1) love of family and desire to strengthen the family as a social unit, (2) fear of tribal land passing into the control of noncitizen whites, (3) determination to prevent intermarriage between Cherokees and their Negro slaves, (4) a strong belief in equality of women, (5) resistance of a portion of the tribe to migration to Arkansas.

Corpus of the Cherokee Written Laws

VI

THE ANCIENT Cherokees gathered yearly to hear their custodian of law, the Unagai, read the wampum and recite the body of tribal custom and regulation which governed the life of the Indian.[1] By the year 1898 not only had the meaning of the wampum been lost but no single individual would have been capable of reciting the vast body of treaties, public laws, federal cases, tribal statutes, cases, and regulations that comprised the laws of the Cherokees.

In the ninety years between the adoption of the first written law (1808) and the abolition of tribal courts (1898) the wampum was supplanted by more than a million pages of legal manuscripts and printed material. By 1896 the Redbird Smith-Keetoowah movement of the Cherokees acknowledged that understanding of the wampum had been lost, and recovery of these ancient laws became one of the cornerstones of this nativistic revival.[2]

In the 1870's William Potter Ross oratorically proclaimed to a group of young ladies at the Female Seminary graduation, "The adoption of the first written law at Brooms Town was for the Cherokees like the signing of the Magna Carta at Runnymede in 1215."[3]

---

[1] Haywood, *History of Tennessee*, 243–56.

[2] Robert K. Thomas, "The Origin and Development of the Redbird Smith Movement" (Master's thesis, University of Arizona, 1953), 119–35.

[3] William Potter Ross, Unpublished Address, Cherokee Documents Collection, Indian Heritage Association, Pensacola, Florida. For an interesting contrast see "Extract from William Henry Drayton's Explanation of the 'Rights of Englishmen' to the Cherokee Indians," in A. E. Dick Howard, *The Road from Runnymede: Magna Carta and Constitutionalism in America*, 448–51. Mrs. William Potter Ross, *Life and Times*, 3–14.

In fact, the gathering at Brooms Town on September 11, 1808, has been celebrated among the Cherokees in much the same manner as the confrontation on that famous meadow among the English-speaking peoples.

The Ross analogy was apt, for the road from Brooms Town, like the road from Runnymede, was a long one. Ironically, the law committed to paper at Brooms Town had been enacted by oral agreement more than a decade earlier.[4] But to men like Princeton-educated William Potter Ross the law was not really law until written out in full and in English. Thus, to Ross and the other Cherokees of his generation, the "civilized Indians" were set apart from their "savage" neighbors.

Despite the significance which Cherokee orators of the 1870's and 1880's attached to the act of recording this first law, their ancestors meeting at Brooms Town issued no manifestoes and, in fact, seemed to have placed little importance upon the act of recording the law. There is no evidence that copies of this act were widely distributed among the Villages.[5] As one of the first Cherokee light-horsemen under the new law recalled, "We had no written (printed) laws."[6] The newly enacted regulations were not, in fact, printed until 1821.[7] In a sense, the Cherokee law might seem to be oral law, but there was the important distinction that the law had been written and could be examined by any Cherokee citizen.

The Law of Abbrogation of Clan Revenge in 1810, the Tribal Reorganization of 1818, and the Constitution of 1822 existed in handwritten manuscripts placed with the tribal chief. When the Cherokee Supreme Court began drafting written opinions, the manuscript copies of the laws were transferred to their care. As late as 1826 the Cherokees enacted a statute which requested four legislators to write in longhand six copies of the Cherokee laws so that they could be distributed among the people.[8]

All early laws, including the manuscript copies, were in English,

---

[4] Benjamin Hawkins to James McHenry, *Letters of Benjamin Hawkins, 1796–1806*, 136.

[5] One of the best accounts of adoption and enactment is McKenney and Hall, *Indian Tribes*, 378–79.

[6] *Cherokee Messenger*, Aug. 1844, 16.

[7] Lester Hargrett, *A Bibliography of the Constitutions and Laws of the American Indians*, 5 (cited hereafter as *Bibliography*).

[8] LCN (1852), 81. Citations are to this edition unless otherwise noted. This is, without doubt the most accessible printing of early Cherokee laws.

for in 1808 there was no written Cherokee language. The task of creating a written language for the Cherokee people seemed an impossible one. Attempts by travelers to write a Cherokee vocabulary using the English characters produced some Cherokee words in a garbled kind of phonetic English which was totally unadaptable for use as a written language. Missionaries and their societies, as well as academic linguists, had worked with the Cherokee language with little success. Development of Christian attitudes and support for the newly emerging legal institutions were severely hampered by the absence of a truly effective Cherokee alphabet.[9]

The Cherokees called the long-awaited creation of their written language "the miracle of the talking leaves," and they have assigned to the illiterate, mixed-blood Cherokee cripple who invented their alphabet a special place in their mythological world as a guardian of tribal spirits.[10] Undoubtedly Sequoyah's development of a usable syllabary was the most significant single event in the history of the Cherokee people.

Linguists have noted that the system was clumsy and missed several Cherokee sounds. Missionaries using English characters developed more sophisticated and workable alphabets for other tribes. But Sequoyah's system possessed what Emerson called "the authentic sign." Cherokees came to love their written language. It was theirs. The syllabary had been invented not by missionaries or government agents but by one of their own. The Kilpatricks, in their field research, noted that many Cherokees assigned full-blood status to Sequoyah while, for example, willingly acknowledging the mixed-blood status of political leaders such as John Ross.[11]

The value of Sequoyah's system in the development of legal institutions was the simplicity with which the written language could be learned. Sequoyah himself could neither read nor write the English language and simply adapted English characters until he had eighty-six symbols representing each of the sounds of the Cherokee

---

[9] One noted Cherokee historian argues that in the eighteenth century "absence of a Cherokee written Language undoubtedly helped them along the white man's road, for they early began to utilize the convenience of the newcomer's writing." Malone, *Cherokees of the Old South*, 15.

[10] Gregory and Strickland, *Cherokee Spirit Tales*, 8. See Grant Foreman, *Sequoyah*, 6–40, and George E. Foster, *Se-Quo-Yah: The American Cadmus and Modern Moses*, 96–178.

[11] Jack Frederick Kilpatrick and Anna Gritts Kilpatrick, *Friends of Thunder*, 196, n. 35.

language. Thus an Indian already speaking the Cherokee language could learn to read and write in a matter of days. Elias Boudinot, in his efforts to secure financial support for a tribal newspaper, reported "the simplicity of this method of writing, and the eagerness to obtain a knowledge of it, are evinced by the astonishing rapidity with which it is acquired and by the numbers who do so. It is about two years since its introduction, and already there are a great many who can read it. In the neighbourhood in which I live, I do not recollect a male Cherokee, between the ages of fifteen and twenty-five, who is ignorant of this mode of writing."[12] In some areas the Cherokees sought to counter mission education, which was English-oriented, with schools conducted in the Cherokee language. The National Committee and Council of the Cherokee Nation West passed a resolution that "Mr. George Guess (Sequoyah) be employed to teach school in the Cherokee language."[13]

Sequoyah's syllabary brought literacy to the Cherokees overnight. From the general introduction of the alphabet in 1822 until the publication of the *Cherokee Phoenix* in 1828, most of the young people had acquired skill with the syllabary. Samuel Worcester, whose dedicated use of the alphabet in religious publications earned him the title "Cherokee Messenger," reported that "a large majority of those between childhood and middle age . . . read and write in the Cherokee language."[14] By 1846 the editor of the *Cherokee Advocate* noted with pride that, "in proportion to population, there are fewer Cherokees who cannot read and write either Cherokee or English, than are found in many states of the union."[15]

There is a theory that Sequoyah's achievement is a kind of Arthurian legend, a hoax created by missionaries to make the new written language acceptable, and that the Cherokees rarely used the syllabary for nonreligious purposes.[16] Studies of the records of the Cherokee court system establish that the Cherokee written language was used extensively in the administration of tribal justice. While English was clearly the primary language of the courts, the bilingual nature of the system continued until the abolition of tribal courts

12 Boudinot, *An Address to the Whites*, 12.
13 Resolution, July 11, 1832, in "Cherokee Agency, West," Letters Received by the Office of Indian Affairs, Microfilm Publications, No. 234, Roll No. 78, National Archives of the United States.
14 *Cherokee Phoenix*, March 10, 1830.
15 *Cherokee Advocate*, Jan. 15, 1846.
16 Letter, Traveller Bird to Rennard Strickland, March 13, 1968.

in 1898. In fact, two of the three justices of the Cherokee Supreme Court during the last term requested a Cherokee interpreter "not being altogether familiar with the English language, and not sufficiently so to fully comprehend the English proceedings of court."[17]

The importance of the Sequoyah syllabary to the study of Cherokee law extends far beyond the general benefit of increased literacy. The language system provided an effective medium for exchange of ideas and the ultimate transmission of the new legal system, which had been created by a mixed-blood minority for the full-blood majority. Laws could be printed in Cherokee native tongue. Court proceedings were therefore able to unite two divergent elements of Cherokee society. Many judges, for example, could not read the English language, but the bilingual nature of the court system enabled them to serve the tribe. Chief Thompson, the last non-English-speaking chief of the Cherokees, estimated in 1877 that three-fifths of the tribe "think, reason, and read in Cherokee."[18]

In short, the use of the Cherokee language through the syllabary legitimized the introduction of a questionable legal system drawn from the English-speaking world. The system was made sufficiently Cherokee to be accepted by the reticent full bloods, who conservatively rejected both white dress and language. Sequoyah was himself a traditionalist, a Cherokee conservative, and is said to have resented the use of his language by the missionaries. However, he was proud of the accomplishment of the Cherokees in building a constitutional legal system and even endorsed the act of union and signed the Constitution of 1839. In his last years Sequoyah was fond of telling visitors of Sam Houston who told him, "Your alphabet was worth more than two handfuls of gold" to each Cherokee.[19]

The final triumph of Sequoyah's system was assured in 1828, when the Cherokee Nation acquired a printing press and type cast in the syllabary.[20] From 1828 to 1907 the Cherokee Nation printed

[17] Minutes of Supreme Court of the Cherokee Nation, 1897. Official Cherokee Records, Vol. 234, 226–28, Indian Archives, Oklahoma Historical Society. See also *Cherokee Advocate*, Nov. 17, 1877.
[18] *Cherokee Advocate*, Sept. 5, 1877. Many legal records are found in the Cherokee language. The Kilpatricks have collected and translated a few of these. Jack Frederick Kilpatrick and Anna Gritts Kilpatrick (eds. and transl.), *The Shadow of Sequoyah: Social Documents of the Cherokees, 1862–1964*, 26, 28, 39, 44, 46 (cited hereafter as *The Shadow of Sequoyah*).
[19] Gregory and Strickland, *Sam Houston*, 15.
[20] LCN (1852), 47, 81, 82, 84, 85; Althea Bass, *Cherokee Messenger*, 78–89; Ralph Henry Gabriel, *Elias Boudinot, Cherokee, and His America*, 106–19.

millions of pages of Sequoyah materials. The official language publications were designed to advance the "civilization" of the Cherokees through the operation of a constitutional government and the court system. Religious material was also printed in the Cherokee language but not as regularly by the official tribal press.[21]

The major written influence in the Cherokee legal system was the official tribal newspaper. The newspaper served as advance sheet, treatise, law school, court record, statute book, and legal conscience. The Cherokee Nation published two official newspapers, the *Cherokee Phoenix* and the *Cherokee Advocate*. The *Phoenix* was published at New Echota in the Cherokee Nation in Georgia from 1829 to 1834. The *Advocate*, the successor paper published after removal from Georgia to the Indian Territory, appeared in two series. The first *Cherokee Advocate* was published from 1844 until the pre–Civil war financial crisis forced suspension. The second series was published between 1870 and 1906, when the tribal government ceased to exist.

The influence of the newspaper in support of the court system was neither incidental nor accidental. The purpose of the newspaper was clearly to advance the level of civilization of the Cherokee Indians through the emulation of white institutions. The legal system of the United States was clearly one phase which both the *Phoenix* and *Advocate* felt worthy of adoption. The "Prospectus" for the *Phoenix* sets forth this goal.[22] The editors of the newspaper attempted to accomplish their goal of promoting a sound and viable legal system in four ways: (1) publication of the text of the laws, (2) strong editorials emphasizing law enforcement, (3) factual reports of crimes and details of punishment, and (4) articles explaining operation of the Cherokee legal system and law-oriented stories reprinted from other papers.

One of the major features of the Cherokee papers, especially the early issues of the *Phoenix*, was the publication of the Cherokee laws, which were generally run on the front page in both English and Cherokee. The English and Cherokee laws were not run in parallel

---

[21] See generally Carolyn Thomas Foreman, *Oklahoma Imprints, 1835–1907* and Lester Hargrett, *Oklahoma Imprints, 1835–1890* which contain an extensive bibliography of Cherokee language publications as does James Constantine Pilling, *Bibliography of the Iroquoian Languages.*

[22] Elias Boudinot, "Prospectus for *Cherokee Phoenix*," Newspaper Collection, Oklahoma Historical Society.

columns as is generally supposed.[23] This newspaper printing was the only publication of many revised statutes. Newspaper copies are often found pasted in the back of Cherokee law books (an example is a Cherokee-language law book in the collection of the Indian Heritage Association; interestingly, both the Cherokee and the English newspaper columns are included).

The newspaper editorial columns regularly encouraged enforcement and support of the laws. Editorials were directed to officers who were slow or unwilling to arrest their constituents. A "Word to Sheriff" from the *Cherokee Advocate* illustrates the use of printer's ink to strengthen the legal system. The editor reports, "Several scenes have occurred from the too frequent use of intoxicating liquors." Then follows the demand that the sheriff "put into exercise the duty required of him by law, and rid the neighborhood of the nuisances of the whiskey shop."[24]

Both the *Phoenix* and the *Advocate* editors believed in teaching by example. The newspaper reports of punishment received by criminals were extensive.[25] Hangings were featured, with the added note of the gallows confession which acknowledged guilt, justness of the court and criminal sanctions including the hanging, and a warning to others not to follow the criminal way.[26] The report of the hanging of Bear-Paw was typical. "This day, I address you, My Uncles, that you may abandon the practice of drunkeness," began the gallows oration. "Forsake all evil, I say, follow that which is good," the prisoner concluded.[27]

During the height of the Cherokee civil war of the 1840's the *Advocate* columns regularly chronicled murders, robberies, and crimes of arson. The steps from crime to arrest to trial to punishment were followed from week to week. More than seventy-five issues of the *Cherokee Advocate* during 1845 and 1846 carried stories of the lawlessness and warfare of the tribal struggle. Most of the issues contained several such stories. It is especially interesting to view the controversial Starr family during their reign from 1844 to 1846. The

---

[23] See for example *Cherokee Phoenix*, March 13, 1828, p. 1., c. 1.

[24] *Cherokee Advocate*, July 10, 1845.

[25] For samples of these stories see the following issues of the *Cherokee Advocate*: Oct. 19, 1844; Nov. 9, 1844; Jan. 23, 1845; Feb. 13, 1845; July 17, 1845; Dec. 25, 1845; April 2, 1846; Oct. 22, 1870; Sept. 13, 1873; June 3, 1876; Oct. 17, 1877; May 11, 1878; Sept. 9, 1893; and Oct. 31, 1893.

[26] *Cherokee Phoenix*, May 14, 1828.

[27] *Ibid.*, May 28, 1828.

accounts began in the *Cherokee Advocate* of November 2, 1844, with the report: "Starr gang runs loose in the Cherokee Nation." Their escapades were followed until the *Advocate* of September 17, 1846, announced that the Starrs appeared after amnesty had been granted them. All the Starrs' alleged robberies, murders, and crimes were graphically described from the viewpoint of the Ross faction in the Cherokee civil war.

When the newspaper purchased a font of italic type, W. P. Ross used it for added emphasis in his report on punishments. The reader can almost feel the suffering of the Cherokee criminals:

Twiged—on tuesday, 25th ult., Young Terrapin A-quo-nie convicted in Flint District, of having stolen saddles were punished with *Thirty-nine* stripes; and, on the day following with *one-hundred and ten* stripes each, for burning the store house of Colonel W. S. Adair.[28]

For fear that some reader might miss the point of the report of punishment, an editorial comment followed, such as, "This teaches the lessons of crime." One editor noted, "This case should serve as a warning to the actual perpetrators of murder as well as those who aid and abet it."[29]

Reading the *Phoenix* and *Advocate* was about all the legal education some early lawyers received. Considering the frequency of reports on trials, explanations of the law, and statutes, it may not have been such a bad education. The editors often chose to reprint legal items from exchange papers. The general reader would be attracted by the sensational facts and also be introduced to the workings of the law.[30]

The newspaper was for the lawyer an early "case-method" approach, as illustrated by the reprint of a judge's charge on "common law murder doctrines." One editor noted that the material "should be read with attention by our lawyers" since "it embodies many principles . . . that will be advantageous to them in their practice."[31] By 1880 the *Advocate* editor had adopted the policy of printing court opinions and wrote, "We publish a decision of the Supreme Court

28 *Cherokee Advocate*, Jan. 9, 1845.
29 *Ibid.*, April 2, 1846.
30 Note the following stories *Cherokee Phoenix*, July 8, 1829 [criminal laws of England so harsh that juries want to let accused escape on technicalities]; *Cherokee Phoenix*, Dec. 10, 1831 [life of John Marshall]; *Cherokee Phoenix*, Jan. 31, 1832 [criminal jurisdiction]; *Cherokee Advocate*, Nov. 9, 1844 [charge to jury in Philadelphia murder trial]; *Cherokee Advocate*, May 26, 1880 [Iowa concept of justice]; and *Cherokee Advocate*, June 13, 1894 [joke about western judge and lawyer].
31 *Cherokee Advocate*, Nov. 9, 1844.

of Iowa, on account of its correct principle laid down, and of its justice; for the information of our courts. We have seen similar cases tried here, and they may come up again."

Full-length explanations of how selected phases of the Cherokee laws operated were printed. Essays appeared on grand juries, contempt of court, demurrers, disqualification of jurors, and duties of officers of the court. The *Cherokee Advocate* was edited almost exclusively by mixed-blood lawyers, who naturally drew upon their own interests for materials to fill the paper. Rarely did a Cherokee editor have an assistant, a reporter, or even a secretary, and since the pressure for copy was great, the lawyer naturally turned to legal issues.[32]

In a sense, the newspapers were an early law review or loose-leaf service not unlike a weekly legal paper—a periodical treatise on Cherokee law. Many issues contained stimulating and highly informative discussions of specific points of view on legal questions of benefit to bench and bar, if not to the general reader.

The first printed volume of Cherokee laws appeared in 1821 under the title *Laws of the Cherokee Nation passed by the National Committee and Council.* The book, printed in English at Knoxville, Tennessee, is the earliest known publication of the laws of an American Indian tribe. An act of each of the council sessions of September, 1808, April, 1810, and May, 1817, plus the acts and resolutions of the regular October sessions of the council for 1819 and 1820 comprise the laws printed therein.[33]

White intruders on Cherokee land constituted, without question, the primary legal problem of the council and committee. Records of the tribal agency are filled with the complaints of individual Cherokees who suffered indignities from white men illegally residing or traveling in the Cherokee Nation. These intruders, noncitizens, beyond the jurisdiction of the Cherokee authorities, provided the immediate motivation for the publication in printed form of the

[32] *Ibid.,* May 26, 1880; Sept. 19, 1877; Nov. 24, 1877; Jan. 18, 1877; Oct. 24, 1877; Sept. 13, 1873; July 10, 1845; March 14, 1877; Dec. 9, 1881; April 1, 1891. Gregory and Strickland, *Starr's History of the Cherokee Indians,* 297.

[33] The title page of the volume is as follows: *Laws of the Cherokee Nation, passed by order of the Committee and Council.* Knoxville Register Office by Heiskell & Brown, 1821. Only two copies are known to have survived and these are in the New York Public Library and the New York Historical Society. Lester Hargrett, *Bibliography,* 5. The same Tennessee printer had, in 1819, printed a Cherokee spelling book of Buttrick, a missionary, using the Roman alphabet which is believed to be the first book printed in the Cherokee language.

Cherokee laws. The immediate impetus behind the initial publication of the manuscript laws was suggested in a letter from chiefs Path Killer and Charles Hicks to Agent Return J. Meigs.[34] Path Killer and Hicks wrote, "You will please to have the laws published in [sic] some of the printers that the law may be well known among our white brethren that none may plead Ignorance." Thus the two great early leaders, whose support guided much of the formation of the written law, outlined the reason why the Cherokees wished their Intruders Law to be printed. (Note that this was before Sequoyah's alphabet and that the publication was to be in English.) The stated purpose of notification to whites could have been achieved only by English-language publication.

The letter, reprinted below, illustrates the manner of enactment of laws as well as containing what appears to be the first order for publication of a Cherokee legal document:

Newtown Nov. 2nd 1819

Friends and Brothers

We have at this Council passed a law that no Cherokee shall employ white persons as farmers or cropers and only millers, Ferrymen & black smiths and school masters or mechanics are allowed to remain in our land only for term, by permission, we desire also that the [sic] be removed by the first of January next. Missionary Schools and white men having Indian families will enjoy the same privileges as they have ever done, and, we would desire likewise that you will please to have the laws published in some of the printers. That the law may be well Known among our white brethren that none may plead Ignorance of those which may concern of the whiskey peddlers & other peddlers of merchandize and we would ask the aid of you in particular in regard of the whiskey and to furnish the nation with fifty printed copys of the laws passed here, and charge the expenses to our Anuity.—

Your Friends & Brothers
his
Path X Killer
mark
C. Hicks

More than two hundred editions of Cherokee laws are believed to have been published. These range from broadside announcements

34 Letter, Path Killer and Charles Hicks to Return J. Meigs, Nov. 2, 1819, Records of Cherokee Indian Agency in Tennessee, National Archives, Microfilm Number 208, Roll 8.

of a single new regulation through the 1893 edition of *Laws of the Cherokee Nation*, which contained more than four hundred pages of regulations. Both Cherokee and English editions of most laws were published.[35]

The process of publication was generally the same. Both the English and Cherokee translation appeared in the tribal newspaper. An excellent example of this procedure was in the publication in 1878 of "Penal Law: An Act for the Protection of the Public Domain, and in Relation to Intruders upon the Same." The law was signed by the principal chief on December 12, 1878, and issued as a quasi-extra number of the *Cherokee Advocate* in a broadside of two columns headed "Weekly Advocate/Published every Saturday by the Cherokee Nation/Official Journal of the Nation/Saturday, Dec. 28, 1878." Following the text of the law was the rather bitter comment of the printer: "This being Christmas week, and according to usage, we did not intend to issue any paper this week; but a penal law over which we had no control compels us to 'publish' this Christmas gift!"[36]

If the publication was not a general revision or if a new edition of the laws was not soon planned, a pamphlet containing the new laws was issued. Upon occasion, the newspaper edition was the only general publication of laws which were of a private nature or of a limited duration or application. After 1893 all copies of Cherokee laws were printed either in a single sheet or a pamphlet. The *Cherokee Advocate* of May 16, 1877, reported that "the laws enacted by the Council will be published in pamphlet form immediately—both in Cherokee and English." The task of preparing these pamphlets placed quite a strain on the limited resources of the newspaper offices.

[35] The Hargrett bibliography lists 87 items classed as Cherokee "constitutions and laws." Hargrett, himself, has located several additional items and the author has examined numerous smaller items and sheets of laws which are not included in general bibliographies. There are probably more than 100 printed versions of Cherokee laws. Hargrett, *Bibliography*, 5–40, see also Lester Hargrett, *Oklahoma Imprints, 1835–1890*, Item 399; Carolyn Thomas Foreman, *Oklahoma Imprints, 1835–1907*, and James Pilling, *Bibliography of the Iroquoian Languages*, 38–44. The author believes from study of contemporary evidence, especially reports in the *Cherokee Advocate*, that if single leaf, legal forms, and pamphlet laws are counted that considerably more than 200 items were published. Use of the broadsheet was common procedure for the Cherokee Nation, especially in printing the rules of procedure which each new senate and council adopted.

[36] The Thomas Gilcrease Institute has preserved the only known copy of this edition of the *Penal Law of 1878*. Hargrett, *Bibliography*, 28. *Cherokee Advocate*, Dec. 28, 1878.

In fact, in 1830 the *Phoenix* suspended publications of "our next paper . . . for the purpose of printing the acts of the last session of the General Council."

Ultimately, most laws were issued in hardback form in editions of approximately 1,000 copies in English and 1,000 copies in Cherokee. Only 500 copies in English and Cherokee of the *Laws of the Cherokee Nation* (1845) and *Laws of the Cherokee Nation* (1853) were printed. As few as 300 copies of *Laws and Joint Resolutions of the National Council* (1871) were ordered, while 2,000 copies of the English edition and 1,500 copies of the Cherokee edition of *Constitution and Laws of the Cherokee Nation* (1893) were issued. Most editions contained an act authorizing publication which set forth the number of copies authorized.

Often the same type was used as that used in the newspaper edition, although some editions were not issued by the official Cherokee Nation Press. Many of the early laws were printed by private firms in Tennessee or Washington, and most of the final laws were the work of job printers in the Indian Territory. More than eighteen separate firms are known to have published the Cherokee laws. When the American Board of Mission Press, at Park Hill in the Cherokee Nation, issued the printed tribal laws for 1839, 1840, and 1841, Samuel Worcester noted in his annual report that the Nation paid the mission press for this work.[37]

Cherokee printed laws were widely distributed. Attorneys were expected to purchase their copies, but the chief was charged with placing the laws in the hands of all public officials and with "posting a copy" in the seven district courthouses. The *Cherokee Advocate* of July 29, 1876, stated requirements of "hanging up the books of law at each of the court houses." The *Cherokee Phoenix* of February 4, 1829, reported the laws and constitution "printed in parallel columns for sale at this office." Cherokee-language copies were free to non-English-speaking readers, and merchants made these editions available in their stores.[38] Supreme courts in other states and territories were provided copies on an exchange basis. All federal government agencies were to receive copies distributed by the executive secretary of the Cherokee Nation.[39]

[37] Samuel Worcester Papers, American Board of Foreign Missions. Houghton Library, Harvard University.
[38] *Cherokee Advocate*, March 11, 1876.
[39] *Ibid.*, July 4, 1877.

The Cherokee Nation generally relied upon the government publication of United States treaties, laws, and regulations. The chief kept the original copies of all treaties and agreements in the public archives, but these were essentially ceremonial or symbolic documents. The *Phoenix* and *Advocate* published the complete texts of regulations, laws, and other government enactments which related to the Cherokee people. Often sections of congressional hearings and debates, presidential messages, and documents were also printed. Elias Boudinot was careful to reprint relevant materials on Cherokee removal during his tenure as *Phoenix* editor. A sampling of congressional documents may be found in the pages of the *Cherokee Advocate* as new legislation was limiting the jurisdiction of Cherokee tribal courts.[40]

Although a pamphlet version of the Trade and Intercourse Act was printed in English, until after 1850 no attempt was made to publish Cherokee-language editions of treaties and regulations. This is understandable since negotiations and correspondence between the United States and the Cherokees after 1800 were almost exclusively in English. After 1850 the Nation published such documents with the regularity of tribal law. An 1884 two-volume edition of treaties and regulations, in both Cherokee and English, was definitive and remained in use until tribal dissolution.[41] In order to make the most significant treaty provisions available, the texts of treaties were printed in the back of the regular editions of the Cherokee laws. As the body of federal regulation and treaty law expanded, only relevant excerpts were included in the law books. These generally concerned land provisions and tribal boundaries.[42]

There is a general impression that the Cherokees produced a number of treatises on Indian law. This is not correct. Only two books which could be described as legal texts were published during the ninety years of the Cherokee court system. These were *The Nut-*

---

[40] See *Cherokee Advocate*, May 16, 1894 [Indian Territory court bill], March 6, 1895 [court bill], Feb. 5, 1898 [Curtis Act]. Almost every issue of the *Cherokee Phoenix* contains these materials. Note the *Cherokee Phoenix*, Aug. 14, 1830; Sept. 4, 1830; Sept. 18, 1830; Jan. 22, 1831; July 30, 1831; Oct. 22, 1831; Jan. 21, 1832; Nov. 24, 1832; and Dec. 1, 1832.

[41] The most readily available edition is probably *Treaties Between the United States of America and the Cherokee Nation from 1785* published in 1870 by the National Printing Office in Tahlequah. Both the Hargrett and Foreman bibliographies have missed these editions which bear the year 1883 on the title page but were not issued until 1884.

[42] CLCN (1892), 407–26.

shell: Cherokee Constitution and the Laws and Rulings Bearing on the Autonomy of the Cherokee Nation Condensed in a Nutshell, published in 1894,[43] and *Cherokee Citizenship and a Brief History of Internal Affairs in the Cherokee Nation,* which appeared in 1895.[44]

Failure to produce a body of interpretative literature is understandable. The legal profession was small. Most judges and lawyers were not full-time legal officers but were ministers, farmers, ranchers, and merchants. The early system was designed to stress simplified pleading and statutes, and questions presented were rarely sufficiently complex to require detailed analysis. There was a deliberate attempt to avoid technical questions. In later periods, when a body of law became complex, as in railroad operations, citizenship, or administration of estates, the highly trained specialist, such as Elias C. Boudinot, Robert L. Owen, or W. W. Hastings, with law-school educations, assumed most of this work. The lawyers' "ads" in the *Cherokee Advocate* often stated specialization. For example, on one occasion the editor noted that "Campbell Taylor, Esq., seems to have pretty much all the practice before the citizenship court, as he is the only attorney who is a regular attendant."[45]

The birth of the Indian law treatise signaled the beginning of change for the tribal legal system. In Cherokee courts there was never a commercial market for published interpretations. Most of the tribal lawyers were familiar with the process of growth and evaluation of doctrines in such a small judicial system, with many lawyers learning their trade in Cherokee law offices. These treatises were an outgrowth of the movement toward termination, not a genuine product, of the Cherokee court system. As more and more non-Indian lawyers began to practice in the congressionally authorized Indian Territory courts, interpretative law books were needed to explain the Indian law which governed land, inheritance, jurisdiction, and citizenship questions. The new books covered laws of all the Five Civilized Tribes, since the

43 Wilson⸱ Otho Bruton and William Christopher Norrid, *The Nutshell: Cherokee Constitution and the Laws and Rulings Bearing on the Autonomy of the Cherokee Nation Condensed in a Nutshell.* Muskogee, Indian Territory: The Phoenix Printing Company, 1894. The only known copy of this treatise is at the Oklahoma Historical Society.

44 W. J. Watts, *Cherokee Citizenship and a Brief History of Internal Affairs in the Cherokee Nation.* Watts and his "Cherokee Citizenship Association" were in the center of tribal controversy. *Cherokee Advocate,* Feb. 4, 1894; Feb. 28, 1894; March 21, 1894; April 18, 1894; April 25, 1894. "John Watts: A Name Engraved in the Cherokee Nation," *Chronicles of Oklahoma,* Vol. 44 (1966), 330–32.

45 *Cherokee Advocate,* July 11, 1877.

Indian Territory lawyer would not be limited to practice under the laws of the Cherokee Nation but would be using Indian laws in federal courts.

Zechariah Chafee, Jr., has observed that the appearance of written opinions was a sign of a maturing judicial system.[46] From the very beginning of an organized appellate court system in 1822, Cherokee Supreme Court justices were required to write an explanation citing the reasons for their decisions. These early judicial opinions were in manuscript form, and no effort was made to publish them.[47] The bar was small, and memory would serve in all but the most complex cases. Pleadings were simple, and the issues raised were rarely complex. The nation was small, with a population of fewer than fifteen thousand persons. Those who appeared as counsel before the courts were, without exception, active in the National Council or government agencies which met in New Echota at the same time as the Supreme Court. The manuscript opinions were kept on file in the courthouse at New Echota and could be consulted if a question arose.[48] Judicial continuity created a situation in the early years in which the bench would be familiar with all decisions rendered at other terms. There was no need for printed opinions by lower courts because the same judges served on district and supreme courts.[49]

The situation became more complicated after removal from Georgia. The circuits were larger, and the lower courts began to acquire their own judges. Population increased, geographic areas expanded, the bar was enlarged, and issues became more complex. As early as 1850 the Cherokee Supreme Court reflected on the need to make printed opinions available.[50]

[46] Zechariah Chafee, Jr., "Delaware Cases, 1792–1800," reprinted in David H. Flaherty, *Essays in the History of Early American Law*, 489–91.

[47] "Record Book of the Supreme Court of the Cherokee Nation, 1823–1835," Tennessee State Library, Nashville, Tennessee. "*Resolved by the National Committee and Council,* That the Judges of the District Courts, shall keep a record of the proceedings of all causes, evidences, and decisions." (LCN 1852), 26.

[48] The specifications for construction of "a court house built at Echota, for the Supreme Court of the Cherokee Nation" are found in a resolution of November 17, 1828. LCN (1828), 114–15. The State of Georgia has rebuilt the Cherokee Supreme Court and restored much of the old capitol at New Echota.

[49] LCN (1852), 18, 26, 28, 90–91, 97, 101–102.

[50] For general tribal developments during this period see Grant Foreman, *The Five Civilized Tribes* 281–426. Most of the legal records for this period were destroyed during the Civil War as is noted in a petition from the Cherokee bar to the Supreme Court. H. E. Reese, Motion to the Honorable Supreme Court of the Cherokee Nation, 1867, Indian Archives, Oklahoma Historical Society.

Again the *Cherokee Advocate* provided valuable service to the legal system. Important opinions were printed, though with no regularity. In 1887 the *Advocate* announced that the justices would publish their opinions from the current term.[51] Apparently no publication of these opinions appeared. A synopsis of opinions, which was also announced as forthcoming from the Supreme Court, did not make print.[52] The courts eventually published a small pamphlet entitled *Rules of Procedure in the Supreme Court of the Cherokee Nation.*[53]

The courts continued to write manuscript opinions. Over five thousand pages of these handwritten reports have survived, dating from 1822 and including the first and last opinions of the Cherokee courts. The occasional written opinion of a lower court was much less significant than the massive body of Supreme Court judicial reports, which were kept on file by the clerk of the court in the Cherokee Nation capital at Tahlequah.

The laws of the Cherokee Nation required complete records of all court proceedings from initiation to completion. Cases appealed were decided on the record and required transcripts of evidence, as well as pleadings, jury charges, and *all* papers in the case. While lower courts produced few written opinions, hundreds of thousands of pages of Cherokee judicial records survive. Ironically, there is no absolutely complete record for any of the seven judicial districts.[54]

The legal system of the Cherokees as set forth in the printed laws had great symbolic value to the tribe. Whenever the civilization of the Cherokees was at issue, the written law was paraded forth as final and indisputable evidence of Cherokee accomplishment. As early as 1828, Elias Boudinot used the recently published laws for this purpose in a speech before a missionary society in New Haven, Connecticut.[55]

The widespread distribution of these laws was a part of the deliberate campaign to influence attitude toward Cherokee achievements. The editor of the *Advocate* was most disturbed when the secretary of the interior had to write for a copy of the laws. He demanded to know "of what use will it be to argue to the good people

[51] *Cherokee Advocate,* Oct. 24, 1877.
[52] *Ibid.,* Dec. 9, 1871, and Jan. 9, 1889.
[53] *Ibid.,* Jan. 28, 1878; Jan. 13, 1882; March 3, 1882.
[54] Rella Looney, "Inventory of Records of the Cherokee Nation." Indian Archives, Oklahoma Historical Society.
[55] Boudinot, *An Address to the Whites,* 10–11, and Letter, Samuel Worcester to William S. Coodey, March 15, 1830, in *Cherokee Phoenix,* May 8, 1830.

of the United States that we have progressed . . . , and are therefore entitled to their respect and intervention against attempts by the greedy and covetous to wrong us, if we do not take the trouble of giving them evidence we have progressed and are progressing?"[56]

[56] *Cherokee Advocate*, July 4, 1877.

Lawyers, Judges, and Sheriffs: Cherokee Courts in Operation

VII

AMONG the ancient Cherokees there were no counselors for those accused of violating tribal laws. "Criminals before a judiciary had no advocate or lawyer," an early informant reported. All cases "were brought forward and explained by an official called *ki wani gali*," and "the criminals then defended their own cause."[1] Lawyers were a new element in the system.

Students of the process of modernization have reported that a most important factor in securing support for new systems and the values they symbolize is the emergence of a "transitory professional elite."[2] Among the Cherokees this class came to be represented by the law profession and the officers of the courts. A group of bright young men trained in the law were drawn to the management of the business of the Nation. These men believed that survival lay in acculturation rather than in resistance to change. They were secular men of affairs who understood—as a religious elite would never have been able to understand—that incantations and indictments could be mixed to create a meaningful and "civilized" system of laws.

Tribal leaders, in their early negotiations with colonial officials, soon began to assume duties not unlike those of the modern lawyer. One of the perennial sources of conflict with Charles Town centered in the crimes committed by Cherokees and against the Cherokees. Thus Indian politicians began to develop legal arguments regarding tribal legal liability which were presented to the colonial governors.[3]

[1] John Howard Payne Papers, Roll 6986.
[2] David E. Apter, *The Politics of Modernization*, 138–78.
[3] Reid, *A Law of Blood*, 247–69.

This produced an individual whom I have described as an "international lawyer, frontier style."[4]

Many of the whites who came to live among the Cherokees were familiar with the legal practices of the colonies and with the common law in England. Among the most outstanding of these were the forebears of the Martin, Hicks, and Taylor families.[5] The most notable of this group of white settlers was probably Joseph Martin, of Virginia, whose descendants served the Cherokee Nation as judges and lawyers for more than 150 years. No doubt these early whites performed many services that we would today consider legal services.[6]

The first generation of native Cherokee lawyers were the mixed-blood children of the early whites, who were attorneys in the sense of many gentlemen of the southland. They were essentially planters, farmers, and merchants who had read law in an office or picked up some knowledge from their own experience, observation, and study.[7] Foremost among this group was Charles Hicks, whose Virginia-born father had sent him to a private school in his native state. Because of his influence among the full-blood leadership, Hicks was an important figure in the period of transition from the older Cherokee laws. After his death the *New York American* observed:

It has been good fortune of the Cherokees to have had born to them some great men. Of these, Charles Hicks, lately a Chief, stood preeminent. Under his guiding council, and aided by the policy of the national government, they have outstripped the other tribes in the march of improvements. They seek to be a people, and to maintain by law and good government, the security of persons and the right of property.[8]

None of these early lawyers had office or Inns of Court education. These men—Charles Hicks, James Bell, Richard Taylor, John Martin—were the authors of the first written laws and were the early jurists.

[4] Gregory and Strickland, *Sam Houston*, 104–109.
[5] Ross, *Life and Times*, 224–29; *Cherokee Phoenix*, Aug. 12, 1829; *Cherokee Advocate*, Nov. 18, 1891; Aug. 6, 1879.
[6] Gregory and Strickland, *Starr's History of the Cherokees*, 292, 493, 543, 647–48, and discussions with Earl Boyd Pierce, Cherokee tribal attorney and descendant of the Martins. Colyer Meriwether, "General Joseph Martin and the Cherokees," *Southern History Association Publications*, Vol. 8 (1904), 443–50; Vol. 9 (1905), 27–41.
[7] See Anton-Hermann Chroust, *The Rise of the Legal Profession in America*, I, 239–329; II, 92–128.
[8] Reprinted in *Cherokee Phoenix*, Aug. 12, 1829; Robert S. Walker, *Torchlight to the Cherokees*, 26, 37, 63, 89, 113, 123.

In the years between 1830 and 1860 these first Indian barristers were followed by a second generation of Cherokee attorneys, many educated in eastern seminaries or universities.[9] Others had followed a program of reading for the law in the offices of prominent practitioners.[10] William Potter Ross, nephew of Chief John Ross, was educated at Lawrenceville, Princeton, and read law.[11] The Reverend Stephen Foreman attended Virginia Theological Seminary and Princeton but received his legal training as translator of the tribal laws for the *Cherokee Phoenix* and as a clerk.[12] Elias C. Boudinot, after preparatory school in the east, was forced by financial circumstances to read law in the office of W. C. Wilson, of Fayetteville, Arkansas.[13] Stand Watie had only limited formal education but served as clerk for the Cherokee Supreme Court.[14]

The finest of the last generation of lawyers to practice in the Cherokee court system were introduced to their profession through study in law schools. Outstanding among this group was W. W. Hastings, whose distinguished career ranged from tribal courts as Cherokee national attorney through statehood as United States congressman from the Oklahoma Second District.[15] Hastings' education was described by another distinguished member of the Cherokee bar, Judge William Preston Thompson. The judge recalled, "We went to the old log school house, . . . to the old Male Seminary, Tahlequah, Oklahoma, . . . to Vanderbilt University, Nashville, Tenn., graduating in the Law Department."[16]

But practical education and experience in the legislative and executive branches of the government remained the most common

[9] Princeton and Dartmouth were the colleges most regularly attended by this Cherokee elite. The general picture can be drawn from Kathleen Garrett, "Dartmouth Alumni in the Indian Territory," *Chronicles of Oklahoma*, Vol. 32 (1954), 123–41.

[10] This was generally in Alabama, Georgia, or Arkansas and more rarely in the Cherokee Nation.

[11] Ross, *Life and Times*, v.

[12] Cooleela Faulkner, "The Life and Times of Reverend Stephen Foreman," (Master's thesis, University of Oklahoma, 1949), 5–7.

[13] John Hallums, *In Memorium: Elias Cornelius Boudinot, 1835–1890*, 17–18, 41; Dewey Whitsett Hodges, "Colonel E. C. Boudinot and His Influence on Oklahoma History," (Master's thesis, University of Oklahoma, 1929), 11–14.

[14] Cherokee Papers, Northeastern State College, Tahlequah, Oklahoma; Foreman Photostats, Grant Foreman Room, Muskogee Public Library, Muskogee, Oklahoma.

[15] Dollye Hefner Cravens, "Standard Bearer of the Cherokees: The Life of William Wirt Hastings," (Master's thesis, Oklahoma A&M College, 1942), 4–8.

[16] William P. Thompson, "W. W. Hastings, 1866–1938," Unpublished Manuscript, Hastings Collection; see also J. Berry King, "Judge William Pressley Thompson," *Chronicles of Oklahoma*, Vol. 29 (1941), 3–4.

training ground for the would-be Cherokee attorney. This was especially true of Cherokee-speaking attorneys, of which the career of Charles Thompson was typical.[17] When William F. Ramus left the chief's office after six years of tribal service, the *Advocate* editor recommended "persons . . . having business before the Executive Department . . . would be lucky to retain his services, as his is thoroughly posted in that department and knows it from 'a to izard.' "[18]

As a visitor to the Cherokees noted in a *Green Bag* report on "A Legal Episode in the Cherokee Nation," there were, in the 1880's and 1890's, several classes of Cherokee lawyers.[19] These included the highly competent "elite" professional bar members who practiced before the Cherokee Supreme Court and in the Federal District Courts, represented the tribe before congressional committees, and were in the employment of the railroads. For example, in 1877 there were five attorneys "in attendance on the Supreme Court."[20] A second group was the Cherokee-language bar, which generally appeared only before the circuit courts and represented the full bloods.[21] Yet another element was what George Foster has called the "travelling Indian lawyer," a circuit rider who went from court to court, picking up business at every stop.[22]

Such diversity is easy to understand when Cherokee restrictions on the practice of law are considered. The Nation never required examination and provided more legislation controlling stud horses and stray pigs than regulating attorneys. The act of November 2, 1849, typical of Cherokee law-practice statutes, required payment of a fee and an oath that the lawyer would "to the best of his knowledge and ability, support and defend all causes that may be entrusted to his care."[23] Article IX of the Compiled Laws of 1892 contained eight sections on "Attorneys," which establish, among other items, license

[17] *Cherokee Advocate*, June 10, 1876.

[18] *Ibid.*, April 14, 1882.

[19] George Foster, "A Legal Episode in the Cherokee Nation," *Green Bag*, Vol. 4 (1892), 486–90.

[20] *Cherokee Advocate*, Oct. 3, 1877.

[21] *Ibid.*, June 10, 1876. See translations of their work in Kilpatrick and Kilpatrick, *The Shadow of Sequoyah*, 26–31, 36, 44, 46–47.

[22] George Foster, "A Legal Episode in the Cherokee Nation," *Green Bag*, Vol. 4 (1892), 486–90. Those familiar with the early legal career of Abraham Lincoln will recall that this sort of practice was common on the frontier. Even the most prominent Cherokee lawyers might appear in court in a number of districts. *Cherokee Advocate*, May 11, 1878, and May 30, 1894.

[23] CLCN (1852), 195–96.

fees, oaths, restrictions on judges and tribal officials practicing before tribal courts, and the grounds for removal of an attorney from practice.[24]

It is doubtful that the lawyer's practice before the tribal courts differed substantially from the practice of his brothers in the bordering states. Probably the most nearly complete record of the cases and clients of an early Cherokee attorney can be reconstructed from the papers of Stand Watie.[25] Watie, like most so licensed, was not a full-time practitioner but operated large farms and maintained considerable mercantile interests. The day-to-day basis of his work was the routine collection of debts, drawing of agreements, and general commercial considerations with only an occasional break for something like his sensational defense of Archilla Smith in a politically charged murder trial.[26]

Regulation of the conduct of the bar was a continual problem for the Cherokee Nation. As early as 1829 the Cherokees refused William Rogers the right to plead a case, more because they considered him a "troublemaker" than because he was a Western Cherokee.[27] The *Cherokee Advocate* of November 16, 1844, reported the trial of "a young half-breed, named Jackson Witt, a 'lawyer.' " He was found guilty of forgery of "a certificate which called for twenty-three dollars, purporting to have been issued by the Clerk of the Supreme Court for services rendered the Nation as a witness." He was sentenced to thirty-nine lashes on his bare back, and the editor, with an almost inexcusable example of humor, reported that "this was undoubtedly the most *feeling* specimen of *cutting Witt*."[28]

There is only one recorded case of a lawyer's disbarment. On December 12, 1891, the Cherokee National Council passed a joint resolution "asking and directing the Supreme Court to cancel the license of J. H. Beck and A. H. Norwood as attorneys practicing law before the Supreme Court for violation of their oath as taken by attorneys to practice law in the Cherokee Nation." Although the

24 CLCN (1892), Article IX, 313–16.

25 Watie Files, Cherokee Papers, Northeastern State College, Tahlequah, Oklahoma.

26 Photostats of Stand Watie trial, Foreman Room, Muskogee Public Library, Oklahoma; Grant Foreman (ed.), *Indian Justice: A Cherokee Murder Trial at Tahlequah in 1840, Passim.* (cited hereafter as *Indian Justice*).

27 *Cherokee Phoenix*, Sept. 4, 1829.

28 *Cherokee Advocate*, Nov. 16, 1844. One senses a general distrust of lawyers as "sharpies" especially white lawyers who came into the Nation. *Cherokee Advocate*, Jan. 23, 1845, March 1, 1876, Dec. 9, 1881, Sept. 28, 1887.

Weekly Advocate.

PUBLISHED EVERY SATURDAY BY THE

CHEROKEE NATION.

Official Journal of the Nation.

SATURDAY, DEC. 23, 1878.

PENAL LAW.

[Published by Authority]

An Act for the protection of the Public Domain, and in relation to intruders upon the same.

Be it enacted by the National Council: That the Principal Chief is authorized and hereby directed, to order the sheriffs of the several districts of the Cherokee Nation to assist the officers of the United States Court for the Western District of Arkansas in the arrest of all persons, charged with tresspass upon the public domain of the Cherokee Nation, and it is hereby made the duty of the sheriffs of of several districts of the Cherokee Nation to arrest and deliver to the authorities of the United States representing the said Western District of Arkansas—any and all persons found tresspassing upon the public domain of the Cherokee Nation—whether the same be in removing timber, salt, coal, wood, lumber or mineral of any kind when such removal is not authorized by the laws of the Cherokee Nation: *provided,* that in all cases where such tresspass shall be committed by a citizen of the Cherokee Nation he or she so tresspassing shall be held for trial before the circuit court for the district in which the offense is alleged to have been committed—and upon conviction of the same the person so convicted shall be, in addition to other penalties already imposed by law, imprisoned in the National prison for a term not less than twelve months, at the discretion of the court trying the same.

Be it further enacted: That it shall be the duty of the Principal Chief to report all intruders, who may so be declared by the National Council, or by the solicitors of the various districts of the Nation, or by any court acting under the authority, or by virtue of an act of the National Council, to the Commissioner of Indian Affairs, and ask the removal of such intruders, *provided;* that in case the Commissioner of Indian Affairs fails to remove intruders, so declared by the first day of August 1879 it is hereby made the duty of the Principal Chief to remove beyond the limits of the Cherokee Nation any and all persons who may be residing in the Cherokee Nation, who may be declared intruders as above provided, for which purpose he is hereby authorized to call upon the sheriffs of the several districts of the Nation, *provided:* that the solicitors of the several districts shall report on the fifth day of July, 1879, to the Principal Chief, all persons who are intruders in their respective districts, and any solicitor so failing to report shall be removed without further process, by the Principal Chief.

Be it further enacted: That from and after the passage of this act, it shall not be lawful for any citizen of the Cherokee Nation to employ any citizen of the United States, not a citizen of the Cherokee Nation, (school teachers, ministers of the Gospel, and missionaries, following their professions excepted) in any capacity—except mechanics working as such, unless such citizens desiring to employ a citizen of the United States, other than as herein provided, shall pay to the clerk of the district in which such citizen may live, twenty five dollars per month, in advance for every citizen of the United States, and not a citizen of the Cherokee Nation so to be hired, and the clerks of the several districts of the Nation are hereby directed to keep a record of all persons so hiring citizens of the United States, as above provided and report the same monthly to the solicitors of the districts in and for which they are clerks, *provided* that all monies so received by the clerks shall be transmitted monthly to the treasurer of the Nation, and any citizen of the Cherokee Nation violating the provisions of this act, shall upon conviction of the same before the district court for the district in which the offence may be alleged to have been committed, shall be deemed guilty of a misdemeanor and be fined one hundred dollars, and upon failure to pay said fine, be imprisoned in the National prison for a period of not less than twelve months at the discretion of the court trying the same, and it is hereby made the duty of the solicitors of the several districts to prosecute all violations of this act, and all laws, and parts of laws, conflicting with this act, (are) hereby repealed.

Tahelquah, C. N., Dec. 12th. 1878.

CHARLES THOMPSON,

Principal Chief.

—This being Christmas week, and according to a long custom, we did not intend to issue any paper this week; but a penal law over which we had no control compels us to "publish" this. Christmas gift—!

This special legal supplement of the *Weekly Advocate* contains the text of the 1878 Penal Law and a closing note from the printer that this "extra" is a "Christmas gift." Courtesy Thomas Gilcrease Institute.

Laying the corner stone of the United States Court House, Muskogee,
June 24, 1889. White and Indian citizens of Indian Territory gathered

in the Creek Nation for ceremonies in preparation for legal changes,
which symbolized the twilight of the tribal court systems.

First United States Court Building, Muskogee, Indian Territory. Authority ov
citizens of the Cherokee Nation was shifted from the courts of the Cherokees to tl
United States courts in preparation for the end of tribal government. Courtesy Okl
homa Historical Society.

Cherokee Indian police, or light-horsemen. Three Cherokee law-enforcement officials are shown in a studio picture. Note that one is wearing traditional Cherokee hunting jacket and another has a gun in a holster on his belt. Gregory-Strickland Collection.

Zeke Proctor, Cherokee lawman. Each of the Cherokee districts elected a sheriff who was the highest law enforcement official in the district. Proctor, a legendary law enforcement and outlaw figure, was believed by many traditional Cherokees to have a guardian spirit or witch who protected him. Courtesy Oklahoma Historical Society.

Sam Sixkiller, Cherokee jailer and lawman. Among law-enforcement offices held by Samuel Sixkiller were Sheriff, High Sheriff, Warden of the National Prison, and Captain of the Union Agency Police. Courtesy Oklahoma Historical Society.

RESOLUTIONS.

Be it Resolved by the Citizens of the town of Muskogee: That the killing of Samuel Sixkiller, Captain of the U. S. Indian police and Deputy U. S. Marshal, on the 24th of December, 1886, was a willful and cowardly assassination. We condemn this awful deed as horrible, worthy of the detestation and execration of all honest and upright men, and we desire it to go on record that we regard this villainous act as unpralelled and infammous in its atrocity.

We have experienced therein a sad and serious loss, not only socially, but to the cause of law and order in this town and the Indian Territory. For seven years he had been Captain of the U. S. Indian Police, for four years Deputy U. S. Marshal, and as such a vigilent, honest and courageous officer, an acknowledged leader in all perilous enterprises, and we regard his unfortunate death as being directly due to his honorable and faithful services against the lawless elements that afflict this country. We deeply regret his untimely end, and hereby tender our heart-felt sympathy to his bereaved widow and orphaned children, and as a practical testimonial of our indebtedness to him for his labors in our midst we have this day taken steps to raise funds for their relief.

A resolution condemning the death of Sam Sixkiller, who was serving as Captain of the United States Indian Police. Courtesy Thomas Gilcrease Institute.

Chief's annual address, Cherokee capital, Tahlequah. The Cherokees were a politically active people who maintained considerable interest in the operation of tribal government. With a constitution dividing powers among an executive, legislative, and judicial body, the chief's annual message was regarded as extremely vital. Courtesy Oklahoma Historical Society.

Cherokee Capitol, Tahlequah. Regular court sessions were held in the specially designed courtrooms in the capitol building. Appellate review took place here where the records of the tribal courts were kept on file. Today this structure serves as the Cherokee County court house for the state of Oklahoma. Courtesy Phillips Collection, Western History Collection, University of Oklahoma.

LAWS OF CHEROKEE NATION.

LUMBER LAW.

AN ACT prohibiting the sale and shipment of lumber or timber to a non-citizen of the United States.

Be it enacted by the National Council, That it shall be unlawful for any citizen of this Nation to saw and ship lumber beyond the limits of the Cherokee Nation, or to sell lumber or timber of any kind to any non-citizen, or citizens of the United States.

Be it further enacted, That every citizen of this Nation violating the provisions of this act, shall upon conviction, before the Circuit Court of the district wherein the offense shall have been committed, be fined in a sum not less than five hundred dollars nor more than five thousand dollars,or be imprisoned not less than one year, nor more than three years, and in default of payment, to be both imprisoned and fined.

Be it further enacted, That all laws or parts of laws conflicting with this act are hereby repealed.

Approved February 1, 1888:

J. B. MAYES,
Principal Chief.

GAMBLING LAW.

AN ACT amending Article XIX. Chapter 4, Revised Laws of the Cherokee Nation.

Be it enacted by the National Council, That Sec. 54, Article 19, Chapter 4, Revised Laws of the Cherokee Nation, be and the same is hereby so amended as to make it the duty of the Court having jurisdiction to imprison for any term not less than one nor exceeding six months, in all cases of conviction when the party convicted shall fail to pay the fine.

Be it further enacted, That Section 55, Article 10, Chapter 4 Revised Laws of the Cherokee Nation, be and the same is hereby so amended as to authorize and make it the duty of all Sheriffs, Town Constables, High Sheriffs, in accordance with Sec. 12. Art. 5, of the Constitution, to search all places known or suspected to be used as gambling resorts or places of gaming, and to seize and destroy all cards, dice, checks or other devices used for the purpose of gambling,or gaming,and to report all parties offending to the Solicitor of the district for prosecution. Providing, that before any cards, dice, checks, or any other device used for the purpose of gaming, as aforesaid, are destroyed, the same shall be in a hearing before the Judge of the district, or the Mayor of the town in which such seizure is made,be condemned by such Judge or Mayor of such town as being cards, dice, checks or other devices of gaming, and in order to carry out the provisions of this act, the Judges of the several districts and the Mayors of the several towns of the Cherokee Nation are hereby authorized and required to call special sessions of the courts of which they are Judges, to be held upon information from the Sheriffs of the district or Constables of the town, that such a seizure has been made, and pass judgment in the matter, and when after a hearing has been had and the articles seized, condemned by the Judge or Mayor aforesaid, it shall be the duty of the Sheriff, High Sheriff or Town Constable to destroy the same.

Be it further enacted, That Section 55, Article 19, Chapter 4, Revised Laws of the Cherokee Nation, be and the same is hereby so amended as to authorize and require the Court having jurisdiction to imprison for any term not less than six months, nor exceeding one year in all cases of conviction where the party convicted shall fail to pay the fine, or by both fine and imprisonment, at the discretion of the Court having jurisdiction.

Approved February 4, 1888:

J. B. MAYES,
Principal Chief.

GRAND JURY LAW.

AN ACT providing for Special Sessions of the Grand Jury.

Be it enacted by the National Council, That Section 77, Page 107, Article 6, Chapter III, Compiled Laws, be and the same as to read as follows, to-wit: "Whenever information of the commission of any felony within his District, shall come to the knowledge of any Solicitor at any time between the regular sessions of the Grand Jury, and the due execution of the law, shall in his opinion, make it unsafe to await for their action at the regular sessions of the Grand Jury, but shall require an immediate investigation of the facts in the case, with the view to prevent the escape from justice of any person strongly suspected or to ascertain and fix the crime upon the guilty party, he shall be required to obtain summons from the District Clerk, commanding the Sheriff to summon the Grand Jury of the Court, already authorized and empowered by law to take jurisdiction of such crimes, to meet at the Court-house in his District at as early a day as possible, to be fixed by the Solicitor, for the purpose of an immediate investigation of such charges as the Solicitor may prefer against any party before them; also the said Solicitor will obtain summons for witnesses as in other cases, made and provided for. Provided, That the Solicitors shall not require the Grand Jury as provided for in this section, to remain in session in the investigation of any one case more than five days."

Be it further enacted, That all laws or parts of laws, providing for the filing of an indictment by the Solicitor before the Clerks of the districts in cases of felonies are hereby repealed.

Aproved Nov. 10, 1888:

J. B. MAYES,
Principal Chief.

FISH LAW.

AN ACT to prevent the destruction of fish in the various lakes, ponds or streams of water in the Cherokee Nation.

Be it enacted by the National Council, That it shall be unlawful for any person or persons, citizens of the Cherokee Nation, to use in fishing giant powder dynamite of any kind that will be the destruction of fish.

Be it further enacted, That any and all persons, citizens of the Cherokee Nation, found violating the provisions of this act shall be deemed guilty of a misdemeanor and be subject to a fine of not less than fifty dollars, nor more than one hundred dollars, and in default of payment of such fine be imprisoned for any term not less than six month nor more than one year at the discretion of the Court having jurisdiction.

Be it further enacted, That twenty-five per cent. of all fines

---

Laws of the Cherokee Nation. The laws are presented in a series of broadsheets taken from the initial printing in the *Cherokee Advocate*. Courtesy Thomas Gilcrease Institute.

NEW JURY LAW.

New Jury Law, an official copy with the certification of W. H. Mayes attesting that the executive department of the Cherokee Nation has approved this printing. Courtesy Thomas Gilcrease Institute.

AN ACT repealing the act of the National Council approved April 21st, 1886, entitled "an act amendatory of Chapter three, Article five of the Compiled Laws of the Cherokee Nation relating to Juries" and amending Section fifty-four, Article five, and Section sixty-one, Article six of the said Chapter three, Compiled Laws of the Cherokee Nation.

Be it enacted by the National Council, That the Act of the National Council, approved April 21st, 1886, and entitled "An Act, amendatory of chapter three, article five, section fifty-one of the Compiled Laws of the Cherokee Nation, relating to Juries," be and the same is hereby repealed.

Be it further enacted, That section fifty-four of chapter three of the Compiled Laws, be amended so as to read after the word "Clerk," in the seventeenth line, of said section, but in all other criminal cases the Clerk shall summon eighteen after the same have in like manner been drawn by the Sheriff who shall be empanneled as above, the prosecution objecting to three, and the accused or Court, selecting the twelve out of the remaining fifteen to try the case. No verdict shall be rendered in any criminal case without the unanimous consent of the whole jury: Provided, That at all special terms of the District and Circuit Courts, for the trial of criminal cases, when there shall be more than one case, to be tried there shall be thirty names drawn and summoned according to chapter three, article five, section fifty-one, of the Compiled Laws, who shall serve as jurymen for that term of of Court.

Be it further enacted, That at least fourteen (14) days before the commencement of the regular terms of the Circuit and District Courts in each year, the Judges of both Courts, shall each furnish to the Sheriff of each District a list of thirteen names of persons, intelligent and who shall have attained the age of twenty one years and are otherwise qualified as jurymen, citizens of the District, who shall be summoned to act as Grand Jurors for that District, during the year, and to sit during the regular terms of the court respectively, unless sooner discharged by the court, and the Solicitors of the several districts shall not be authorized to convene a Grand Jury between the regular terms of the court except in cases for capital offenses, or cases of felony, and only when there is apprehension that the accused will escape beyond the jurisdiction of the Cherokee Nation in such cases of felony. No person, summoned to serve as Grand Juror, shall be exempt from service, except on account of personal sickness, severe or dangerous sickness in his immediate family, or recent death, and before the burial of any member thereof. In case of the absence of any person summoned as Grand Juror, his place shall be filled by some competent person who shall, if necessary, be summoned by special writ.

Be it further enacted, That Section sixty six, of said Article six, is hereby amended, so as to read, "No indictment shall be found by the Grand Jury unless voted for by a majority of their number;" And provided further, That all Jurors shall receive two dollars per day's service as juror.

Approved Nov. 28th, 1892.

C. J. HARRIS.
Principal Chief.

Executive Department C.
Dec 3? 1892
I W H Mayes Asst Executive Secretary do hereby certify that the foregoing is a true and correct copy of the Original

W H Mayes
Asst Executive Secty

Thomas Mitchel Buffingham,
Delaware District Judge.

William Pressley Thompson,
Illinois District Judge.

JOSEPH M. HILDEBRAND.
CHEROKEE.

Joseph M. Hildebrand,
Coowescoowee District Judge.

Henry Clay Crittendon,
Goingsnake District Judge.

W. W. Hastings was among the most distinguished lawyers from the
Cherokee Nation. He was a graduate of the Law Department of Vanderbilt University, who served as Attorney General for the Cherokee Nation
and later served as United States Congressman from Oklahoma. Courtesy
Oklahoma Historical Society.

"Hanging" Judge Isaac C. Parker, United States Judge for the Western District of Arkansas and the Indian Territory, felt that the Cherokees were a very lawful people and told a United States congressional committee that there was not as high a percentage of crime committed in the Indian country as in southern and western states. Gregory-Strickland Collection.

record is not clear about cause, the case probably involved duplicity in the sale of land, since Beck was known for dealing in tribal property. The Supreme Court, however, reversed the disbarment since the proper statutory procedure providing a hearing was not followed. *In the Matter of J. H. Beck* the court concluded that the right to practice law was a property right and reinstated Beck because his disbarment involved taking property without due process of law.[29]

One may get a sense of what it must have been like to practice law in the Cherokee Nation from the comments of the lawyer-editors of the tribal newspaper and from the "Professional Ads" proclaiming the specialized services of the members of the Bar. The *Advocate* reported on one court session that "lawyers on hand were more numerous than clients—a circumstance less fortunate for themselves than the country."[30] Earlier an editor similarly noted that "we understand that the lawyers have a heap of fun and a fine time generally, down in Sequoyah District [with] few cases and no money; but, at the same time they have fun, and lots of it."[31]

Judged by reports of the day, lawyers had taken on much of the pomposity of the Victorian master of the courtroom.[32] A correspondent covering the trial of Butler and Bennett, indicted for the murder of Dick Chicken, warned that "there being about half dozen lawyers on each side—for prosecution and defense—it is hard to tell how long the trial will last."[33] For, as noted of the 1892 Supreme Court session, there were always "quite a number of lawyers in attendance anxious to spout and shoot forth eloquence and oratory thereby creating awe and shaking of the dry bones."[34]

In final analysis how should these Cherokee lawyers be judged? A study of the briefs and arguments which they presented indicates a remarkably high standard of practice, especially for the frontier.[35] The cogent arguments of William Potter Ross, Dennis W. Bushy-

[29] *In the Matter of J. H. Beck* (1894) "Opinions of the Cherokee Supreme Court," Cherokee Nation Papers, Indian Archives, Oklahoma Historical Society (cited hereafter as OCSC with the Oklahoma Historical Society Microfilm number). See also Chapter Five, especially note 69.

[30] *Cherokee Advocate*, Sept. 22, 1882.

[31] *Ibid.*, March 16, 1878.

[32] See the oral arguments of W. P. Ross, in Ross, *Life and Times*, 7, 29, 82.

[33] *Cherokee Advocate*, Oct. 3, 1877.

[34] *Ibid.*, Feb. 10, 1892.

[35] A marvelous collection of actual courtroom presentations, briefs, and petitions is in the trial records of the Cherokee Nation in the Indian Archives, Oklahoma Historical Society.

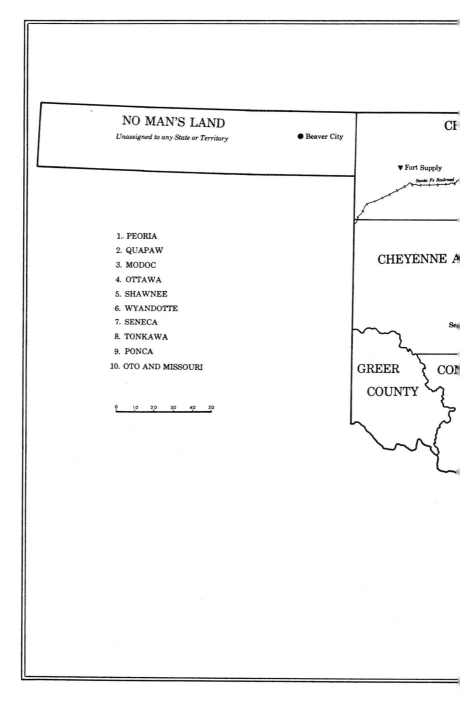

NO MAN'S LAND

Unassigned to any State or Territory   ● Beaver City

CH

▼ Fort Supply

Santa Fe Railroad

CHEYENNE A

1.. PEORIA
2. QUAPAW
3. MODOC
4. OTTAWA
5. SHAWNEE
6. WYANDOTTE
7. SENECA
8. TONKAWA
9. PONCA
10. OTO AND MISSOURI

Se

GREER   COD
COUNTY

0   10   20   30   40   50

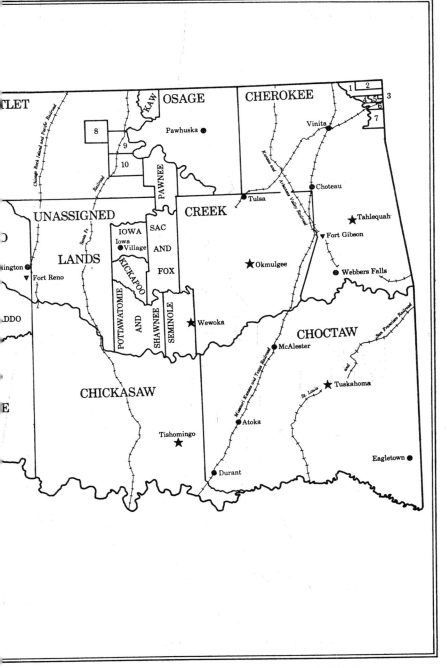

Indian Territory, 1866–89. From *Historical Atlas of Oklahoma.*

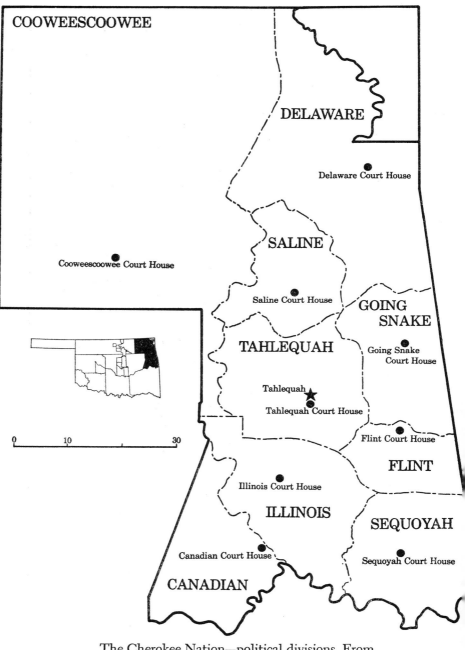

The Cherokee Nation—political divisions. From
Historical Atlas of Oklahoma.

head, W. A. Duncan, Robert L. Owen, W. W. Hastings, Elias C. Boudinot, and William Penn Adair not only compare favorably with the surrounding bars of Arkansas, Texas, Kansas, and Missouri but are on a par with their adversaries before congressional committees and the United States Supreme Court.[36] The achievements of the Cherokee-language attorneys are even more remarkable. The few surviving examples of their drafting and pleading show a clear grasp of legal issues and even technicalities.[37]

From the time of the first reported Cherokee murder trial, a businesslike approach and a respect for the tradition of the law are apparent.[38] Similar court records that have survived from all periods of the Cherokee legal system are an eloquent testimony to the achievement of the Cherokee bar.[39] The praises of this small group of mixed- and full-blood Indians trained in the profession of justice were often sung by fellow attorneys in many jurisdictions.[40]

To detail extensively the development of the intricacies of Chero-kee written law would be tedious and contribute little to an under-standing of broad changes. The story of Cherokee legal history is one of gradual evolution from simple regulations to relatively complex codes. Chief John Ross had suggested laws which were "short, plain & suitable to the condition of the people" so that "the mode for conducting suits in courts should be free from all complicated for-malities, and no other *form* should be required than, to let both parties know distinctly, what is alleged."[41] Originally the tribe knew that "they were not in a position to adopt the whole . . . system of the whites" but needed laws so simple in administration as to "require

[36] Cherokee Nation Papers, Indian Archives, Oklahoma Historical Society. Note the brief in *Cobb* v. *Cherokee Nation* reprinted in *Cherokee Advocate*, Aug. 29, 1894, and Sept. 5, 1894.

[37] Cherokee Nation Papers, Indian Archives, Oklahoma Historical Society.

[38] *Cherokee Phoenix*, Nov. 20, 1830.

[39] A rather complete picture of the operation of the court system could be drawn from the following issues of the *Cherokee Advocate*, Oct. 5, 1844; May 29, 1845; Oct. 14, 1871; Sept. 26, 1877; Nov. 17, 1877; Jan. 28, 1878; May 26, 1880; June 23, 1880; Jan. 13, 1882; May 12, 1882; May 19, 1882; Dec. 15, 1882; Aug. 24, 1883; Nov. 13, 1885; Nov. 10, 1886; Jan. 9, 1889; Oct. 10, 1894.

[40] See, for example, the praise of W. W. Hastings in the *Gainesville* [Texas] *Daily Register*, reprinted in the *Cherokee Advocate*, Jan. 17, 1894 and similar com-ments on E. C. Boudinot in Halum, *In Memorium: Elias Cornelius Boudinot, 1835–1890*, 37–71 and William Penn Adair in *Cherokee Advocate*, Nov. 10, 1880.

[41] *Cherokee Phoenix*, Oct. 22, 1828.

no great stretch of judicial acumen to determine the best methods of applying their remedies and securing the ends of justice."[42]

Yet the legalistic pleadings of the "educated" Cherokee lawyers had emerged by the 1890's, when the court system was abolished. The major shift began when a "New Code of the Cherokees" went into effect in 1876. At that time one Cherokee observed that "in borrowing and adopting a civilized form of Government . . . in place of the savage customs, . . . the Cherokees were compelled to adapt what they borrowed to their condition and stage of advancement" so "much [that] was left out because it was difficult then [is] easy now."[43]

The ancient clan law was a peculiarly personal status-oriented system in which the tribe had little function. At a second stage in Cherokee development the machinery of the state was initiated by private action; there were no public prosecutors, and all actions were filed by individual citizens. Thus in the intermediate state from clan to court a unique combination of the traditional and the modern merged. Finally the Cherokee Nation concluded that to rely upon private action to punish public wrongs was decidedly inefficient and adopted a public prosecution system.[44]

Until the end of the national court system, individuals were free to bring indictments. Most permit and resource violations were prosecuted on the basis of a fixed percentage of fines collected being paid to the individual responsible for obtaining the information upon which conviction was based. Eventually the Cherokees determined to give sheriffs and solicitors a share in their collections as an incentive to enforce statutes such as the timber and mining regulations.[45]

One of the major law reforms, the grand-jury system, served to make the courts more responsive to the community standards but nonetheless exasperated the most literal-minded advocates of strict law enforcement. The grand jury came to stand as a symbol of the vigilance of the law. The warning—"offenders against the law, and those inclined to be offenders, have good reason to bear this Grand Jury in mind"—reflects the symbolic importance of this institution, whose "business is to . . . make careful inquiry whether the law has

[42] *Cherokee Advocate*, March 28, 1877.
[43] *Ibid.*, Aug. 5, 1876.
[44] *Ibid.*, Oct. 11, 1873.
[45] CLCN (1892), Ch. I, Art. VI, 76–78. *Cherokee Advocate*, March 19, 1879; Oct. 19, 1881; Nov. 16, 1881.

in any instance been violated."[46] The willingness of these grand juries to adapt the law to meet the individual standards of an actual case is reflected in many of their actions. One suspects that the jury members must have known the wife in question when they refused indictment in the following case. The *Cherokee Advocate* reported that "a certain man knocked his wife on the side of the head with his law book." The grand jury examined the case, "parleying awhile they decided that it was lawful because it was done with the law and constitution and they dismissed the case."[47]

Once in actual operation the Cherokee court system under the Revised Code differed little from the typical state court. This similarity is demonstrated by following a criminal case from arrest to punishment. In the extended report of the Archilla Smith murder trial were examples of the indictment, the selection of a jury, the examination and cross-examination of witnesses, the final summation of counsel, the judge's instruction to the jury, the verdict, the appeal, a new trial, the requests for pardon, and finally the hanging.[48] The one distinguishing feature which makes the case uniquely Cherokee was the bilingual nature of the proceedings. While English could be considered the official court language, testimony was taken in whichever tongue was most familiar to the witness, and this, plus all oral features of the trial, was then translated. The process of translating was described by an American journalist visiting a Cherokee Court. George Foster noted: "All the jurymen could speak English save one. An interpreter was sworn in for his benefit, and all the evidence was given twice,—first in English."[49] John Howard Payne recorded the instruction of Judge Price that "great heed must be taken in translating . . . neither to over-state nor under-state the slightest particular."[50]

The most important members of the Cherokee legal system were the district officers—the light-horsemen, the sheriff, the solicitor, and the judge. Upon their shoulders fell the daily operation of the machinery of justice. The formal authority vested in these men was

[46] *Cherokee Advocate*, Oct. 3, 1877; Sept. 19, 1877.

[47] *Ibid.*, Feb. 1, 1879.

[48] Foreman, *Indian Justice*. A number of sample forms have been gathered in the Appendix to T. L. Ballenger, "The Development of Law and Legal Institutions Among the Cherokees," (Ph.D. dissertation, University of Oklahoma, 1938). Other collections rich in these materials are found in the Indian Archives, Oklahoma Historical Society and the Phillips Collection, University of Oklahoma.

[49] Foster, "A Legal Episode in the Cherokee Nation," *Green Bag*, Vol. 4 (1892), 486–90.

[50] Foreman, *Indian Justice*, 14.

great, but their significance extended far beyond their powers and duties enumerated in the tribal statutes. These "grass-roots" public servants were the center of the informal authority and decision making which smoothed the path of order.

While the name light-horseman conjures up a romantic image of early officers, the corps eventually degenerated into private groups of vigilantes, such as those suspected of executing the political vendettas of Chief John Ross.[51] After several years of granting police power to this group of regulators, the Nation formally created the office of sheriff (and later marshals) with jurisdiction in each of eight districts, with duties ranging from arresting and carrying "to be tried, all persons who may be charged with criminal offenses" to supervising the public domain and mineral resources of the nation.[52]

As a rule the Cherokee sheriff tended to be the same kind of gun-toting, free-wheeling, whisky-drinking arbiter of justice as that generally pictured as the western peace officer. The Cherokee Nation was, for many years, the wildest of frontiers. Hanging Judge Isaac C. Parker, whose legendary fame struck fear into the Cherokees, sat in judgment over all white men who committed crimes in the Indian Territory. Yet white intruders still joined with renegade Indians to wreak havoc in the Cookson Hills and on an essentially peaceful Cherokee people.[53]

The Cherokee Advocate was filled with the stories of such crimes. Some of the items are humorous. On June 23, 1882, the editor noted in a pious tone: "Our High Sheriff had some prostitutes, who had been a nuisance to our town for some time taken down to Agent Tufts for removal from the Nation."[54] This editor later warned of the "smoke house bandits" and stated that "the rogues are about the people had better lock their meat houses . . . or else they will wake up some of these fine mornings without any meat for breakfast."[55] But the general state of lawlessness the sheriffs faced was not comic.

[51] The Internal Feuds Among the Cherokees, April 13, 1846, Senate Document 298.

[52] For the final form see CLCN (1892), Ch. I, Art. IV, 62–68.

[53] Students of the gangster era of the 1920's and 1930's will remember that many famous gangs took cover among the Cherokees in this Cookson country. The most famous account of these early days is Gregory and Strickland (eds.), Hell On the Border.

[54] Cherokee Advocate, June 23, 1882.

[55] Ibid., April 4, 1888.

The cases of murder, cattle theft, rape, and drunken assaults are legion.[56]

Further complicating the sheriffs' duties of regulating violent crimes was the responsibility of enforcing the laws regulating public morals. Compounding these difficulties were a number of seemingly unenforceable ordinances on gambling, drinking, and carrying weapons.[57] The inappropriateness of such laws to the Cherokee frontier did not concern the self-righteous proponents of these programs backed by the missionaries. What was a sheriff, who sought to encourage the peaceful recreation of the ancient tribal stick-ball game, to respond to the obviously conflicting cultural viewpoint reflected by the puritan author of the following letter? The writer begins, "I am told that the greater part of the players are usually entirely naked, some of them always—and that multitudes of women, as well as men attend and look on as shamelessly as if all the men were in decent apparel."[58]

The extent to which sheriffs enforced, or failed to enforce, these laws was always an issue. Sheriffs were investigated and removed more often than were any other tribal officers.[59] Some, no doubt, "looked upon the wine when it was red," while others simply felt that law was intended "only for whiskey peddlers," not "those who sometimes bring it in and deal it out to their friends."[60] It would be safe to say that, as a rule, the sheriff did not devote much of his time to the liquor, gambling, or gun-control crimes. This is probably fortunate, considering the number of murders and the extent of cattle theft. In fact, communities were granted the right to form "patrols" to search out "the evil distilled spirits."[61] Many, including an early *Advocate* editor, saw the failure to enforce these public morals laws as the *cause* of the more serious crimes. The editor warned, "The remissness of

[56] Louise Welsh, "The Development of Law and Order In the Cherokee Nation, 1838–1907." (Master's thesis, University of Oklahoma, 1932), 94–118. The Cherokees contended that the state of lawlessness was exaggerated and regularly wrote in their defense. For the Cherokee position see *Cherokee Advocate*, May 20, 1874, and March 2, 1878.

[57] See Arrest Warrants, Cherokee National Papers, Indian Archives, Oklahoma Historical Society.

[58] *Cherokee Advocate*, Oct. 16, 1845.

[59] *Ibid.*, March 16, 1883; Aug. 20, 1879; June 11, 1879; Aug. 22, 1877; Aug. 15, 1877; Jan. 18, 1884.

[60] *Ibid.*, Oct. 10, 1888; March 16, 1883; Sept. 26, 1888.

[61] LCN (1852), 24-25.

the Sheriffs in enforcing . . . the laws prohibiting the introduction and vending of Ardent Spirits in the Nation has been productive not only of much complaint but also of much crime and suffering among the people."[62]

Working closely with the sheriff was an elective officer, the solicitor. In the Cherokee government he was not unlike a prosecuting, state, or district attorney. His chief statutory duties were to prosecute all crimes, defend the district in court, and collect fines and fees. The office was an exceedingly important one, especially in view of the discretionary powers and the tremendous opportunity for prosecution of noncitizen permit violations.[63]

Evidence points to the fact that this office was rarely staffed with competent prosecutors. One Cherokee, styling himself "Pro Bono Publico," wrote:

It is only too plain to all who have noticed that in too many instances the Solicitor is elected on *other* grounds than personal fitness for the responsible position. *Intelligence* and *some little knowledge of the law* should be insisted on. Far too many who have filled this office, have been altogether deficient, or nearly so, in both these particulars.[64]

Another concluded, "We hear from all sides complaints of the inefficiency of solicitors."[65]

The difficulty of the honest Cherokee-speaking district solicitor, attempting to enforce the strangely foreign regulations against the pressures of growing white intrusions and the legalistic tactics of their mixed-blood attorneys, is reflected in the translation of the hauntingly simple resignation of a Goingsnake District officer:

Goingsnake District
Cherokee Nation
March 9, 1877

Now! Friend Utsale;dv (Chief Thompson), I just wrote you a few lines today.

---

62 *Cherokee Advocate*, Jan. 29, 1846. This is a theme echoed from the earliest law enforcement efforts. *Cherokee Phoenix*, Aug. 27, 1828. "It is to be wished that the officers . . . were more vigilant and more attentive to their duties. Unless they do speedily go to work, they will make themselves liable to public reprehension: and these frequent thefts and murders will go to confirm the world in the opinion that we are still savages." *Cherokee Phoenix*, June 25, 1828.

63 CLCN (1892), Ch. I, Art. VI, 76–78: *Cherokee Advocate*, May 9, 1884; Dec. 5, 1894; Jan. 2, 1895.

64 *Cherokee Advocate*, Nov. 16, 1881.

65 *Ibid.*, Oct. 19, 1881.

Now I have just relinquished the District Solicitorship, and now this is why it has just come about: My head is simply too small for official work, and the new law is very difficult to interpret rightly. That is the reason why I have decided that it would be good to get a replacement.

Personally, I do not desire to keep the job just because of the salary. I know my capabilities in enforcing the law. It has become desirable to do the right thing, and to ask someone to finish out my unfinished year.

Beloved Principal Chief, since it has become necessary to write you, I will be greatly hoping to hear that you have asked someone to become Solicitor. All of this has become very difficult, finding the . . . homes of white intruders. Now I have made it known three times, and we do not know the reason why it has become this way. For I do not have the authority to remove them firmly in my hand, and I cannot continue to do the work of two persons. Since it has become difficult, I have just decided that those who live in the District should think that I have done right.

Now! That is all that I just wrote you, beloved Utsale;dv, Principal Head of the Cherokee Nation, and officials at the National capital.

I now relinquish the commission that you bestowed upon me.

I, Gane:ne:li:sgi Ne:wadv

I greet you, Utsale:dv.[66]

The legal training and the standard of practice of solicitors was often so inadequate that private attorneys were hired to prosecute in trials,[67] and the Nation was compelled to issue special printed forms for use by district solicitors whose bungling indictments were freeing many criminals.[68] A "Plea to Solicitors to Enforce Law" was issued,[69] and an aroused public complained of solicitors who were "learning law at the expense of the Nation."[70] There were, of course, notable exceptions, such as "the present solicitor of Cooweesooowee District who has collected 450 fines for violation of permit laws."[71] Apparently most solicitors followed the lead of the sheriff on questions of drinking, gambling, and disorderly conduct, although there was a period in which the number of gun-violation prosecutions was surprisingly high.[72]

The solicitors' position, of all tribal law-enforcement offices,

[66] Jack Frederick Kilpatrick and Anna Gritts Kilpatrick, *The Shadow of Sequoyah*, 26–28.

[67] *Cherokee Advocate*, June 20, 1882.

[68] *Ibid.*, Feb. 24, 1882.

[69] *Ibid.*, Feb. 28, 1877.

[70] *Ibid.*, May 9, 1884.

[71] *Ibid.*

[72] See Inventory, Cherokee Tribal Records, Indian Archives, Oklahoma Historical Society.

seems to have become the most political and the most lucrative in terms of use of influence, since the regulation of permit fees was exceedingly important to large-scale cattlemen and farmers.[73] Temptations to abuse were many. The misuse of discretionary powers of prosecution was noted in an *Advocate* editorial charging racial discrimination in the case of Henry Seales, "who formerly kept a barber shop . . . hung . . . at Greenleaf Court House . . . for the murder of another colored man." The editor asked the question, "Why is it that none but colored men are dealt with thus? The Cherokee country is overrun with murderers, but none of them are ever molested unless it is a negro."[74]

Too much discretionary power was not generally an evil of the Cherokee legal system. In fact, one of the most valuable features was this flexibility which the eight district governments provided. The tribal makeup varied from section to section, reflecting, in part, original settlement patterns dictated by political considerations. This organization allowed district judges to adapt their rulings to the consensus of a smaller unit of the tribe.

This ability and willingness to consider the circumstances of each case was, in my view, the most important contribution of district officers, especially the trial judges. One gets the feeling of being in a modern juvenile court when reading about cases in which these men were faced with young offenders and noting that in one case "the Judge . . . was quite overcome by the (apparent) penitence of the young offender" and that in another "his honor very kindly told the young gentlemen that they should not disturb the peaceful slumber of citizens, and [then] fined them 'V' [a $5.00 gold piece] each, for so doing."[75]

The strict letter of the law was often modified to prevent unreasonable results, as in the interpretation of the rigid alcohol prohibition. Judge Stuart was highly praised for ruling "that a man is not guilty of a misdemeanor for introducing liquor in small quantities for medicinal purposes." The injustice of the opposite position was likewise noted in the "case of a man being arrested in this city for having on his person one pint of whiskey which he was taking to his father . . . who was supposed to be dying."[76]

[73] See Papers of Cherokee Solicitors, Cherokee National Collection, Indian Archives, Oklahoma Historical Society.
[74] *Cherokee Advocate*, Nov. 11, 1876.
[75] *Ibid.*, July 10, 1885.
[76] *Ibid.*, May 27, 1893.

An added safety valve often used was voluntary arbitration by officials selected with the approval of the parties in a dispute. These arbitrators used in civil controversy were free-wheeling in their decision and were bound to no formal procedure or rules.[77] Perhaps the most famous arbitration case was "the controversy between our fellow citizen Mr. E. C. Boudinot and Mr. Joe Henricks as to right of possession on grounds lying on the water front of the town of Tahlequah." The decision was reached after several days of hearings "by arbitration [of] Prof. Smith, Mr. James Stapler, and Mr. James W. McSpadden acting as the Court in the premises."[78]

It was in regard to questions such as pardon, parole, appearance bonds and executive clemency that the Indians' remarkable legal informality became apparent.[79] This was an era before "mass production justice," an era in which, especially in Cherokee district courts, the individual could be seen and judged on his own merit or, at least, on the community's general impressions of his merits. An unpleasant suspicion must be entertained that this personal element could, and in some cases did, become far too influential for the best workings of the system. The pardon was an especially clear case of such abuse wherein juries came to request almost as a matter of policy that the sentence they had just imposed be commuted, and chiefs casually accepted these inconsistent recommendations, freeing armies of recently convicted criminals.[80] This breakdown became acute in the

---

[77] CLCN (1892), Ch. XII, Art. XVIII, 335–36. The arbitration procedure was upheld by the Cherokee Supreme Court in *Dameron v. McGee*, OCSC, 8736, 71.

[78] *Cherokee Advocate*, Nov. 3, 1882.

[79] Most of the records in pardon and parole cases may be found in the Phillips Collection, University Library, University of Oklahoma. For a general picture of the procedure see *Cherokee Phoenix*, Oct. 21, 1829; and *Cherokee Advocate*, April 23, 1846; Aug. 22, 1877; Sept. 21, 1881; Oct. 12, 1881; June 23, 1882; Sept. 19, 1884; June 22, 1887; Aug. 31, 1887; Nov. 18, 1893.

[80] As one editorial in the *Cherokee Advocate* noted: "it looks a little strange to us to see a man sent down to our National Prison convicted of larceny . . . and the very jury, judge, solicitor and all who were the court that convicted him, sign a petition asking the Executive to pardon him. But stranger still is that the petition . . . got here before the prisoner did." *Cherokee Advocate*, Jan. 13, 1882. Louise Welsh has argued that a major reason for lawlessness was the free granting of pardons. She concludes that "all that was necessary to secure a pardon was to circulate a petition, asking clemency in the convict's behalf, for any of a number of various reasons—the convict was suffering from poor health or insanity, he came from a good and respectable family, he was unjustly convicted, there was a flaw in the indictment, the term was about to expire and the criminal wished to secure his citizenship." Louise Welsh, "The Development of Law and Order In the Cherokee Nation, 1838–1907," (Master's thesis, University of Oklahoma, 1932), 133–34.

closing days of tribal courts, when all inmates in the national prison were freed.[81]

A strength of the Cherokee court system rested in the elective office of appellate judge. As for qualifications of these judges, there were no "examination[s] whatever [nor was] it necessary that they . . . should be known to have become familiar with [the] small volume of Statutes."[82] Because of the elective nature of the office, the traditional full-blood Cherokee-speaking districts tended to elect district judges who spoke the native tongue, but mixed-blood centers such as Tahlequah elected English speaking justices. As described by W. P. Boudinot, while "all that is required . . . of aspirants to Judicial honors is that they should be of a certain age and they should get enough votes" on the whole "the men selected to fill the Supreme Bench particularly are picked from the class of respectable and well informed citizens who are induced more by the honor than the compensation to undertake the onerous duties of their office."[83]

The fact that appellate justices most often came from the same class of closely intermarried whites whose cases constituted the bulk of litigation created one of the most difficult problems in early judicial administration. Further complicating the situation was the fact that families and clans tended to live in the same geographic areas which became the local judicial districts. Therefore, even district judges sat in trials of their kinsmen and clan brothers and were thus purportedly slow to pronounce judgment.[84] The *Journal of the Cherokee Legislative Council* contains an extended discussion of a bill to suspend Circuit Judges "when connected with either party by affinity, or consanguinity." The bill, originally rejected, was finally adopted after an "eloquent speech by Bark of Chatooga."[85] This danger was eliminated by a constitutional guarantee found in Article V, which disqualified such judges.[86]

The original light-horsemen served both a police and a judicial function, being empowered to capture and try criminals.[87] The case of Bear Paw illustrates the difficulty and confusion which a Cherokee officer faced in performing a duty he did not fully understand. Bear

[81] Official Record Book, Cherokee National Prison, Cherokee Tribal Records, Indian Archives, Oklahoma Historical Society.

[82] *Cherokee Advocate*, Oct. 19, 1881; Feb. 17, 1877.

[83] *Ibid.*, Nov. 16, 1881; March 19, 1879.

[84] For detailed discussion see the courts interpretation OCSC, 8736, 148–57.

[85] Typescript of speech in Cherokee Collection, Indian Heritage Association.

[86] CLCN (1852), 12–14.

Paw is said to have tried to force a thief into promising to "be a good man in the future." When the criminal refused redemption, "Bear Paw struck him dead with an axe." When the officer fled, he was "permitted to run unmolested" with no "effort . . . made to bring him to justice."[88] However, after a series of editorials in the *Phoenix* on "the indifference of our officers in regard to this murder," Bear Paw surrendered and stood trial. He appears to have been either acquitted or pardoned.[89]

Such judicial problems are known to have continued even after the election of regular judges. In one of the first cases of murder tried by a Cherokee judge, the defendant was questioned by the magistrate. "How do you plead?" The prisoner answered, "Guilty," and the judge with equal dispatch pronounced that he would be hanged on the spot. Observers are reported to have had great difficulty convincing the judge of the necessity of following the procedures required by law.[90]

The single most common route to the bench was from the office of district clerk. This position was extremely important because "judges were often unacquainted with English, and were consequently more or less dependent [upon the Clerks] whom they selected and were compelled to confide in."[91] Biographical sketches of individual judges published in the *Advocate* show that many of these men were formerly clerks who had been educated in the Cherokee Male Seminary but that relatively few attended schools outside the Nation.[92]

The exemplary dedication and conciliatory attitude of the Cherokee-speaking district judge is nowhere more apparent than in the correspondence concerning the enforcement of a Cherokee language contract. E:lini, with whom the contract was made, died, and

---

[87] LCN (1852), 3–5, 44; *Cherokee Phoenix*, Jan. 21, 1829.

[88] *Cherokee Phoenix*, March 6, 1828; April 3, 1828.

[89] *Cherokee Phoenix*, May 28, 1828. See also Malone, *Cherokees of the Old South*, 164.

[90] The most complete compilation of such stories is William P. Thompson, "An Address Delivered Before the First Annual Meeting of the Oklahoma State Bar Association in 1910," *Chronicles of Oklahoma*, Vol. 2 (1924).

[91] *Cherokee Advocate*, Nov. 17, 1877.

[92] For judicial biographies and background see the *Cherokee Phoenix*, Nov. 19, 1828; *Cherokee Advocate*, Sept. 26, 1844; April 18, 1874; March 11, 1876; July 15, 1876; Sept. 9, 1876; March 7, 1877; Nov. 17, 1877; Jan. 5, 1881; Dec. 9, 1881; March 17, 1882; Dec. 1, 1882; Nov. 13, 1885; Nov. 10, 1886; April 29, 1891; March 7, 1894; July 11, 1894.

Digui(e)dinsgi threatened court action against E:lini's heirs, who sought the help of the judge for the Goingsnake District. The judge's advice that "you two talk it over together" reflects the desire to prevent destruction of long friendships and family ties. The judge concluded "You two should just forgive each other. The way that you will have unburdened yourself will be exceedingly joyful. You two make this right."[93]

The qualifications most esteemed on the bench are reflected in comments on Justices Adair and Ketcher. Adair was praised for a session in which he "presided with suitable dignity, impartiality, and intelligence" and honored as "a good judge who does not suffer partisan predilictions to swerve his judgment of what is right."[94] Ketcher received acclaim for "his charge to the jury [which] was an able and impartial effort; and displayed a mind conversant with the principles of law and equity."[95] The evaluation of another judge by a Cherokee attorney is especially revealing. Judge Benge was commended for being "fair in his rulings" and for granting "all attorneys a chance to have his reasons for them put into the record."[96]

Service on the bench was not generally a goal of the practicing attorney. Judges might as likely come from the Christian ministry, as in the case of Jesse Bushyhead, or from the National Council, as did Roach Young or Richard Fields.[97] One major reason attorneys were not attracted was that judges could not practice law before the tribal courts and were paid "like Masons . . . by the Day," and, as one advocate of judicial reform noted, "there is a [great] deal of actual service —of hard study—expected of them to prepare them to make correct decisions upon law points for which they are not paid at all."[98] Therefore, it is understandable that court sessions might be postponed "in consequence of the failure of the Judge to attend."[99]

Justice John Martin, first chief justice of the Supreme Court of the Cherokee Nation in the West, set a pattern of excellence in devotion, education, and personal training which few who followed were able to match. His education, like his father's, began in Virginia but continued through extensive reading. Most other judges had

93 Kilpatrick and Kilpatrick, *Shadow of Sequoyah*, 46–48.
94 *Cherokee Advocate*, March 17, 1882.
95 *Ibid.*, Jan. 5, 1881.
96 *Ibid.*, Sept. 26, 1888.
97 *Ibid.*, Nov. 10, 1886; Sept. 9, 1876.
98 *Ibid.*, Oct. 14, 1871.
99 *Ibid.*, Sept. 26, 1844.

followed a program of self-education.[100] The obituary of Judge A. Thornton typified Cherokee justices: "His school education was meager but he was a man of fine natural parts, and acquired his book knowledge by his own industry and self-instruction. His habits of life were always methodical, temperate, and exemplory."[101]

On the whole the office of judge seems to have been filled by competent and often highly creative public servants who strove honestly to interpret the law in an equitable manner, adapting, whenever possible, the strict letter of the law to the conditions of the individual tribesman. Even before removal a white observer noted that "in the courts instituted by the written laws, intelligent judges presided."[102]

[100] See *Cherokee Advocate*, Nov. 18, 1891, for a general view of the family. For a brief sketch of Justice Martin see Earl Boyd Pierce and Rennard Strickland, *The Cherokee People*, 81.

[101] *Cherokee Advocate*, April 21, 1882.

[102] John Howard Payne Papers, Roll 6986, 5.

Cherokee Supreme Courts Apply
Their Law, 1867–1898
VIII

WITH THE surviving mass of tribal appellate court opinions as evidence, one is hard-pressed to deny the common belief that the Cherokees were one of the most litigious peoples in the history of the world. Appeal from Cherokee district court decisions was a matter of right and was regularly undertaken by litigants as a matter of course.[1] The result was chronically overcrowded appellate dockets, further burdened by questions of original jurisdiction resting within these same tribal courts. As one official report complained, "The aggregation of causes at law before the Supreme Court . . . are gradually being piled up until the court is unable to dispose of them within any reasonable time. . . . Many are of several years' stand."[2]

This body of material provides a clear picture of the Cherokee courts' interpretation and application of their law. Changes in the legal system are reflected in the surviving court records for the period 1867 to 1898.[3] The first of the post-American Civil War reports are more lengthy than any of the earlier preremoval opinions written in Georgia but continue to discuss the facts of the case in elaborate detail to the virtual exclusion of legal theory. In the mid-1880's a more sophisticated and better-reasoned series of opinions began to appear. Legal reasoning reached an apex which was as clear and in-

[1] *Cherokee Advocate*, June 1, 1892; Feb. 28, 1894; March 7, 1894.
[2] *Ibid.*, Nov. 11, 1893.
[3] Cherokee Supreme Court Records for the period from removal in 1839 to the end of 1865 were destroyed or scattered during the American Civil War in the Indian Territory. "Report of the Clerk of the Court to the Honorable Supreme Court of the Cherokee Nation," OCSC, 8736, 23.

cisive as any found in the opinions of state court justices.[4] In the final years of tribal courts the opinions began to sink to a level not distinguishably better than those of the late 1870's and early 1880's.[5]

Opinions of judges of the Cherokee Supreme Court in this period before the American Civil War consisted of little more than statements of the names of the parties, denominations of the nature of the actions, and decisions of the parties in whose favor the court had ruled.[6] This was also the pattern in the period immediately following the war. The first fairly complete decision, in the modern sense, involved one of the justices as party plaintiff. No doubt, with the verdict in favor of their colleague, the judges who decided the case felt called upon to develop their reasoning more fully.[7]

The overwhelming majority of cases decided by the Cherokee Supreme Court involved statutory interpretation. The judges systematically applied the language of an act to the facts of a case. Like the seamstress who places the pattern upon the cloth, the sections in question were measured against the dimension of the incident giving rise to the controversy. *Percival v. Bryant* demonstrated the workmanlike manner in which the task was often approached:

It is evident from the language of the Constitution that an improvement must be a fixture or a permanent attachment to the soil. The term used is, "improvement made thereon." The law in reference to improvements alludes to a "house, field, or other improvement." Abandoned improvements reverts to the nation as Common property—The phrase improvements of the Common Domain implies or rather discloses that the improvement is a portion of the common domain improved by *labor*. All of our laws made upon the subject recognize this construction as the true one.

Is then, the Mill Machinery attached in this case an improvement as defined? We think not, and was never intended to be classed as such by the framers of the Constitution and laws. The machinery of a Steam Mill is often called a Steam Engine so is a locomotive or the machinery of a Steam Boat. All of which belong to the same class subject to be removed

[4] See OCSC, 8736 and OCSC, 8740.

[5] An explanation of this is probably the return to the bench of the Cherokee language justices. For example, in the 1897 session Justices Benge and Redbird required an English language interpreter. "Minutes of the Cherokee Supreme Court," Vol. 234, p. 226–28 in Indian Archives, Oklahoma Historical Society.

[6] "Record Book of the Supreme Court of the Cherokee Nation, 1823–1835," Tennessee State Archives, Nashville (cited hereafter as RBSC).

[7] Martin Case, RBSC.

at any time and cannot be called a fixture or an improvement to the common domain.[8]

The written laws of the Cherokees were clearly the primary basis for decisions by the tribal courts. Yet even with the most sophisticated legislation, written rules are never adequate to cover all possible legal questions and changing circumstances. Undoubtedly in a newly emerging legal system, problems will arise for which the precise statements of the legislature will be inadequate. Where then did the Cherokees turn under these circumstances? What weight was given to the ancient customs, common-law concepts, statutes of the United States, case law from other jurisdictions?

In the earliest days of the new court system the customary law of the tribe was most important. *Fields & Hicks* v. *Ross* discusses the traditional clan revenge system and provides an excellent example of use of tribal custom. The Supreme Court in this case considered the Negro woman in question to be a Cherokee citizen because "she was received by D clan and by the authorities agreeable to the Indian Law and Usage."[9] Extensive use of tribal custom was necessitated by a decision that "the Courts of Justice have cognisance of causes transpiring as far back as the year one-hundred & eight-hundred. 1800."[10]

The Cherokees chose to apply customary tribal law to the extent that it was applied during that year in which a controversy arose. Fortunately the committee and council always carefully avoided retroactive legislation so that laws were written "from this enactment" and new enforcement bodies were restricted to violations occurring after the date of the new law. Many times a statute creating an offense would provide a waiting period of a year before enforcement. Penal legislation did not take effect until ninety days after enactment and until the new law had appeared in the tribal newspapers for a specified period of time. Typical of legislation designed to prevent retroactive application is the Act Confirming Former Decisions approved by the Western Cherokees in 1831.[11]

The courts of the Cherokee Nation, formed by the union of Eastern and Western Cherokees in 1839, were forced to interpret and apply laws enacted by former separate tribal branches in addition to

8 *Percival* v. *Bryant*, OCSC, 8736, 167. See also *Cherokee Nation* v. *Nash*, OCSC, 8736, 205; *Lipe* v. *Mayes*, 8736, 39; *Chandler* v. *Ritter*, 8740, 31–34.
9 *Fields & Hicks* v. *Ross*, RBSC, October Term, 1827.
10 *In the Matter of Jurisdiction of Cherokee Courts*, RBSC.
11 LCN (1852), 173.

the laws of other tribes, the Delawares and Shawnees, who were incorporated into the Cherokee Nation. In *Morgan v. Bushyhead* the court ruled:

The adjudication of all questions shall be according to the provisions of the respective law under which they originated. Cases arising under the laws and usage of the Cherokees previous to their removal West— shall be adjudicated under such laws and usages—also cases originating under the laws and usages in existence among the Western Cherokees previous to the Act of Union July 12th 1839 shall be adjudicated under said laws and usages.[12]

Thus in the 1878 case of *Woodall v. Woodall* the court interpreted a law passed in 1814 to determine whether or not an intermarried white man could transfer his rights to improvements within the Cherokee Nation. The conclusion was that since "there was no marriage law in existence, the first law of that nature having been passed in November 2nd 1819" the party was "living in the nation by the . . . old customs and laws" and according to old usage had no rights of transfer.[13] Similarly in 1892 the validity of a marriage of Delaware Indians was upheld because of old Delaware tribal customs, even though they conflicted with current Cherokee law.[14]

In the years following the American Civil War, customary law came to play a smaller and smaller role in Cherokee ways as the old usage was nullified in conflicts between ancient custom and statutory law. The retreating usage of primitive law ways is illustrated by the case of *Lesher v. Lesher*:

The evidence in this case shows that the Plaintiff and Carter Lesher, decd., did live together and cohabited for a period of several years, and it is argued that such living together and cohabiting constituted marriage between the parties according to the customs of the Cherokee people. Whatever may have been the custom among the Cherokees the law of 1875 regulating marriage like all other general laws applies to all classes of Cherokee citizens and supercides and annuls customs. Cohabiting for any period does not, under the laws of the Cherokee Nation, constitute marriage.[15]

In the early Cherokee Supreme Court decisions no reference is

---

[12] *Morgan v. Bushyhead*, OCSC, 8736, 284.
[13] *Woodall v. Woodall*, OCSC, 8736, 89.
[14] *Arlie Washington v. Edson Washington*, OCSC, 8736, 228, 138 (1889).
[15] *Lesher v. Lesher*, OCSC, 8736, 254–55 (1886).

made to previously decided court cases. Numerous instances of decisions involving precisely the same legal issues in similar factual contexts establish the assertion that the first Cherokee justices acted in a manner typical of nonrecord courts, by deciding each case in a vacuum seemingly unrelated to earlier actions. However, the tribe early recognized restrictions binding parties by decisions in the same case. As early as October, 1868, the court ruled:

On examination of the case and on motion of defendant counsel to dismiss, the court finds evidence that this case has been in litigation many years ago whereupon the rights of the property in question has been settled and that a final decision imenating from this court has been had and executed by the authority of the proper officer. To review a case that has been decided by this court would contravene outside its jurisdiction and in opposition to the law establishing the judiciary.[16]

Clearly by the mid-1870's Cherokee judges and lawyers were no longer familiar with events that had transpired in the Cherokee courts of the 1820's and 1830's. This fact is reflected in reports of the lawyers who were also editors of the *Cherokee Advocate*. In a news report attention was called to a slander case and a conspiracy to overthrow the government of the Cherokee Nation case as being especially interesting because no indictment had ever been brought under these statutes. In fact, cases involving both slander and conspiracy had been tried in Cherokee courts during the period before the American Civil War.[17]

Yet the court had developed a philosophy of being guided, if not bound, by former decisions as early as *Smith* v. *Smith*, reported in 1871. In that case the court noted that "the demise of both Plaintiff & Defendant . . . presents a situation unprecedented in the history of our Courts." The opinion which follows sets forth a ruling that was to be binding on all courts of the Nation:

In the decease of either of the parties to a suit we find the Court has universally sustained a motion to dismiss . . . but the Court is of the belief there should be remedy for such cases and feel authorized to go further than former decisions by giving the following as their decision—That where a Suit is pending before any of the Courts of this Nation and one, or both principals decease before the final termination of the matter at

16 OCSC, 8736, 15.
17 *Cherokee Phoenix*, March 8, 1834; *Cherokee Advocate*, May 26, 1882; April 9, 1846; Sept. 13, 1873.

law, such suits shall be sustained and continued under the representation of a legal administrator.[18]

The Cherokee Supreme Court clearly felt restrained by previous decisions. As soon as briefs of lawyers began to make reference to earlier cases, citations to specific cases began to appear in court opinions. In the 1886 decisions in *Dawson* v. *Dawson*, the court cited an 1871 case of *Cherokee Nation* v. *Nancy Rogers* and concluded that, since "fifteen years have lapsed since this date of this decision and the National Council has not by legislation changed [our interpretation], . . . the court sees no good reason for change."[19] Hereafter use of precedent as a basis for decision became the pattern and the court evidenced concern that particular decisions would "lend aid to establish . . . precidents."[20]

Soon after decisions of Cherokee courts began to be cited, reported cases from other jurisdictions were referred to as evidence in the interpretation of the provisions and doctrines of Cherokee law. The most frequently cited cases were those from neighboring Arkansas, where many tribal attorneys read law and whose courts were the sites of controversies between Cherokees and white men.[21] Arguments were, however, drawn from the decisions of many states and the opinions of the United States Supreme Court.[22]

Hastings v. *Walker*, probably the most elaborate and painstakingly written opinion in the history of the Cherokee Nation, is filled with United States Supreme Court opinions from Justice John Marshall forward and tedious statutory analogies among state officials, national executives, and the officers of the Cherokee Nation.[23] One should not be surprised at the involved use of jurisprudential theory and United States and British history when the nature of the

---

18 *Smith* v. *Smith*, OCSC, 8736, 74 (1871).

19 *Dawson* v. *Dawson*, OCSC, 8736, 257 (1886).

20 *Auschutz* v. *Nelson*, OCSC, 8740, 233, 176–78; *Breedlove* v. *Dawson*, OCSC, 8740, 234, 40–41; *Brewer* v. *Cannon*, OCSC, 8740, 233, 125–27; *Bales* v. *Vann*, OCSC, 8736, 68–69; *Davis* v. *Ross*, OCSC, 8740, 230, 90; *Kelly* v. *Fielson*, OCSC, 8740, 106–107.

21 Arkansas opinions were often the basis for Cherokee decisions as in the Cherokee case *Harris* v. *Fuller*, OCSC, 8740, 230, 98–104 (1893), in which the court cites *Johnson* v. *Clark*, 5 Ark. 321 concluding that "the Arkansas case . . . is an elaborate opinion and all the reasoning seems to justify the above distinction."

22 *Boudinot, Thompson and Hastings* v. *Barnes*, OCSC, 8740, 233, 64 (1894); *E. E. Starr, rep. of Cherokee Nation* v. *Arch McCoy et. al.*, OCSC, 230, 75–76 (1893); *Hastings* v. *Walker*, OCSC 8740, 233, 55–60.

23 *Hastings* v. *Walker*, OCSC, 8740, 233, 55–60.

case—the right to the office of Cherokee attorney general—is considered. However, equally sophisticated arguments were developed in cases such as *Audmain v. Wyly & Davis* and *Ex parte James W. Williams.*[24]

Cherokee lawyers were fond of noting that their judges were "guided by opinions of justice, and on account of the peculiarity of our laws and practices of our laws and practices of our courts, the considerations of equity."[25] On the many questions for which there was no specific legislative act or Cherokee case law, the courts turned to what was denominated in *Woodard v. Wilkerson* as "civilized law . . . recognized as such in all civilized Nations."[26]

Most commonly the court simply declared, as in *Buchanon v. Blackstone*, a case with an astonishingly appropriate name, that "as we have no special statute providing for the foreclosing of mortages . . . we must determine the question under the common law rule of constructing contract."[27] Whereupon the court would generally pronounce without authority or reference what it conceived to be *the* common law on the subject in doubt. Statements such as the following were typical of the nature of these pronouncements: (1) a conveyance of real estate made in writing must be taken to embrace the contract in full;[28] (2) secondary evidence [is] admissible when sustained by other facts in [the] case [and] hearsay evidence admitted so far as sustained by positive evidence;[29] (3) the sanctity of marriage is protected and encouraged by all civilized law;[30] (4) it is a matter of common knowledge that statutes of limitations do not run against the state.[31] While most of the interpretations seemed eminently sound—occasionally even supported by reasoning—Cherokee attorneys sought a more systematic and certain method of determining the common law.

In August, 1876, W. P. Boudinot made an impassioned plea for uniformity in decision making and reliable and consistent procedural rulings. He argued that "unless this practice is followed the adminis-

[24] *Audmain v. Wyly & Davis*, 8740, 230, 121–24 (1893) and *Ex parte James W. Williams*, 8740, 223, 40–46 (1893).
[25] *Cherokee Advocate*, May 19, 1882.
[26] *Woodard v. Wilkerson*, OCSC, 8736, 65.
[27] *Buchanon v. Blackstone*, OCSC, 8740, 223, 181–86 (1894).
[28] *Buchanon v. Blackstone*, OCSC, 8740, 223, 181–86 (1894).
[29] *Cherokee Nation v. John Welsh*, OCSC, 8736, 21 (1876).
[30] *Woodard v. Wilkerson*, OCSC 8736, 65.
[31] *E. E. Starr, rep. of Cherokee Nation v. Arch McCoy, et al.*, OCSC 8736, 230, 75–76 (1892).

tration of law can never become uniform and will always be more or less unequal and unjust." His proposed solution was heavy reliance upon the legal treatises of the day. Boudinot concluded that "there are standard works published to explain and assist the operation of the system of laws" and expressed a hope that "our courts will not make a merit of ignorance of standard works, but will upon all suitable occasions encourage reference to such works as part of the system of law."[32]

Again, as with case law, the courts began to use "standard works" as they were introduced into arguments and briefs by members of the bar. In 1879 the *Advocate* editor stated that "the evidence was not what Greenleaf calls good circumstantial evidence" and in later cases, "Attorney's . . . quoted Hurd on Criminal Procedure and . . . also read from Cooley on Constitutional limitations."[33] The following paragraph from *Audmain* v. *Wyly & Davis* illustrates the widespread use of the encyclopedic and dictionary law resources:

The title must in general . . . be fully and particularly alleged. See: Stend on Civil Pleading page 222. . . . Thus in a complaint for personal property the complaint must allege ownership either special or general, and the Statement of a mere legal conclusion that the Plaintiff is entitled to possession is not sufficient: See: Boon on Code Pleading page 25. In an action for the destruction of property the allegation of ownership in the Plaintiff is material, and a failure to deny it in the answer is an admission of its truth: *St. Louis and Iron Mountain Road Co.* v. *Strecht*, 38 Ark., Rept., p. 357. . . . Lawful Possession is defined in Bouviers Law Dictionary to be equivalent to peaceably possessed.[34]

The commonly held belief that United States statutes were applied in controversies between two Cherokee citizens within the Cherokee Nation is erroneous. This use remained a highly controversial issue and was the subject of much litigation and several advisory opinions of the attorney general of the United States.[35] The Cherokee courts decided that United States statutes did not apply and were not part of the common law of the tribal court system, but United States courts thought otherwise.[36]

[32] *Cherokee Advocate*, Aug. 19, 1876.
[33] *Ibid.*, Jan. 4, 1879, and Oct. 7, 1893.
[34] *Audmain* v. *Wyly & Davis*, OCSC, 8740, 230, 121–24 at 123 (1893).
[35] See Manuscripts, Cherokee-Federal Relations, Vertical Files, Indian Archives, Oklahoma Historical Society.
[36] *Cherokee Advocate*, Oct. 28, 1893; Nov. 18, 1893; Jan. 10, 1894.

The issues exploded in a series of habeas corpus cases in the 1890's.[37] The arguments were summarized in the *Advocate*. "The [the Cherokee Nation] denied that the legislature had provided for the issuance of the Writ. The applicants contended it was a constitutional remedy to which every man in the United States and Cherokee Nation was entitled to, and the omission of the legislature could not prevent him invoking the Writ."[38] The decision of the Cherokee Supreme Court acknowledged the desirability of such a statute but concluded:

The matter complained of in this petition could be reviewed only, if we are to be guided by the U. S. Reports, on Writ of Error, and in the U. S. and State Courts, this Writ is authorized by Statute, and in this Nation we have no such statute. We are fully persuaded that we need some law on this subject and these Writs of Error and Habeas Corpus and authorizing Appeals in Criminal Cases, but it ought not to be expected of this Court to supply the lack of legislation in these matters by such a wonderful stretch of its judicial powers.[39]

The appellate courts were simply unwilling, in the modern sense, to legislate judicially. Although ready to stretch a point to encompass the equities of a case, they would not step across the boundaries constitutionally separating the three branches of government. Case after case bears the message that courts adjudicate, legislatures enact laws, and executives administer the government and enforce the laws. A wall existed between these functions, and the court did not intend to knock it down.[40] A typical opinion supporting this position concluded that "the court . . . is at a loss to adopt rules to cover the whole grounds complained of. . . . The court view the misfortune that is now complained of [of] such magnitude . . . would respectfully suggest to the parties that the National Council at an early day may have the matter fully brought before them and that a law be passed for the benefit of the courts to act in the promises whereby Justice may be [maintained?] to all."[41]

[37] The most notable of these was the controversial opinion of Judge Parker. The Cherokee Bill cases created considerable excitement in the Indian Territory. For discussion of jurisdiction in criminal cases see *Famous Smith* v. *United States*, 151 U.S. 50 (1894).

[38] *Cherokee Advocate*, Oct. 7, 1893.

[39] *Ex parte James W. Williams*, OCSC, 8740, 223, 46 (1893).

[40] See CLCN (1852), Constitution, Art. II, III, IV, V. This theme appears in many of the decisions in OCSC. See especially the discussion of jurisdiction of the court in OCSC, 8736, 106.

[41] *Cherokee Nation* v. *George W. Johnson*, OCSC 8736, 24.

This is not to suggest that the appellate courts felt no obligation to provide assistance to the other branches. A highly effective means of co-operation rested upon the use of the advisory opinion. The court could ask a legislative committee the intended meaning of a specific piece of legislation, or the executive, lower courts, or legislature might ask for a similar interpretation of a regulation from the court.[42] The judiciary had no requirement of a case in controversy.[43] In fact, one of the most important functions of advisory opinions of the Supreme Court was the promulgation of rules of evidence and procedure for the lower courts.[44]

[42] This procedure was used most extensively following the adoption of the Code of 1876.

[43] OCSC, 8736, 39, 106.

[44] "Rulings of Cherokee Supreme Court," typescript, Indian Heritage Association; "Rules adopted and Established for the More Uniform Practice of the Lower and Special Supreme Court of the Cherokee Nation," OCSC 8736, 79.

Criminal Punishment: A Case Study of Tribal Change

IX

THE DEVELOPMENT of criminal punishments reflects the emergence of new Cherokee standards and values. The evolution of punishment for criminal conduct is illustrative of the whole changing legal process. In this specific area we can view a transformation in philosophy from clan revenge to public reform.

Revenge was the cornerstone of traditional regulation of criminal behavior. Among the ancient Cherokees, the greatest of all public disgraces was to fail to avenge a crime, for "the man who would not revenge the murder of a relative was called by way of reproach *ku tsa*."[1] The traditional Cherokees had developed an elaborate system of punishments avenging the exact nature of the offense. Women, for example, assigned the duty of inflicting the penalty for violation of certain marriage regulations and taboos, used "whipping and cropping [the ears or nose]."[2]

The range of permissible retributions is astonishing. For example, "if in fighting, one bruised the other, the same kind of a bruise was made on his flesh." Revenge in kind was the rule extending to scratching, gouging, or knocking out teeth. This might include having someone "killed in a similar manner . . . but more generally the murderer was taken to the top of a steep and high precipice . . . and cast off head long and dashed to pieces on the rocks below."[3]

Whipping and hanging became the accepted forms of public punishment and remained so until the 1870's, when the national jail

[1] John Howard Payne Papers, Roll 6987, 524, and Roll 6986, 4–5.
[2] John Howard Payne Papers, Roll 6987, 401.
[3] *Ibid.*, 525.

was constructed at Tahlequah.[4] Building a prison was an old dream of the Cherokees dating from a proposal of Standing Turkey, who in 1761 proclaimed that "we are now building a Strong House, and the very first one of our People, that does damage to the English, shall be put there until the English fetch them."[5] Whipping was undoubtedly the most common punishment under the early Cherokee written laws. Sentences ranged from one hundred lashes for "any persons who shall bring into the Cherokee Nation, without permission . . . a white family" to "fifty-nine stripes on the bareback" for any "male Indian or white man marrying a negro woman slave."[6]

The purpose of this punishment was originally more the infliction of pain than the hope of reform through humiliation. There was also the hope that those witnessing the whipping would be deterred from crime. One observer noted that "whipping was no disgrace to an Indian . . . the Cherokees have no marks of public disgrace."[7] Explaining the use of lashes, an advocate of reform concluded that "whipping for offenses . . . was adopted as a punishment . . . because that or some other equally repulsive mode of administering justice was at the time the only available means . . . they had not the means to build a penitentiary; they flogged because they could not confine."[8]

The practice of public whipping, administered by public officers, was difficult to justify in the minds of many of the traditional Cherokees. Even the light-horsemen, appointed to administer the sentences, were not the smooth operating group which the Cherokees might have wished them to be. An incident recorded in the journals of the American Board of Foreign Missions is illustrative of the difficulties in punishment during the transition period of Cherokee law:

On our way from Turkey Town yesterday, we rode to the door of a house and were saluted by a man partially intoxicated. In a few moments, a company of lighthorse rode up—dismounted, seized the man—bound him and led him away to a tree and tied him for the purpose of whipping him

---

[4] The Cherokee denied using whipping as a means to collect debt as is suggested in Gregg's *Commerce on the Prairie*. Cherokees were sensitive to charges of barbaric punishments. *Cherokee Advocate*, Oct. 19, 1844, and Dec. 21, 1878.

[5] Cited in John Dickson, "The Judicial History of the Cherokee Nation from 1721 to 1835." (Ph.D. dissertation, University of Oklahoma, 1964), 74 n. 75.

[6] LCN (1852), 10–11, 38.

[7] *Cherokee Advocate*, Jan. 23, 1845; June 9, 1845; July 17, 1845; June 3, 1876. John Howard Payne Papers, Roll 6987, 527. Contrast with Reid, *A Law of Blood*, 229–45.

[8] *Cherokee Advocate*, Oct. 22, 1870.

for theft. We rode on, however, before the punishment was inflicted. This company of lighthorse was composed of well dressed and apparently lonely young men. After punishing the man above mentioned they came on to Grimmets, got to drinking, and took Grimmet and whipt him sixty lashes. Being perhaps a little ashamed at what they had illegally done the commenced whipping one another fifty lashes each. . . .

About noon the Captain of the lighthorse rode up to the door, bruised and intoxicated. He said that others had bound & whipt him that he might know how it felt to be whipt or to that effect. About sunset one of the lonely young men who yesterday shown as the brightest gem, rode up, bruised and almost deranged by liquor. I was much distressed at this sight. Soon others rode up, and accompanied him from the house. . . .

During meeting a man came in and seized one of the young men I have mentioned and took him out, saying it was known that Grimmet whom the light horse last whipt was not guilty and it was determined that they should all be at his house that day (probably to answer for this conduct.)[9]

A note in the missionary journal of the following Saturday explained that "we're informed that the difficulty with the light horse was amicably settled." There was no hint what the solution might have been.

In addition to whipping, the first written laws retained traces of earlier forms of punishments. The most obvious of these was "cropping" or defacing for sexual crimes. Llewelyn and Hoebel have documented this practice of removing an ear or slashing the nose as practiced among the Plains tribes.[10] John Howard Payne's informants recorded this as a Cherokee custom.[11] The first published statute on rape provided this seemingly barbaric revenge for what the Cherokees regarded as an even more barbarous crime. In the language of the statute a person found guilty of rape "shall be punished with fifty lashes upon the bare back and the left ear cropped off close to the head; for the second offense, one hundred lashes and the other ear cut off; for the third offense, death."[12]

The most important traditional survival element was the institution of outlawry, or placing individuals guilty of specified crimes beyond the protection of the tribe. This procedure, existing among

[9] Buttrick Papers, Mission Papers, 1822, American Board of Foreign Missions, Harvard University Library, Cambridge.

[10] Karl Llewelyn and E. Adamson Hoebel, *The Cheyenne Way*, 187–88.

[11] John Howard Payne Papers, Roll 6987, 401.

[12] LCN (1852), 53–54.

the ancients, was revived by Chief John Ross for "political crimes," such as the sale of tribal lands. What the custom did, in practice, was to declare that all citizens privately selling or making treaties concerning the public domain should be punished by death and that individuals so accused who refused to surrender themselves for trial might be killed with no state reprisal. The murderer became, in effect, the public executioner.[13] This practice, denounced by the military officers assigned to protect the Cherokees as vicious and vindictive, ultimately escalated into the Cherokee civil war of the 1840's.[14]

Cherokee punishments were cumulative. Second and third offenses produced progressively more severe treatment and could lead to hanging if the conduct became habitual.[15] That the Cherokees came to view this increased severity as an instrument of criminal rehabilitation is shown by a case in which an individual was tried for a second offense of stealing. The issue in this case was whether or not the more severe second penalty should be applied, since the theft in question occurred before the infliction of the first punishment. The better reasoning seemed to be that the stiffer penalty was not required, since the justification for the harsher action was that the first punishment had not had the chance to succeed in making the criminal a better citizen.[16] The *Cherokee Advocate* of August 22, 1877, reported the sentencing of "Willis Pettit (colored) convicted of disturbing a religious meeting while intoxicated . . . the second offense of a similar nature to his account, and it is hoped the penalty may be the means of reforming him."

The campaign to secure construction of a national penitentiary, which began before removal from Georgia, reflected the emerging philosophy of rehabilitation and punishment. Tribal funds were limited, and many objected to such a large expenditure on convicted criminals. The fight was a long one. The arguments put forward for the construction of the facility are persuasive in both economic and humanitarian terms. Cases of individuals whipped in error are cited

---

[13] The ancient custom was reaffirmed with specific reference to the murders of the Ridges and Elias Boudinot. Wardell, *A Political History of the Cherokee Nation, 1838–1907*, 16–19.

[14] See generally *The Internal Feuds Among the Cherokees*, April 13, 1846, Senate Document 298.

[15] LCN (1852), 53–54; CLCN (1892), Chapter IV, 158–207.

[16] *Cherokee Advocate*, Feb. 28, 1874.

with the conclusion, "If a man . . . is whipped by mistake, there is no way to make amends."[17] The "practice of whipping" was assailed as "altogether too barbarous for a country that pretends to the enlightenment that this country does."[18] The rehabilitation potential and the saving in money expended to guard prisoners were further justifications presented.[19]

Once constructed, the national jail was conceived of not only as a place of incarceration for the dangerous criminal but as a center in which the wayward soul could "learn a trade" to enable himself to "make an economic contribution."[20] As one Cherokee explained, "Our national prison is a good place to get drunken men sober, and to bring them to reason."[21] The *Cherokee Advocate* chronicled that "convicts of the National Prison are to be taught mechanical arts, such as shoe making, blacksmithing, wagon making &c" and that "the W.C.T.U. has given the convicts at the National Prison both English and Cherokee Bibles and Testaments and some other literature."[22] Thus the Cherokee prisoner was given a chance at an earthly skill and eternal salvation while paying for his past misadventures.

Furthermore the convict was given a chance to perform good works for the Nation, "filling up gullies in . . . Streets," "cutting wood, . . . preparing for cold weather," putting up a fence around the prison, and constructing a national lime kiln.[23] The results of these activities, if the contemporary accounts are to be believed, was prisoners who "want to profit by their confinement, they say, and had rather work than be idle."[24]

The Cherokees took great pride in the operation of the prison and the conduct of their "zebra coated brigade."[25] The annual report of the medical superintendent continually showed "the health of the prisoners good" and "the rooms kept as clean as circumstances will permit and disinfected as required."[26] For contrast the tribal

[17] *Ibid.*, May 27, 1876.

[18] *Ibid.*, May 13, 1876.

[19] *Ibid.*, Oct. 22, 1870; June 3, 1876; Nov. 11, 1876; Dec. 21, 1878.

[20] *Ibid.*, Aug. 22, 1877.

[21] *Ibid.*, Dec. 8, 1880.

[22] *Ibid.*, Jan. 5, 1878, and Sept. 26, 1888.

[23] *Ibid.*, Aug. 31, 1881; Oct. 26, 1881; April 11, 1877; Oct. 5, 1878.

[24] *Ibid.*, April 11, 1877.

[25] *Ibid.*, Oct. 20, 1882.

[26] *Annual Report, Medical Superintendent, Cherokee Nation*, 1894.

newspaper printed stories of the inhuman conditions in the federal prison at Fort Smith.[27]

The Indians firmly believed that "the prisoners in our jail have a kind and intelligent but firm and resolute keeper and guard, and both the class of prisoners and the manner of their confinement is different from what is in older countries where they have well-defined criminal classes and the handling of them is more severe."[28] The Cherokee opinion seems to have been confirmed by independent reports.[29]

The success of the national prison stimulated a movement to build district jails to hold prisoners prior to trial. None were ever constructed, and marshals and sheriffs paraded about the country, guarding prisoners who accompanied them on horseback in this Indian form of police custody. There was a good deal of truth in the argument that these lines of equestrian criminals drew so much attention that their romanticized image encouraged others to follow outlaw paths. Some argued that "the practice of paying able bodied men to run after every prisoner while he is going, and to pass the time in idleness or gambling when he is stationary, is mischievous in itself [and] the jail system would undoubtedly operate to lessen the expense."[30]

Hanging became the approved method of execution in capital cases. The Cherokees self-righteously considered themselves far more civilized than their Creek and Choctaw neighbors, who executed by firing squad and suffocation. An amusing story which survives in Cherokee folklore from what was purportedly the first public execution in the Cherokee Nation West tells of the hangmen who were unfamiliar with the exact procedure to be followed and who, after much delay, asked the prisoner to jump from the hanging tree with the rope around his neck. The convict is reported to have obliged his executioners.

The making ready of the gallows became the signal for a public gathering. Few Cherokee citizens missed the socially approved object lesson of an evil man dangling from the end of a rope.[31] An Indian

27 *Cherokee Advocate*, March 9, 1881, [federal jails]; April 29, 1891 [Creeks have no jails]; June 29, 1898 [Indian Territory jails].

28 *Ibid.*, May 2, 1877.

29 St. Louis newspaper editor's report as reprinted in *Cherokee Advocate*, Dec. 14, 1878.

30 *Cherokee Advocate*, March 23, 1877.

31 T. L. Ballenger, *Around Tahlequah Council Fires*, 45–46; *Cherokee Phoenix*, April 24, 1828; *Cherokee Advocate*, Nov. 9, 1844; Feb. 13, 1845; April 2, 1846.

who was to be hanged might be allowed to go home, plant his crops, and make arrangements for his family.[32] The family often attended and picnicked on the lawn with the assembled crowd.[33] Not surprisingly, many vivid accounts of hangings, gallows confessions, and the redeeming virtues of the occasions have survived.

The Cherokees hoped that their public executions would produce a state of "Christian sensibility" in all citizens. The looming presence of *the Structure*, however, offended the sensibilities of some citizens, who argued that "we would express a hope that the gallows may not be allowed to stand where it now is. Instead of rearing its hideous form over the town and haunting with its frightful associations the most beautiful of the surrounding eminences, it should be consigned to some less conspicuous situation."[34]

[32] There is no provision in the law allowing for this, but such procedure was apparently an early practice.

[33] The author was told of this custom by a Cherokee who worked for the author's family. The Indian had attended his own father's hanging and the victim had lunched with wife and children within the shadow of the gallows.

[34] *Cherokee Advocate*, Feb. 13, 1845.

The End of Cherokee Law

X

THE CLERK of the Cherokee Supreme Court noted on the ledger pages for 1898 the absence of the three tribal justices. The record book for that year opened with the miscellaneous federal orders closing the Cherokee courts; then the pages were blank.[1] In 1898 the formal use of Cherokee law ended. Cherokee judges were no longer allowed to enforce tribal regulations.

What had formally begun at an Indian council at Broom Town in 1808 was suspended by federal legislative fiat at Washington in 1898. Most unceremoniously the Cherokee courts ceased to function. Only a ghost of native government survived, presiding over the dismantling of tribal existence and preserving tribal integrity in alloting common lands directly to individual Cherokees.

The process of abolishing tribal courts had begun in 1889, when the Fiftieth Congress passed a statute "to establish a United States court in Indian Territory."[2] The new court was given "exclusive original jurisdiction over all offenses against the laws of the United States committed within the Indian Territory." Section 6, however, specifically exempted "controversies between persons of Indian blood only." In 1896, Congress proclaimed it to be the duty of the United States "to establish a government in the Indian Territory which will rectify the existing inequalities and afford needful protection to the lives and property of citizens and residents therein."[3]

[1] Minutes of the Supreme Court, Cherokee Nation, 234, 299–301. Indian Archives, Oklahoma Historical Society.

[2] Charles Kappler (ed.), *Indian Affairs: Laws and Treaties*, I, 39–44. (Cited hereafter as *Indian Affairs*).

[3] *Ibid.*, I, 90.

The final blow to the court structure came in 1897, when the United States Congress restricted jurisdiction of tribal courts in Indian Territory. The act provided that after January 1, 1898, the United States courts in the Indian Territory would have "original and exclusive jurisdiction and authority to try and determine all civil causes in law and equity . . . and all criminal causes." The law also provided that the statutes of the United States and the laws of the state of Arkansas would be in effect and "apply to all persons of all races."[4]

Some question remained whether the tribal courts would be continued in operation to complete business already initiated and for cases arising before January, 1898. This question was answered by the Curtis Act, which clearly outlined the procedures to be followed in ending tribal courts. Section 28 provided that after July 1, 1898, "all tribal courts in Indian Territory shall be abolished, and no officer of said court shall . . . have any authority whatever to do or perform any act."[5]

A summary end for a system that had survived so very much. In less than ninety years the tribal courts had faced six major crises and had weathered five of them surprisingly well. The first two had been confrontations with traditionalists, Doublehead and White Path, who had opposed adoption of the new legal system.[6] Doublehead was executed,[7] and the White Path faction, never able to build solid tribal support among dissident full bloods, died away.[8] The three remaining tests—Georgia removal, Cherokee Civil War, and American Civil War—were in a sense all related to the same basic tribal conflict from which emerged a consensus that the legal system must survive.

The final crisis, which the system could not withstand, was the white onslaught which followed the American Civil War.[9] For all the apparent sophistication and the complex codes, the Cherokee courts had evolved in a protected environment far away from the disruptive forces of large bodies of whites. An end to this protected

[4] *Ibid.*, I, 86–89.
[5] *Ibid.*, I, 90–100.
[6] Cherokee Tribal Papers, Indian Heritage Association; Robert F. Berkhofer, Jr., *Salvation and the Savage*, 138 and n. 33.
[7] Malone, *Cherokees of the Old South*, 196.
[8] Primary material on White Path is available in the Cherokee Mission Papers, Andover Library, Harvard University, Cambridge.
[9] See Margaret Louise Barnes, "Intruders in the Cherokee Nation, 1834-1907." (Master's thesis, University of Oklahoma, 1933.)

atmosphere came with the Treaty of 1866, terminating Cherokee participation as a Confederate ally in the American Civil War. The terms of the treaty were dictated by government officials determined to open tribal sanctuaries to systematic development by railroads and farmers.[10] When the plan of Colonel Ely Parker, himself an Iroquois, ended the policy of treaty making with Indian tribes, the Cherokees were thrown upon the mercy of the United States Congress, whose position in a contest between Indian rights and expansion of railroads and white settlement was never in doubt.[11]

The presence of white intruders created considerable pressures on the Cherokee legal system. The first of these was jurisdictional. Thousands—eventually upward of one hundred thousand whites— were not subject to Cherokee law enforcement. Further complicating this crisis was the fact that any controversy between whites and Cherokee citizens fell outside the jurisdiction of tribal courts. The second problem, closely related to the first, was the strain of determining who was a Cherokee citizen. Determination of this elusive right was given, in the final analysis, to the Cherokee tribunals. Federal courts, nonetheless, continued to decide the issue. The benefits of tribal citizenship were great and many a land-hungry white was willing to claim Indian blood to gain a share of the tribal domain.[12]

The coming of the railroad, intensified mining and timber exploitation, and the building of towns and cities severely dislocated the people of the Cherokee Nation.[13] Tribesmen were subjected to the pressures of rapid change. All the elements of the lawless frontier were present. Intruders were almost as numerous as citizens—and most claimed that they were citizens.[14] Minimum consensus of shared values necessary to preserve public order was under severe strain. Not only was the pressure of outside white interference

---

10 Wardell, A Political History of the Cherokee Nation, 1838–1907, 177–207; Kappler, Indian Affairs, II, 942–50, 996–97.

11 As of March 3, 1871, the Congress prohibited treaty making which was alleged to acknowledge Indian tribes as sovereign states. Wardell, A Political History of the Cherokee Nation, 1838–1907, 255–56.

12 Cherokee Advocate, Jan. 12, 1878; Feb. 10, 1882; Sept. 14, 1883; Feb. 23, 1887; Nov. 18, 1891; March 23, 1892, Jan. 31, 1894.

13 V. V. Masterson, The Katy Railroad and the Last Frontier, 98–119; Walter A. Johnson, "Brief History of the Missouri-Kansas-Texas Railroad Lines," Chronicles of Oklahoma, Vol. 14 (1946), 340–58; Grant Foreman, Muskogee: The Biography of a Town; Cherokee Advocate, July 27, 1881; June 2, 1882.

14 Cherokee Advocate, Dec. 4, 1885; May 7, 1886; Aug. 24, 1887; Aug. 26, 1893.

uncontrollable but tribal disagreement on a solution encouraged the intruders and "territorializers."

The Indian country was a dangerous place in which to be. The Cherokees argued that, if white men were removed, as their treaties and federal law required, their own courts could handle all problems relating to Cherokee citizens. The settlers' lobbies demanded that the Indians be "protected" by opening tribal land to the settlers' own "civilizing influence." Judge Parker acknowledged the magnitude of the lawlessness but exonerated the Indians.[15] In the end, the territorializers won, and Congress passed the series of acts closing tribal courts and opening Indian lands.[16]

When the land speculators finally won, the propaganda of a lawless and ungovernable Cherokee Nation came to be accepted as fact. The Cherokee position, that whatever lawlessness existed was essentially a product of white intruders, has, even until this time, been largely ignored. W. A. Duncan, a tribal delegate, presented a most persuasive argument on behalf of the Cherokees:

> The evidences of successful government are to be found in the prosperity of the people. Tried by this standard the Cherokee government will compare favorably with other governments. While we admit that imperfections and failures have more or less frequently presented themselves in the operation of our government, we are confident in the assertion that it has been quite as successful as other governments in promoting the well being of the people. . . . As in every State of the Union, there are two governments, namely, the Federal and State governments; so in Indian Territory there are two governments, the Federal government and the Indian government. There are also two classes of crime committed in Indian Territory, one class falling within the jurisdiction of the Indian courts, and the other falling within the jurisdiction of the Federal courts. Hence, from the conditions of the case it follows that if an omission

[15] *Ibid.*, May 20, 1874; March 2, 1878; May 9, 1884; Sept. 26, 1888; Feb. 28, 1894; Aug. 15, 1894; Nov. 7, 1894; Nov. 14, 1894; Feb. 13, 1895. The following sources present a fairly accurate picture of the Cherokee Nation during this period. J. H. Beadle, *Western Wilds and the Men Who Redeem Them*; Fred Harrington, *Hanging Judge*; C. H. McKennon, *Iron Men: United States Marshalls Who Rode the Indian Territory*; and Glenn Shirley, *Law West of Fort Smith: A History of Frontier Justice in Indian Territory, 1834–1896* and James Oakley Murphy, "The Work of Judge Parker in the United States District Court for the Western District of Arkansas," (Master's thesis, University of Oklahoma, 1939), 10–72; Gregory and Strickland (eds.), *Hell on the Border.*

[16] Charles Wayne Ellinger, "The Drive for Statehood in Oklahoma, 1889–1906," *Chronicles of Oklahoma*, Vol. 41 (1963), 15–37; *Cherokee Advocate*, May 16, 1894; March 6, 1895; Feb. 5, 1898; Kappler, *Indian Affairs*, I, 39–44, 86–89, 90–100, 967–84.

on part of the Indian courts to enforce law in some instances proves that the Indian governments are failures, similar omissions on part of the United States court would prove the United States Government a failure. It is not at all fair to blame the Indian government for not suppressing crime in persons over whom they have no jurisdiction, while many of the greatest crimes committed in the Territory are chargeable to that class of persons. Hence, if there be blame to attach to the governments in Indian Territory, let the party to which it is due be charged with it.[17]

Truly the pressures of outside white interference would have tested a firmly established legal order. The tribal court system was simply not prepared to deal with the intruder crisis. The failure of the United States to expel the white intruder doomed the Indian nations. Management of Cherokee cases was still a challenge to the tribal court where vestiges of the ancient Cherokee clan revenge systems still remained. Alleged witches were occasionally shot by the superstitious, and protective rings modeled after the ancient system of clan revenge were clandestinely operating until the final days of tribal courts.[18]

Yet the legal system, for all these failures, served the tribe remarkably well. One has only to contrast the peaceful passing of the Cherokee state with the slow and bloody death of many other Indian cultures to conclude that the tribe was given valuable time in which to prepare for the end. Among those who benefited most from the development of the court system were, without doubt, the intermarried Indians who initiated the courts to provide an institutional framework for their newly acquired wealth. Furthermore, these citizens were able to make the transition from tribal state to actual statehood with the same ease with which they guided the tribe from clan to court. Many of their numbers became leaders of the new state of Oklahoma.[19]

Nonetheless, it would be an error to suggest that the mass of full bloods were exploited by the legal system or even that it was a form of colonialism imposed from above by their own people. The traditional Cherokee-speaking citizen helped create the stable government in which he actively participated. It was this traditional Cherokee

[17] Cherokee Tribal Documents, Earl Boyd Pierce Collection, Fort Gibson, Oklahoma.
[18] See especially the reports of the organized ring of avengers. *Cherokee Advocate*, April 20, 1892; April 27, 1892.
[19] Gregory and Strickland (eds.), *Starr's History of the Cherokees*, 489–672.

who was the real victim of the abolition of tribal courts and government. He was not ready, as was the mixed blood, to "move into the cultural mainstream of life in a white community."

Roach Young, a Cherokee full blood, argued, "My country has been charged with considerable lawlessness . . . and that our government was a failure, but as far as I know it is not that way." Speaking through an interpreter, this native delegate pleaded with a congressional committee. He refused to accept the position that "people were held in terror down there." He concluded that "we have different officers down there throughout the nation, who execute and enforce the laws and make arrests in case of violation of law just like any other country."[20]

These full bloods and the non-English-speaking mixed bloods, who had played important roles in tribal government as sheriffs, committeemen, lawyers, and judges, retreated in the face of statehood. Hundreds who might have been leaders in the Cherokee district courts or prominent in the National Council chose not to participate in the transformation to statehood.[21]

The frustration which the full blood faced is conveyed in a memorial they submitted to Congress in 1897. In this document they argued that "we could not understand the white man's laws which are in big books and that we cannot read English; but that our children, who are now attending school, are learning English, and will, after awhile, be prepared to live under the whiteman's laws."[22]

The potential damage to the full blood was one of the major points of "An Appeal: By the Delegates of the Five Civilized Nations of Indians to the Congress at the United States for Justice." The message was presented as follows:

> To the full-blood Indians the United States courts will be, indeed, a foreign tribunal. They understand neither the English language nor the laws and practices of the white man's courts and consequently they will be led to look upon these courts as places of hardship to them rather than sources of protection. Their ignorance of the English language and also their ignorance of the laws that are to be administered by these courts will render them ready prey for designing sharpies who never fail to pervert and trifle with the rights of the ignorant and helpless.[23]

[20] Cherokee Tribal Documents, Earl Boyd Pierce Collection, Fort Gibson, Oklahoma.
[21] Gregory and Strickland, *Starr's History of the Cherokees*, xi.
[22] *Cherokee Advocate*, June 26, 1897.
[23] *Ibid.*, Feb. 27, 1895.

The full blood was thrust into a world ready to prey upon his weaknesses. This traditional Cherokee, without doubt, suffered most by the abolition of his tribal courts and native government. Judge Parker had warned a congressional Indian committee of the dangers and had predicted the tragedy, which came to pass:

A destruction of [the Cherokee] system of government at this time and the establishment of Territorial government over them, with free access of white men, would have precisely the same effect as our action toward the California Indian has had upon those people there; it would send them out as beggars without a dollar. The man who has a blanket mortgage would rush in there and persuade them that they needed money to build a house or improve their lands, and in six months, if left with the ownership over the soil, they would not have a place to lay their heads in that country. It would be, in my judgment, absolute cruelty. They are shielded by their government. . . . They protect their own people, so that there is not a pauper Indian in the whole Five Civilized Tribes.[24]

Angie Debo chronicled the plight of these Indians in her moving narrative *And Still the Waters Ran*. Perhaps, as the full-blood memorial argued, another generation could have made the difference. We will never know. But a few tragic facts are apparent.

Today the children of the Oklahoma Cherokee settlements are less well educated and are more poverty-stricken than their grandparents. Thousands of Cherokees have retribalized and have moved beyond the fringes of Oklahoma society. The numbers participating in a separate Cherokee society appear to be increasing. Cherokee ghettoes are hidden in the hollows of the Cookson Hills. Too often to these Cherokees the "laws" are hostile white men looked upon with suspicion. These communities and their people are more distant from the Oklahoma courts than they were from the operation of the Cherokee courts.[25]

Perhaps such a disappointing end was inevitable. But the 1808 enactment of a written law had been, in a very real sense, a declaration of faith in the rule of law, a faith to which the Cherokees tenaciously held through expropriation of their lands by the state of Georgia, removal under the federal bayonet, bloody tribal civil war, and the repercussions of the white man's Civil War. Yet from the moment it

[24] Cherokee Tribal Documents, Earl Boyd Pierce Collection, Fort Gibson, Oklahoma.

[25] Albert L. Wahrhaftig, "The Tribal Cherokee Population of Oklahoma," *Current Anthropology*, Vol. 9 (1968), 510–18.

became apparent that Justice Marshall was unable to enforce the Court's decision in the Georgia controversy, the end could have been predicted.

The original adoption of written laws was viewed as a step in the "civilization" process preparing the Indian for that ultimate of all nineteenth-century achievements—United States citizenship. It was unfortunate for the United States Congress, bitterly ironic, that in the process the Cherokees learned too well these lessons from their white mentors and that they should have had the arrogance to believe red men were entitled to govern themselves in their own territory under their own laws. In the end, even their simple dream of Sequoyah—the Indian state with a Cherokee name—came to naught.[26]

26 See generally Amos Maxwell, *The Sequoyah Convention* and Annie H. Abel, "Proposals for an Indian State, 1778–1878," *Annual Report of the American Historical Association for 1907*, I, 87–104. For a discussion of some of the Indian influences on law in the state of Oklahoma see Rennard Strickland and James C. Thomas, "Most Sensibly Conservative and Safely Radical: Oklahoma's Constitutional Regulation of Economic Power, Land Ownership, and Corporate Monopoly," *Tulsa Law Review*, Vol. 9 (1973), 167–238.

Survival of Traditional Cherokee Ways

XI

To THE Cherokee Nation the transition from priestly theocracy to trial by a jury of peers was decidedly different from an American jurisdiction adopting the Uniform Commercial Code or abolishing capital punishment. Traditional Cherokee thought on laws and legal institutions survived long after the adoption of written laws. To a people who felt that every rock and every living thing involved an earthly manifestation of a spirit world, conceiving of law as "social engineering" was impossible.[1]

Cherokee historians have mistakenly concluded that once the new written laws were adopted traditional Cherokee elements soon disappeared. This was not true. A unique characteristic of the Cherokee people has always been their adaptability. When the priestly religious complex ceased to function as a tribal governing force, lesser "medicine men," with purported powers to bring divine assistance and to heal, assumed many of the new social and legal roles in the life of the individual Cherokee.[2]

A unique intermingling of newly written laws and the ancient spiritual culture emerged. As late as the mid-1960's, Cherokee ethnologists Jack and Anna Kilpatrick discovered the survival of the use of magical legal incantations (*idi:gawe;sdi*) "to 'remake' tobacco . . . to weary judges, to create indecision in juries, to raise dissension in the prosecuting team and to addle witnesses."[3] Specific formulas reported

[1] Jack Gregory and Rennard Strickland, *Cherokee Spirit Tales*, 1–3.
[2] Mooney, *The Swimmer Manuscript*, 83–116.
[3] Jack Frederick Kilpatrick and Anna Gritts Kilpatrick, *Run Toward the Nightland: Magic of the Oklahoma Cherokees*, 101 (cited hereafter as *Run Toward the Nightland.*)

by the Kilpatricks included those for minor crimes and for homicides and to assist prisoners escape, aid fugitives from the law, and protect peace officers.[4]

This process of acquiring spirit help was, in fact, a long, complex one with roots in the mystical mind of the Cherokee. For example, a Cherokee charged with murder would think the following chant four times a day and drink water for thirty days from a glass containing a bullet he had found. The chant must be thought exactly as follows:

Now! Fishinghawks!
Ha! Very quickly You have just come down to the
very middle of the Thicket.
You have just come to give him life.
Then you great Wizard, You can fail in nothing.
Now this is his name, _____. and
this is his clan, _____.
You have just come raise up his soul.
You released him alive![5]

Such rituals were designed for "curing" or "remaking" tobacco to be smoked in the vicinity of and within the courtroom. Deviation from the prescribed form was fatal to the spell. In a typical formula the recitation was a simple four-line verse:

My Soul is not to return.
The Little Person is not to return.
The Wizard is not to return.
Now! Listen! At night their feet will be pointed
toward the Seven Clans, never to be traced.

But the sorcerer must go at midnight to running water, sing the song, recite the incantation four times, wash his face, throw water over his head seven times, and finally roll the tobacco. The ritual was enacted in this manner four times at intervals so spaced as to conclude at dawn. The sorcerer fasted the next day and then with the defendant smoked the tobacco at the courthouse, if possible during the trial.[6]

It is interesting to compare the magical-spiritual use of tobacco today with the account of an early observer of the Cherokee court systems. George Foster reported on a day he spent in a Cherokee tribal court in the early 1890's:

[4] *Ibid.*, 101–112.
[5] *Ibid.*, 102.
[6] *Ibid.*, 103–104.

As the case proceeded, and evidence grew more complicated, the jury dropped into apparently deep meditation. Finally one drew out a long pipe, filled it with tobacco, and commenced to smoke. The interested audience outside the bars also lit their pipes, and at length the judge, five of the jurymen, and nearly the whole audience were smoking. [T]his assemblage [was] blue with smoke of tobacco.[7]

In many Cherokee communities there was a peculiar mixture of the ancient religion and the statutory white-based legal system. Law-enforcement officers were often drawn from among the conjurers or were said to possess special knowledge and power in the supernatural. Rarely even today does one ever speak to a Cherokee who has not heard of or used some magic formula or incantation to enforce the written law. Special tobaccos were often used to protect the light-horsemen or sheriffs, who would often rub themselves with the cured tobacco plant to make themselves invisible.[8]

One of the most famous of all Cherokee sheriffs was Zeke Proctor, who was reported to have been under the protection of a guardian witch. This witch was said to have enabled Proctor to track and find escaped prisoners or tribal enemies.[9] Proctor has become an important figure in Cherokee tribal folklore. The story, as told by a Cherokee informant, emphasizes his supernatural powers:

One of the most beloved men of the old Cherokee Nation was the famous lawman-outlaw Zeke Proctor. They say that Uncle Zeke had a charmed life. He was shot several times and his horse fell off a cliff while he was riding it. He was never hurt. This was more than a charmed life, Zeke Proctor had a good witch to guard him and keep him safe from all danger. One day Zeke was sitting eating at a friend's house when he jumped up from the kitchen table, pulled out his colt and shot through the back door. When the door was opened, they found a member of the Starr Gang with his gun in his hand who had been ready to kill Uncle Zeke. At the famous Goingsnake Massacre, Zeke told the sheriff and his friends to come prepared for bloodshed. During the trial a large armed band of men came prepared to kill Zeke Proctor. Many men were killed on both sides of the battle. Uncle Zeke Proctor's witch protected him again and he was spared death. At the time of Zeke's death several years later, the

[7] George Foster, "A Legal Episode in the Cherokee Nation," *Green Bag*, Vol. 4 (1892).
[8] Rennard Strickland, Unpublished Field Notes; Interview, Cecil Dick, June 18, 1969; Kilpatrick and Kilpatrick, *Run Toward the Nightland*, 108–110.
[9] Strickland, Field Notes; Edward A. Burbage, "The Legend of Zeke Proctor," (Master's thesis, University of Tulsa, 1950).

witch was transferred to one of his kin. Even today they say that this very powerful witch protects one of the Proctor clan.[10]

Some law-enforcement officers such as the famous Andy Dick were reported to have been powerful witches capable of transforming themselves into birds and flying away from possible danger.[11]

Any Cherokee law officer (*di:da?:ni:vi:sgi*—"one who apprehends them") whether or not a witch himself could call upon a medicine man to use one of any number of (*idi:gawe:sdi*) sacred rites for "remaking" tobacco to strengthen the power of the law.[12] The following is typical of the ritualistic formulas for protecting and aiding peace officers:

> Now! Little Wolves! Very quickly all of You bark
> so that nothing can climb over.
> They cross your Path at the treetops.
> Now! Big Wolves! They just come trailing you.
> Now! "They will corner you right now in the
> Wolf-places," I will be saying![13]

In 1829 the Reverend Samuel Worcester wrote that Cherokee traditions "are fading from memory, and only a few aged men can give much information respecting them."[14] This man of God would have been shocked to learn that "aboriginal culture went underground before the onslaught of Christianity but did not die."[15] Worcester accepted as an article of his faith that "the printed constitution and laws . . . show progress in civil polity."[16] He never suspected that one of the principal forces in support of the "civil polity" of the newly adopted tribal codes was the traditional incantation of the local conjurers.

In truth many of the ancient tribal customs survived because the

10 Gregory and Strickland, *Cherokee Spirit Tales*, 35.

11 Interview, Cecil Dick, June 18, 1969.

12 For use of tobacco by the Cherokees see Mooney, *The Swimmer Manuscript*, 31–32, 74–75, 91, 151, 170–171, 224, 230, 241, 285, 289, 301, and Kilpatrick and Kilpatrick, *Run Toward the Nightland*, 8–12, 101–113.

13 Kilpatrick and Kilpatrick, *Run Toward the Nightland*, 109.

14 *Cherokee Phoenix*, April 1, 1829, reprinted in Jack Frederick Kilpatrick and Anna Gritts Kilpatrick (eds.), *New Echota Letters: Contributions of Samuel A. Worcester to the Cherokee Phoenix*, 43 (cited hereafter as *New Echota Letters*).

15 Kilpatrick and Kilpatrick, *New Echota Letters*, 43.

16 Worcester defended the operation of the Cherokee court system in a letter to the editor of the *Charleston Observer* reprinted in the *Cherokee Phoenix*, Oct. 28, 1829.

new statutes attempted only limited regulation. The laws operated in a variety of situations, for the new statutes were of two basic types. The first were the *substantive* regulations, that is, those declaring murder to be a crime. The second were the *procedural* regulations, those providing the mechanism for healing a breach, as in a trial for the crime of murder. As for the lives of the Cherokees four patterns may be suggested:

1. Situations in which there was little or no existing tribal law and the council was free to adopt regulations

2. Situations in which the council was changing mechanisms for healing the breach but retaining the essential rules of substance

3. Situations in which both substance and mechanism were being changed

4. Situations in which no attempt to regulate was undertaken

By far the largest number of the early statutes were designed to regulate new economic activities and are within situation 1, since there was little or no existing tribal law. Examples of this kind of legislation were the elaborate regulation of public roads and live-stock.[17] Murder is an excellent instance of situation 2 in which the breach itself, homicide, already existed but the mechanism for healing the breach was changed.[18] Inheritance and transmission of wealth required a change in both substantive law and in procedure, as in situation 3.[19] Almost all situations which the white man would have considered social custom, such as marriage and clan obligations, were instances of situation 4 and were not regulated by the earliest laws.[20] Polygamy was also such an instance, in which change was specifically encouraged but was not mandatory.[21]

In the period immediately following the enactment of the new written codes much of the ancient custom survived. One of John

[17] See these kinds of regulations in LCN (1852), 6, 7–8, 12, 13, 19, 20–23.
[18] See Rennard Strickland, "Development of Control of Homicide in the Cherokee Nation," Unpublished Paper, 1965, Law School Library, University of Virginia. See Chapter Two.
[19] See Rennard Strickland, "Tribal Goals Reflected in Cherokee Law of Inheritance," Unpublished Paper, 1965, Law School Library, University of Virginia.
[20] An excellent example of this is the tribal regulation of marriage within the clan structure. These regulations, not enforced by tribal written law, survived into the twentieth century. See Benny Smith, "The Keetoowah Society of the Cherokee Indians," (Master's thesis, Northwestern State College, Alva, Oklahoma, 1967).
[21] LCN (1852), 10.

Howard Payne's informants reported that "although the excellent laws and regulations . . . were regularly executed . . . yet the influence of the patriarchs in their respective towns was considerable; especially in matters of minor importance wherein they presided and made decisions which the parties saw proper to obey." Yet in criminal matters and "important cases" the new written law is said to have "triumphed over the old barbarious customs."[22]

Even more significant than actual survival of traditional elements was the appearance of survival of the ancient forms. The unique employment of existing institutions and personalities deserves additional examination. For, without doubt, the use of old clan and town organization as the framework for new administration, combined with the freedom given early light-horsemen and marshals, accounted for the personal identification which many Cherokees came to feel for the system of enforcement of their laws. The importance of the gradual adoption of foreign elements and the actual survival of ancient magical practices cannot be overemphasized.

Documented case studies suggest that among traditional Cherokees clan regulation survived into the late nineteenth and early twentieth centuries. One noted Indian historian remembered the murder of a witch in the late 1930's. The Kilpatrick work shows the continued use of magical powers within the legal system of the state of Oklahoma. Among the most traditional groups, such as the Redbird Smith Keetoowahs, there is today a studied effort to keep to the old ways. The ancient Cherokee way of law did not end with the adoption of written laws in 1808 but lived on in many ways through the period of Anglo-American adaptations. It is ironic that the written laws adopted in 1808 ceased to function in 1898, while informal magical and spiritual aspects have survived into the twentieth century.[23]

The magic is not all that remains. Much of the spirit of the written law and the traditional rule of law survives. No other Indians have been able to use white man's law and white man's courts with the success of the twentieth-century Cherokees. But that is yet another story—the story of millions of dollars in judgments won in recent litigation before the Indian Claims Commission and the United States Supreme Court. The roots of modern legal victories

22 I. P. Evans, John Howard Payne Papers, Roll 6986, 4.
23 Interview, Carolyn Thomas Foreman, July 3, 1964. Strickland, Unpublished Field Notes.

which could lead the way to another golden age of the Cherokee can be traced deep into the past, to a time when the Cherokees began to move from clan to court.

But even to this day the spirit lives. Every year the traditional Cherokees gather to dance in the bright flame and dark shadows of the eternal fire and to ask for the help of the fire and the spirits. This fire of the Cherokees is believed to be eternal. When the world was young, this sacred fire was stolen by a conjurer and transformed into small white crystals in which the future might be seen. When the thief held the stones in his hand, the flames of the sacred fire came forth and revealed the way for the Cherokees. The Cherokees sent a warrior to recover the fire. The boy tricked the conjurer by asking to see the future in the stones. As the flames burst forth, the boy threw tobacco onto the blaze, and the flames consumed the evil one.

It is said that, as long as the flame of the sacred fire burns, the Cherokee people will survive. Evil has been imprisoned in the fire, and the fire burns for the Cherokee people. The story of the Cherokees is told by the eternal fire. The blaze dies down, appearing to die, but again bursts forth even brighter. The flame of the Cherokees burns. The Cherokee people, like their fire, seem to have an eternal spirit.

J. A. Scales, Chief Justice of the Cherokee Supreme Court and Solicitor General of the Cherokee Nation. Courtesy Thomas Gilcrease Institute.

Members of the Council Branch of the National Council of the Cherokee Nation, Tahlequah, 1889–90.

NAMES OF SENATORS.

1. L. B. Bell, President of Senate.
2. William Rogers.
3. Henry Ross.
4. Walter Agnew.
5. S. H. Mayes.

6. Wash Swimmer.
7. William P. Ross.
8. John Meigs.
9. Johnson Whitmere.
10. David Faulkner.

11. William Triplett.
12. Stephen Tehee.
13. Roach Young.
14. Jackson Christie.
15. Rabbit Bunch.

16. W. P. Henderson.
17. William Mayes, Interpreter.
20. John Welch, Ass't Interpreter.
18. A. H. Norwood, Clerk
19. T. E. Downing, Ass't Clerk.

Members of the Cherokee Senate, Cherokee Nation, Tahlequah, 1889-90.

The Cherokee National Supreme Court Building, Tahlequah. Courtesy
Oklahoma Historical Society.

The Delaware District Court House, painting by Hazel Barnett, Grove, Oklahoma, 1971.

The old jail, Tahlequah. Courtesy Oklahoma Historical Society.

The Gallows of the Cherokee Nation, Tahlequah, 1891. The tribal laws provided for the death penalty by hanging for a number of crimes. Courtesy Oklahoma Historical Society.

Lawmen and executioner standing by the Tahlequah gallows.

Court day in the Cherokee Nation, April, 1901. When the tribal courts ceased to function, most legal issues were shifted to the United States courts. This picture shows the building in which the United States court met when in session in Tahlequah.

Cherokee National Prison. Courtesy Oklahoma Historical Society.

NAMES OF PRISONERS.	NATURE OF OFFENSE.	FROM WHAT DISTRICT RECEIVED.	TIME OF IMPRISONMENT.	AMOUNT OF FINE.	TIME Expires.	REMARKS.
Charles Clark.	Felony.	Tahlequah.	5. Years.	—	1881. Sept. 28th	was Pardoned by Principal...
Dirt.	Felony.	Tahlequah.	15. Years.	—	1891. Nov. 1st	was Pardoned by Principal...
Young Wolf Peter.	Felony.	Saline.	5. Years.	—	1881. Nov. 24th	was Pardoned by Principal...
Walt. Drake.	Felony.	Saline.	5. Years.	—	1881. Nov. 24th	Died of Congestive chill November...
Skeyosty.	Felony.	Saline.	5. Years.	—	1881. Nov. 24th	was Pardoned by Principal...
Tom Turkey.	Misdemeanor.	Tahlequah.	1. Month.		1877. April 12th	Served out time, and was released...
Coony Chinubbee.	Felony.	Tahlequah.	5. Years.		1882. April 11.	Escaped the jail 22 day of January...
Nat.	Felony.	Tahlequah.	5½ Years. 3. additional for Escaping		1885.	Escaped guard while at labor outside...
Willie Gritt.	Misdemeanor.	Tahlequah.	30. Days.		1877. June 5th	Served out time...
Manuel.	Misdemeanor.	Tahlequah.	30. Days.		1877. June 5th	Served out time...
	Murder in the 1st Degree	Saline.	Sentenced to be hung.	on the	1877. October	Sentence Executed...

Register of Prisoners, National Prison, Cherokee Nation. The question of building a tribal jail was considered for almost three-quarters of a century. When the jail was finally built at Tahlequah, the tribe kept this record of prisoners. Courtesy Indian Archives, Oklahoma Historical Society.

An Indian Territory posse. A group of citizens of Indian Territory, including Cherokees and whites, captured the famous Cherokee Ned Christie. Informal groups served as law-enforcement agents during the period of the breakup of tribal government.

Appendices

1. Cherokee Legal History: Chronology 1540–1907

Frontier Contact (1540–1785):

1540 De Soto expedition is first white party to visit "Province of Chelaque."

1671 Guns introduced by this date; traders record Cherokees using muskets.

1673 Itinerant traders from English settlements begin to operate trade routes among the Cherokees.

1684 First recorded Cherokee treaty is signed.

1690 Alexander Dougherty, Virginia trader, is first white man reported to marry a Cherokee.

1693 Cherokee delegation protests seizure of Indians to be sold to British as slaves.

1711 Account of Baron deGraffenreid is first recording of aboriginal Cherokee trial.

1711 Eleazar Wiggan, or "Old Rabbit," considered first white trader to settle permanently in Cherokee country.

1715 Cherokee uprising against South Carolina promotes reforms.

1717 Cherokees and Indian commissioners establish exchange rate for trade goods.

1721 The Charlestown Treaty with Governor Francis Nicholson of the Carolinas is purported to be first Cherokee concession of land.

1730 Cherokees go on official visit to London and sign Treaty of Dover.

1731 Treason trial of Cherokee delegate to London is first recorded action for unauthorized land sale in action based on treaty signed at Dover.

1736 Christian Gotelieb Priber, European philosopher, establishes Cherokee Kingdom of Paradise and crowns Chief Moytoy as "Emperor of Kingdom."

1738 First major smallpox epidemic which eventually reduces population of Cherokees by half.

1746 Kingdom of Paradise ends with British imprisonment of Priber.

1760 John Daniel Hammerer, a teacher from Georgia, moves into Cherokee Nation, where he teaches some Cherokee youths to read and write.

1760–1761 Henry Timberlake accompanies Cherokee delegation to London.

1761 Cherokee and English border clashes lead to devastating campaign by Captain James Grant; significant reduction in Cherokee population results from conflict.

1773 Date given for first conversion of Cherokee to Christianity.

1776–1785 Cherokees provide military support for English during the Revolutionary War.

1777 Dragging Canoe and 1,000 dissident Cherokees remove to Chickamauga in present Tennessee.

1783 Smallpox again decimates major areas of Cherokee population.

1785 Treaty of Hopewell, first treaty between U.S. and Cherokee Nation.

White Ascendancy (1786–1828):

1791 Treaty of Holston; fourteenth article states U.S. policy to advance civilization among the Cherokees.

1797 Light-horsemen appointed by Cherokees to assist Benjamin Hawkins in preserving peace on borders and in nation.

1797 Official implementation of "civilizing policy" by designation of Silas Dinsmoor as U.S. Temporary Agent to Cherokees "to improve them in civilized pursuits."

1801 Appointment of Return Jonathan Meigs as Cherokee Indian Agent.

1801 Establishment of first permanent Christian mission in Cherokee Nation, Moravian Mission at Springplace.

1802 Georgia Compact of 1802 lays foundation for ultimate removal of Cherokees.

1803 Major Ridge refuses to sanction ancient clan retaliation in substitution of brother's life for escaped murderer.

1807 Doublehead killed for treason in land treaty case; provides impetus for abrogation of clan revenge law.

1808 First written law of Cherokees provides for establishment of light-horsemen regulating companies.

1810 Act of Abrogation of clan revenge enacted.

1817 Treaty provides exchange of eastern lands for equal land area in Arkansas.

1817 Steps toward establishing Cherokee Republic with creation of Standing Committee by Council of Chiefs and Warriors.

1817 Inauguration of U.S. mail service through the Cherokee Nation with first post office at Ross's Landing (near present Chattanooga, Tennessee).

1817–1823 Extensive migration to Cherokee West areas in Arkansas; U.S. recognition of government of Cherokee Nation West.

1820 First oral law of Western Cherokees establishes light-horsemen to "preserve peace and good order."

1820 Division of Cherokee Nation into judicial districts; provisions for district courts, judges, and officers.

1821 Approximate date for completion of Sequoyah's syllabary and widespread acceptance of writing in Cherokee language.

1822 Cherokees require by law that "courts . . . keep records of proceedings of all causes, evidence, and decisions."

1822 First Cherokee law book is printed.

1824 First written law of Western Cherokees.

1825 National Council passes act providing for use of "five disinterested men" as jurors.

1825 Authorization for establishment of Cherokee capitol at New Echota (near present-day Calhoun, Georgia).

1826 Call for tribal constitutional convention is issued.

1827 Emergence of modern Cherokee Nation with the establishment of the Cherokee Constitution by an elective constitutional convention.

1827 Georgia resolves to "extend authority over Cherokee country" unless U.S. assists as provided in Compact of 1802.

1828 First issue of *Cherokee Phoenix* appears on February 21. This bilingual Cherokee national paper publishes important Cherokee documents including laws.

1828 First laws published on Cherokee Nation press are circulated in pamphlet form.

Tribal Dislocation (1829–1846):

1828–1830 Series of acts by Georgia legislature abolishing Cherokee tribal government and authority while extending Georgia sovereignty over Cherokee country; oppressive laws enacted against Cherokees including restrictions on rights in Georgia courts.

1829 Construction of court house at New Echota for the Supreme Court of the Cherokee Nation.

1831 Committee and Council of Cherokee Nation adopt resolution to continue court system despite Georgia laws and orders judges "to hold court where convenient."

1832 United States Supreme Court decision in *Worcester v. Georgia* supporting Cherokees ignored by President Jackson and state of Georgia.

1832 Attempted assassination of Chief John Ross.

1832–1833 Violence following lottery to transfer ownership of Cherokee lands claimed by state of Georgia.

1834 Last issue of *Cherokee Phoenix* appears on May 31.

1835–1836 Treaty Party negotiates and signs Treaty of New Echota which exchanges southern lands for new areas in Indian Territory (now Oklahoma).

1836–1838 Chaos in Cherokee Nation; breakdown of Ross government in opposition to removal is climaxed by arrival of federal troops commanded by General Winfield Scott.

1838 National Committee and Council declares that "sovereignty of the Cherokee Nation, together with the constitution, laws, and usage" are to remain in full force during migration and in new country.

1838–1839 "Trail of Tears" or enforced removal of Cherokees to lands of the Cherokees in the West; more than 4,000 die during removal.

1839 Assassination of Major Ridge, John Ridge, and Elias Boudinot for alleged violation of ancient laws on sale of tribal lands.

1839 Convention uniting Eastern and Western Cherokees followed by Constitutional Convention and ratification of Constitution written by William Shorey Coodey and patterned after 1827 Eastern Cherokee constitution.

1839–1846 Period of Cherokee civil war, lawlessness, and reversion to clan revenge in protest of murder of Ridges and Boudinot; dissatisfaction with a constitution alleged to be fraudulent by Western Cherokees and Treaty Party.

1844 Cherokee Supreme Court opens term in "new and comodius brick court house."

1844 Light-horsemen companies reinstituted because of breakdown of judicial system; Colonel Matthew Arbuckle attacks "misuse of light-horse."

1845 Report of Captain A. Cody, 6th Infantry, on an examination of Cherokee laws is highly complimentary of legal structures but critical of some practices.

1846 Cherokees attempt to use laws preventing "conspiracy to overthrow constitution and laws of Nation" through "regular system of robbery and murder" to control crime.

1846 Treaty of Washington unites Eastern Cherokees, Western Cherokees, and Treaty Party in new Cherokee National Government.

Struggle for Self-Government (1847–1860):

1846–1847 Amnesty extended to all charged with violating laws before the Washington Treaty.

1847 As symbol of relationship between newly founded educational academies and law, *Acts of National Council* and *Laws of Cherokee Nation* placed in cornerstone at Cherokee Female Seminary.

1849 Cherokee law enacted to license "persons engaged in the practice of law . . . before any of the Courts of the Cherokee Nation."

1853 Largest contested wills case in Cherokee courts ($60,000) results in setting aside will and dividing estate among heirs.

1856 Shortage of funds reaches chronic stage as tribe is forced to close both Cherokee Male and Female Seminaries.

1859 "Keetoowah" reorganized from full-blood Cherokees as conservative secret society to perpetuate tribal traditions and fight slavery.

Cherokees in American Civil War and Reconstruction (1861–1867):

1860–1861 Mounting tension between Union Cherokees and pro-Confederate forces.

1861 Tribal struggle climaxed by treaty between Cherokee Nation and Confederate government signed at Park Hill in October of 1861.

1861–1865 Cherokee Nation scene of border warfare; tribal courts are unable to function and Confederate congress fails to appoint or confirm justices for Confederate courts in Cherokee Nation. Martial law prevails.

1865–1866 Negotiation of peace treaty between Cherokees and the United States at Council of Fort Smith ending participation in American Civil War; Cherokees sign agreement limiting tribal land rights and admitting former Negro slaves to tribal membership.

Establishing the Cherokee Nation (1867–1892):

1867 Capitol building of Cherokee Nation built at Tahlequah; still in use as Court House of Cherokee County, Oklahoma.

1867 Constitution amended to provide for direct election of judges of circuit court by their people.

1872 District Court Judge suspended by chief for refusing to try a murder case.

1873 Cherokee trial for "conspiracy to overthrow government" is held.

1875–1876 Public debates and legislative reaction against public whippings.

1876 Cherokee laws codified and new code adopted.

1876 Judicial "conference and consultation" held at Tahlequah to "consider powers under new code."

1876 Cherokee national prison at Tahlequah is opened.

1876 In recognition of tribal achievements, missionaries propose to use Cherokees and Choctaws to "educate and civilize" plains Indian tribes.

1877–1878 Movement to have prisoners in national jail learn a trade.

1878 Cherokee Citizenship Commission created to relieve strain of testing tribal membership controversies in courts.

1878 Distribution of *Rules and Regulations for Lower Courts* issued by Cherokee Supreme Bench.

1879 First published rules for national prison appear in *Cherokee Advocate.*

1880 Indian police force appointed for entire Five Civilized Tribes areas becomes operative.

1881 Office of Attorney General for Cherokee Nation is created.

1882 Establishment of Cherokee Supreme Court National Library.

1882 *Procedural Rulings of Supreme Court* published in 12 page pamphlet.

1882 Cherokee judges assist Osage tribe in "framing constitution and laws" based upon Cherokee experience.

1883 Printed blank forms of indictments prepared by executive for use by lower courts and district solicitors.

1883 Removal of sheriff who "look upon the wine" is apparently first such instance in Cherokee Nation.

1883 Last documented killing justified on grounds of victim's use of witchcraft.

1887 Chief issues executive proclamation to sheriffs ordering enforcement of laws against intruders.

1889 Courts begin to hire stenographers, expert "in joting down testimony" at trial.

1892 Survival of private Cherokee retaliatory law enforcement group is discovered.

Tribal Termination (1893–1907):

1893 Railroads and land speculators increase pressure to open Cherokee lands to noncitizen.

1893 Federal courts delay execution of murderers convicted by Cherokee Supreme Court.

1894 United States reaffirms willingness to prosecute whites who violate Cherokee laws if Nation requests in writing; crime continues to increase.

1894 Executive order from chief to all officers to suppress "gambling, drinking."

1895 Judge Isaac C. Parker ("Hanging Judge") of Western District of Arkansas testifies before Congressional Committee that intruders and not Cherokees are responsible for lawless condition in Indian Territory.

1897 Memorial to United States Congress by full-blood Cherokees protesting abolition of tribal courts because "we could not understand the white man's laws which are in big books."

1898 Cherokee tribal courts are abolished by Curtis Act, replaced by United States District Courts for Indian Territory.

1907 Cherokee Nation ceases to exist and joins the Indian Territory and Oklahoma Territory to form the state of Oklahoma.

2. Summary of Early Laws of the Cherokees (1808–1829)*

1. *A Resolution passed September 11, 1808.* Organization of regulating parties to suppress "horse stealing and robbery" and to protect "heirs to their father's property." Sets punishment and outlaws clan revenge against regulating company. LCN 3–4.

2. *A Resolution passed on April 10, 1810.* Agreement among the seven clans to abrogate previous blood debts, recognize justifiable homicides, and acknowledge murder within clan structure. LCN 4.

3. *A Resolution passed on May 6, 1817.* Resolution creating a "Standing Committee" to handle the affairs of the Cherokee Nation with the approval of chiefs of the council. Excludes from common property rights all who remove themselves from the Cherokee Nation. Protects property of maternal line. LCN 4–5.

4. *A Resolution passed on October 26, 1819.* Provision to grant permits to reside in Cherokee Nation with specified rights to "schoolmasters, blacksmiths, millers, salt petre and gun powder manufactures, ferryman and turnpike keepers, and mechanics." LCN 6.

5. *A Resolution passed on October 28, 1819.* Regulation of commerce including limiting license to trade to Cherokee citizens, regulating noncitizen peddlers and restricting the sale of "spirituous liquors." LCN 6–7.

6. *Resolution Settling Dispute and Act of October 30, 1819.* Committee hears evidence and decides case over establishment of turnpikes in Cherokee Nation, then establishes limitations on new turnpikes. LCN 7–8.

7. *Resolution Settling Dispute and Act of November 1, 1819.* Committee rules on dispute over horse traded by Negro slave and then estab-

* All citations from *Laws of the Cherokee Nation Adopted at Various Periods* (1852).

lishes that "no contract or bargain entered into with any slave . . . without approbation of their master shall be binding [on the master]. LCN 8–9.

8. A *Resolution passed on November 1, 1819*. Persons employing or instigating others to steal are equally guilty and subject to punishment. LCN 9.

9. A *Resolution passed on November 1, 1819*. Emigrants to Arkansas cannot reclaim property in possession of Cherokee citizens not enrolled for the Arkansas country. LCN 9–10.

10. A *Resolution passed on November 2, 1819*. White men must obtain marriage license from national clerk and be formally married by minister before acquiring rights of citizenship. Property of Cherokee women not subject to husband's control. White man loses citizenship when "parting from wife" and may be subject to pay wife a sum fixed by national committee. Whites limited to one wife, "recommended to all others." LCN 10.

11. A *Resolution passed on October 20, 1820*. Establishment of Court system with eight district courts presided over by district and circuit judges assisted by marshals and light-horsemen. LCN 11–12.

12. A *Resolution passed on October 25, 1820*. Single men may be employed with permit in Nation but white families are not to be brought into the Nation to work or rent land with penalty of $500 and 100 stripes on the bare back. LCN 10–11.

13. A *Resolution passed on October 25, 1820*. Appointment of ranger in each district to handle stray horses in accordance with the procedures of this act. LCN 12.

14. A *Resolution passed on October 25, 1820*. Establishes a poll tax. LCN 12–13.

15. A *Resolution passed on October 25, 1820*. Provisions for a "National turnpike gate . . . on the Federal road" with regulation and repair bonds. LCN 13.

16. A *Resolution passed on October 26, 1820*. Mission regulations, including right of schools to demand payment of expenses of "runaway scholars" by parents, with provisions for apprentice training. LCN 13–14.

17. A *Resolution passed on October 28, 1820*. Regulations concerning Negro slaves establishing liability of masters, restrictions on purchases from, and authorizing formation of patrolling companies to limit Negro vending of liquor. LCN 24–25.

18. A *Resolution passed on November 2, 1820*. District representation in National Council allotted with provisions for officers and salaries. LCN 14–15.

19. A *Resolution of uncertain date in 1820*. The boundaries and dates for meeting of each of the eight council or court districts are set forth. LCN 15–18.

20. A *Resolution passed on October 26, 1821.* Provided that "a court be convened at the present session, to be composed of the Circuit and District Judges, and the Marshals of the several districts, to adjust and settle all such cases as may be submitted to them by the committee. LCN 18.

21. A *Resolution passed on October 27, 1821.* Any person migrating to Arkansas who sells any improvement and any person who buys an improvement from such person shall each pay a fine of $150. LCN 19.

22. A *Resolution passed on October 27, 1821.* District and circuit judges shall check on all stray and stolen horses and return any belonging to U.S. to the Cherokee Agent. LCN 19.

23. A *Resolution passed on October 27, 1821.* Persons who "resist and kill any of the Marshals or light-horsemen" shall be apprehended or killed by the Marshals and light-horsemen. LCN 20.

24. A *Resolution passed on October 28, 1821.* Regulation of use of white ferrymen by Cherokees living on ceded lands. LCN 20.

25. A *Resolution passed on October 28, 1821.* An authorization with regulations and rates for a private group of Cherokee citizens to open and keep in repair specific toll roads. LCN 20–21.

26. A *Resolution passed on November 2, 1821.* Fixing pay of circuit judges at $55 and district judges at $25 per annum. LCN 22.

27. A *Resolution passed on November 2, 1821.* An authorization with regulations and rates for a private group of Cherokee citizens to open and keep in repair specific toll roads. LCN 22–23.

28. A *Resolution passed on November 8, 1821.* Establishing interest rates on promisory notes. LCN 23.

29. A *Resolution passed on October 23, 1822.* Statement that "the Chiefs of the Cherokee Nation will not meet any Commissioners of the United States to hold a treaty with them on the subject of making cession of land." LCN 23–24.

30. A *Resolution passed on November 1, 1822.* Raising circuit judge pay to $80 a year. LCN 22.

31. A *Resolution passed on November 2, 1822.* An authorization with regulation and rates for a private group of Cherokee citizens to open and keep in repair specific toll roads. LCN 25.

32. A *Resolution passed on November 8, 1822.* A requirement that "Judges of the District Courts, shall keep a record of the proceedings of all causes, evidence and decisions;" also provides clerks and their salaries for district courts. LCN 26.

33. A *Resolution passed on November 8, 1822.* Restrictions on sale of "ardent spirits" and "gaming at cards." LCN 26–27.

34. A *Resolution passed on November 10, 1822.* Establishing penalty

for persons who "wilfully embezzle, intercept and open any sealed letter." LCN 27–28.

35. A *Resolution passed on November 12, 1822*. Superior Court created to meet annually during session of National Council "to be composed of the several Circuit Judges, to determine all causes which may be appealed from the District Courts." LCN 28.

36. A *Resolution passed on November 12, 1822*. District judges authorized to nominate light-horsemen companies in their respective districts. LCN 28.

37. A *Resolution passed on November 13, 1822*. Tax collection procedures for the districts with detailed operations to marshals. LCN 29.

38. A *Resolution passed on November 13, 1822*. Duties required of specified turnpike companies. LCN 29–30.

39. A *Resolution passed on November 13, 1822*. Reduction of taxes on citizen merchants and noncitizen peddlers. LCN 30.

40. A *Resolution passed on October 4, 1823*. Suspending council and private business on the Sabbath. LCN 30–31.

41. A *Resolution passed on October 9, 1823*. Resolutions require concurrence of both National Committee and Council to be effective. LCN 31.

42. A *Resolution passed on October 17, 1823*. Removing National Committee and Council from adjudication of "claims of a private nature" by requiring these "be submitted to that court of the district where the parties reside" and "all causes . . . appealed from the decision of the District Courts, should be submitted to the Supreme Court in session for a decision agreeable to law and equity." LCN 31–32.

43. A *Resolution passed on October 30, 1823*. "Business pending between individuals" is "laid over to next general Council for a final adjustment." LCN 32.

44. A *Resolution passed on January 27, 1824*. For vending or disposing ardent spirits at "ball games, all-night dances, and other public gatherings . . . penalty of having all liquor wasted." LCN 36.

45. A *Resolution passed on October 12, 1824*. Collection of judgments, summoning of witnesses, and punishment of perjury. LCN 32–33.

46. A *Resolution passed on October 25, 1824*. Sale of shares to lowest bidder to open and repair certain ferries in the Cherokee Nation. LCN 35–36.

47. A *Resolution passed on November 8, 1824*. Procedure to follow in contract to supply beef for the general council. LCN 42.

48. A *Resolution passed on November 9, 1824*. Restrictions on digging for salt and salt wells. LCN 33.

49. A *Resolution passed on November 11, 1824*. Duties of marshals, sheriffs, constables and light-horsemen defined as "to take cognizance of

every violation of Law . . . and to give information of, and bring to justice, according to law, persons so offending" with penalty for breach of duty. LCN 37.

50. A *Resolution passed on November 11, 1824.* Free Negroes in Cherokee Nation are intruders and may not reside without special permit. LCN 37.

51. A *Resolution passed on November 11, 1824.* Robbery shall be prosecuted in any of the district courts "subject to such . . . any punishment . . . the Court may impose . . . not [to] extend so far as to inflict death." LCN 38.

52. A *Resolution passed on November 11, 1824.* Marriages "between negro slaves and Indians, or whites shall not be lawful" and subject to fine by the slaves master and 25 to 59 lashes for the slave. LCN 38.

53. A *Resolution passed on November 11, 1824.* Negro slaves may not possess specified property and must dispose of items subject to confiscation. LCN 39.

54. A *Resolution passed on November 11, 1824.* Fines set for noncitizen "bringing spiritous liquors in to the Cherokee Nation" and for Cherokee citizens purchasing from noncitizen. LCN 39–40.

55. A *Resolution passed on November 12, 1824.* Creation of register's office at national capitol for "estray property" and procedures for handling all stray livestock. LCN 34–35.

56. A *Resolution passed on November 13, 1824.* Limitations upon employment of U.S. citizen or slave of U.S. citizen without Cherokee Nation permit with punishments for violations. LCN 34.

57. A *Resolution passed on November 12, 1824.* Restricting settlement and improvements within one-fourth mile of "field or plantation of another" under penalty of "forfeiting the whole of their labor for the benefit of the original resident." LCN 40–41.

58. A *Resolution passed on November 12, 1824.* Size of light-horsemen companies reduced from six to four and pay increased. LCN 40.

59. A *Resolution passed on November 12, 1824.* Defines lawful fences and obligations of owners of stock "breaking into field of a person having a lawful fence." LCN 41.

60. A *Resolution passed on November 12, 1824.* Fine for setting woods on fire before the month of March. LCN 41.

61. A *Resolution passed on November 12, 1824.* Payment procedure for "skinning a dead cow brute." LCN 43.

62. A *Resolution passed on November 12, 1824.* Appointment, procedure and payment for a Cherokee Nation census and inventory with "a general report of the manner of living and the state of agricultural improvements." LCN 43–44.

63. A *Resolution passed on November 13, 1824.* The light-horsemen

shall serve as jurors in each district with the judge acting as foreman of the jury. LCN 39.

64. *A Resolution passed on November 13, 1824.* No claims paid by National Treasurer from public monies without approval of National Committee. Further "it shall be the duty of every Light Horse to obey the orders of the principal chiefs, when called upon to perform any public business of the Nation." LCN 42.

65. *Article of Fixed and Irrevocable Principle by which the Cherokee Nation Shall Be Governed: of June 15, 1825.*

Art. 1st. Lands are common property of the Nation. Improvements are exclusive and indefeasible property of the citizens.

Art. 2nd. Annuities are public property and with tax revenues shall be funded in National Treasury.

Art. 3rd. Legislative Council alone has legal power to manage and dispose public property.

Art. 4th. Principal Chiefs may not dispose of public property without express authority of Legislative Council in session.

Art. 5th. Members of National Committee and Council may not act officially on any public affairs except as expressly authorized in session.

Art. 6th. Citizens of Nation have exclusive rights to their improvements but possess no right or power to dispose of their improvements to citizens of the United States.

Art. 7th. Courts have no jurisdiction over cases before their organization when case was acted upon by chiefs and council.

Art. 8th. Chiefs have no power to arrest judgments of the courts or National Committee and Council; the judiciary shall be independent and their decisions final and conclusive if in conformity with these principles and the laws of the Nation. LCN 45–46.

66. *A Resolution passed on October 14, 1825.* Light-horsemen companies shall no longer serve as jurymen but "the circuit Judges shall have power to order the Marshals, Sheriffs, Constables, to select and empanel five disinterested men of good character and judgment, to act as jurors." Restrictions and procedures enumerated. LCN 44.

67. *A Resolution passed on October 14, 1825.* District judges shall not serve as jurors to Supreme Court but the four circuit judges "shall compose the Supreme Court, to review and decide all cases appealed from the District Courts" with judges disqualified in cases appealed from their own district. LCN 46.

68. *A Resolution passed on October 15, 1825.* Provisions for financing and obtaining English and Cherokee type. LCN 47.

69. *A Resolution passed on October 15, 1825.* Suspension of poll tax. LCN 48.

70. *A Resolution passed on October 17, 1825.* Supreme Court judges authorized "to summon any of the Marshals, Sheriffs or Constables . . . who may be at New Town to perform their official duties during each term." LCN 48.

71. *A Resolution passed on October 17, 1825.* General two year statute of limitations on "all contested claims." LCN 49.

72. *A Resolution passed on October 27, 1825.* Special act "remitting fine imposed by the court on Samuel Henry" for sale of brandy after Henry entered bond against future violations and "under penalty of making good the fine herein remitted." LCN 49.

73. *A Resolution passed on October 31, 1825.* Declaring "all gold, silver, lead, copper or brass mines" discovered in the Nation to be public property with the discoverer entitled to receive one fourth of net proceeds." LCN 50.

74. *A Resolution passed on November 5, 1825.* Authorization and procedures for the treasurer of Cherokee Nation to loan surplus public monies to Cherokee citizens. LCN 50–51.

75. *A Resolution passed on November 8, 1825.* Light-horsemen companies replaced by a marshal, sheriff, deputy sheriff and two constables whose duties are "to make collections of all just debts, notes, liquidated accounts and judgments, and to arrest horse thieves and other rogues and murderers for trial." Act details procedures, jurisdiction, etc. LCN 51–52.

76. *A Resolution passed on November 9, 1825.* A statute on written and nuncupative wills and intestate distribution. LCN 52–53.

77. *A Resolution passed on November 10, 1825.* Declaring rape and false accusation of rape crimes and establishing the following penalties: first offense, fifty lashes and "the left ear cropped off close to the head; second offense, one hundred lashes and "the other ear cut off"; and death for the third offense." LCN 53–54.

78. *A Resolution passed on November 10, 1825.* Use of rangers and assistant rangers to protect from "injury . . . from citizens of the United States, feeding and keeping their stock on Cherokee lands." LCN 54–55.

79. *A Resolution passed on November 10, 1825.* Tax on citizen merchants suspended. LCN 55–56.

80. *A Resolution passed on November 10, 1825.* Law prohibiting sale and purchase of land of Arkansas Cherokees. LCN 56.

81. *A Resolution passed on November 10, 1825.* Light-horsemen appointment legislation repealed. LCN 56.

82. *A Resolution passed on November 10, 1825.* Acknowledgment of rights of the children of Cherokee men and white women as equal "to all

the immunities and privileges enjoyed by the citizens descending from the Cherokee race, by the mother's side." LCN 57.

83. A *Resolution passed on November 10, 1825*. Making it unlawful for all persons, Cherokee or white, to have more than one wife. LCN 57.

84. A *Resolution passed on November 10, 1825*. Redefines lawful with respect to obligations of hog owners.

85. A *Resolution passed on November 10, 1825*. Duties formerly assigned to light-horsemen will be performed by officers superceding the companies except express service. LCN 58.

86. A *Resolution passed on November 10, 1825*. Bond and salary for Treasurer of the Cherokee Nation. LCN 58–59.

87. A *Resolution passed on November 10, 1825*. Improvements of party removing to another area are considered abandoned after three years and subject to possession by others. LCN 59.

88. A *Resolution passed on November 12, 1825*. Providing that "all lawful contracts" shall be binding, collecting of judgments on debts, and setting forth property exempt from execution. LCN 59–60.

89. A *Resolution passed on November 12, 1825*. Admitting well skilled "mechanics of the several branches of trade, of good character and sobriety" to residence in Cherokee Nation with procedures by which district courts bind out apprentices to mechanics. LCN 60–61.

90. A *Resolution passed on November 12, 1825*. Procedure to summon witnesses to courts with penalties for refusal "to appear and bear evidence." LCN 61–62.

91. A *Resolution passed on November 12, 1825*. Preparing land lots in a town "to be known and called Echota." LCN 62–63.

92. A *Resolution passed on November 12, 1825*. Appointment of commissioners to "superintend the laying off the lots in . . . Echota." LCN 63.

93. A *Resolution passed on November 12, 1825*. Provisions for adjustment "of the improvements made, and now occupied by individuals, on the public ground selected for the jurisdiction of the town of Echota." LCN 63–64.

94. A *Resolution passed on November 14, 1825*. Request for interest on annuity due from United States and request that U.S. "coerce [non-Cherokee] turnpike company to comply with the articles of agreement [in] Treaty of 1819." LCN 64–65.

95. A *Resolution passed on November 14, 1825*. Individuals appointed to draft memorial in behalf of Cherokee Nation to Congress, a communication to United States Agent for Cherokee Nation, and to "arrange and prepare the revision of the laws of this Nation for press." LCN 65.

96. A *Resolution passed on November 14, 1825*. Payment for Echota Commissioners. LCN 65–66.

97. *A Resolution passed on November 14, 1825.* Individual granted permission to raise a crop on land destined to become public lots in the town of Echota. LCN 66.

98. *A Resolution passed in 1825.* Elections to fill posts of resigned judges and a removed member of council. LCN 66–67.

99. *Public Bonds of National Official Submitted November 9, 1825.* Amounts and conditions. LCN 67.

100. *A resolution passed on October 13, 1826.* A call for a constitutional convention with recommended delegates. The proposed constitution "shall not in any degree go to destroy the rights and liberties of the free citizens of this Nation, nor to effect or impair the fundamental principles and laws, by which the Nation is governed." LCN 73–76.

101. *A Resolution passed on October 13, 1826.* Oath required of all officers including jurymen. LCN 77.

102. *Oath of Office Administered to Cherokee Officers.* "Swear in name of the Holy Evangelists of Almighty God." LCN 68.

103. *A Resolution passed on October 13, 1826.* Exclusion from office and testimony in court of any person "who disbelieves in the existence of the Creator, and of rewards and punishments after death." LCN 77.

104. *A Resolution passed on October 14, 1826.* Manner and persons for administering oath of office. LCN 77.

105. *A Resolution passed on October 14, 1826.* Minors under twelve and lunatics and idiots are not criminally responsible but "any person counselling, advising, or encouraging . . . shall be prosecuted . . . as principal." LCN 78.

106. *A Resolution passed on October 14, 1826.* Punishment established for abortion and infanticide and for slander with accusation of the same. LCN 79.

107. *A Resolution passed on October 18, 1826.* Provisions for printer and journeyman with salaries and duties. LCN 84–85.

108. *A Resolution passed on October 18, 1826.* Provision for establishment of a "newspaper at New Echota, to be entitled, the 'Cherokee Phoenix'" and the hiring of an editor who shall also "translate matter in the Cherokee language for the columns of said paper as well as to translate all public documents . . . submitted for publication." LCN 85.

109. *A Resolution passed on October 21, 1826.* Establishment of office of national marshal with regulations. LCN 91.

110. *A Resolution passed on October 28, 1826.* Ten days notice required for delivery in "case of all contracts and debts payable in property when the contracting parties have not specified any fixed period for payment." LCN 79.

111. *A Resolution passed on October 28, 1826.* Improvements unoccu-

pied for one year which are left by persons removing to another place are to be considered abandoned and subject to possession by another citizen. LCN 80.

112. A *Resolution passed on November 2, 1826*. Order for "house . . . for a printing office." LCN 81.

113. A *Resolution passed on November 4, 1826*. Order "to translate eight copies of the laws of the Cherokee Nation . . . into the Cherokee language, written in characters invented by George Guess, and also to translate one copy of the New Testament into the same characters." LCN 81.

114. A *Resolution passed on November 4, 1826*. Private bill "to purchase at public expense, a sledge hammer and a screw plate for Kallo-noohasgih." LCN 82.

115. A *Resolution passed on November 15, 1826*. Appropriation of funds for and provisions for erection or building of the printing office at Echota. LCN 82.

116. A *Resolution passed on November 16, 1826*. All persons not citizens without lawful permit are defined as intruders and ordered removed from the Nation. LCN 83.

117. A *Resolution passed on November 16, 1826*. Treasurer to accept U.S. annuity payment only in specie, treasury or notes of the United States Bank. LCN 83.

118. A *Resolution passed on November 16, 1826*. License and fee provisions for "person . . . to erect or establish a billard table in the Cherokee Nation" with penalty for violation. LCN 84.

119. A *Resolution passed on November 28, 1826*. Owners of stray property sold by the Nation may recover profits within specified period. LCN 80.

120. 1827. Constitution [see Appendix 3].

121. A *Resolution passed on October 18, 1827*. Reduction of tax on noncitizen peddlers. LCN 88–89.

122. A *Resolution passed on October 20, 1827*. Rejecting compromise offer of private turnpike company in controversy over revenues due the Nation. LCN 86–87.

123. A *Resolution passed on October 24, 1827*. Resolution suspending poll tax and merchant tax extended. LCN 87.

124. A *Resolution passed on October 24, 1827*. Suspending loan of public funds with details of methods of repayment and collection of outstanding loans. LCN 87–88.

125. A *Resolution passed on October 26, 1827*. Payments for election officials. LCN 88.

126. A *Resolution passed on July 3, 1828*. Declaring criminal with punishment of one hundred stripes on the bare back the act of "forming

unlawful meetings, with intent to create faction against the peace and tranquility of the people or to encourage rebellion against the laws and Government of the Cherokee Nation." Duties and procedures under this law prescribed. LCN 117.

127. *A Resolution passed on October 16, 1828.* Funds to erect a partition or railing in the committee chamber because "much inconvenience has arisen and the business in the Committee retarded in consequence of visitors mingling with members." LCN 89.

128. *A Resolution passed on October 16, 1828.* Noncitizens "who may bring into the Cherokee Nation at the seat of Government during the sitting of the General Council, any show or shows, such as wax figures, or such as play actors" shall pay a tax. LCN 89.

129. *A Resolution passed on October 18, 1828.* A private bill to provide National funds "for the purpose of purchasing a set of Blacksmith tools" for a native apprentice learning a mechanical trade. LCN 90.

130. *A Resolution passed on October 18, 1828.* Circuit judges shall no longer constitute the Supreme Court but special Supreme Court judges shall be elected to take "complete cognizance of all cases appealed from the . . . Circuit Courts . . . and shall also have power to act and decide upon criminal cases without reference to appeals from the Circuit courts." LCN 90.

131. *A Resolution passed on October 19, 1828.* Additional regulations and duties associated with the *Cherokee Phoenix* and the newspaper staff. LCN 85–86.

132. *A Resolution passed on October 20, 1828.* Supreme court session, docket, and compensation for judges. LCN 90–91.

133. *A Resolution passed on October 22, 1828.* Requirements for bonds of elected officials and certification of election. LCN 92.

134. *A Resolution passed on October 22, 1828.* Specifics and modifications on recall of loans from the national treasury. LCN 92.

135. *An Undated Act* [October 1828?] Appropriation of national funds as reward to a Cherokee for apprehending horse thief. LCN 93.

136. *A Resolution passed on October 28, 1828.* Appropriation of money as a loan to individual Cherokee citizen. LCN 93.

137. *A Resolution passed on October 29, 1828.* Extension of act suspending poll tax and merchants tax. LCN 93–94.

138. *A Resolution passed on October 30, 1828.* Appointment of committee in each judicial circuit "to visit the different schools in the Nation . . . at the public examination . . . once a year, and to report to the General Council annually, on the number of scholars, progress of education, &c." LCN 94.

139. *A Resolution passed on November 4, 1828.* Unlawful "to exact

toll, or ferriage, at any of the turnpikes, tollbridges, or ferries within the limits of the Cherokee Nation from citizens of the Nation." LCN 94.

140. A *Resolution passed on November 4, 1828.* Rates of ferriage at Edward Gunter's Ferry on the Tennessee River. LCN 94–95.

141. A *Resolution passed on November 4, 1828.* Provisions "making trade debts recoverable on certain conditions" and outlining contract judgment procedures. LCN 95–96.

142. A *Resolution passed on November 4, 1828.* Earlier act forbidding gaming at cards amended so that "no person . . . shall be allowed to game at dice, roulette, or thimbles." LCN 96.

143. A *Resolution passed on November 6, 1828.* Providing that the Cherokee National Treasurer shall keep and attend an office at New Echota during the general council sessions. LCN 97.

144. A *Resolution passed on November 8, 1828.* Establishing district courts "which shall sit twice a year . . . , to be composed of a District Judge, six Jurors and a Clerk" with "full and complete jurisdiction over all civil cases [which do not] exceed one hundred dollar" and all criminal cases except murder and setting out court procedure. LCN 97–99.

145. A *Resolution passed on November 8, 1828.* Establishing that "the Judges of the several courts in the Nation shall have power to adopt such rules and regulations, as shall be necessary to preserve good order in their Courts" and providing that new evidence shall not be admissible before the Supreme Court except where "it was impossible for the evidence to have been obtained and produced before the Circuit Court." LCN 101.

146. A *Resolution passed on November 8, 1828.* Requirement that "any person . . . not a public officer, who shall undertake to prosecute any criminal . . . shall be required to give bond and security . . . for faithful performance of prosecuting the criminals." LCN 99.

147. A *Resolution passed on November 8, 1828.* Regulation of non-citizen-employee and mechanics permits. LCN 99–100.

148. A *Resolution passed on November 8, 1828.* Treasurer shall "purchase one iron chest for the better security of the public funds of the Nation" and shall maintain certain specified office hours. LCN 100.

149. A *Resolution passed on November 8, 1828.* Providing for attachment of property of debtor if "he is about to abscond, or dispose of his property, so as to be beyond the reach of the law." LCN 101.

150. A *Resolution passed on November 10, 1828.* Death penalty provided for murder, procedures for execution, definition of justifiable homicide, and definition and penalty for assaults. LCN 104.

151. A *Resolution passed on November 10, 1828.* Compensation to individuals "for translating the laws of the Nation from English into the Cherokee language." LCN 105.

152. *A Resolution passed on November 11, 1828.* Declares unlawful for citizens to open public roads or ferries without permission of general council with provisions for closing illegal roads and penalties. LCN 105–106.

153. *A Resolution passed on November 11, 1828.* Appointment of special site commissioners for holding court in Hickory Log District. LCN 116.

154. *A Resolution passed on November 11, 1828.* Appointment of special site commissioners for holding court in Tahquohee District. LCN 117.

155. *A Resolution passed on November 12, 1828.* Procedure to fill vacancy in general council created by death or resignation. LCN 106–107.

156. *A Resolution passed on November 13, 1828.* Proposals for bids on two national turnpikes on the federal road with rates of tolls. LCN 108.

157. *A Resolution passed on November 13, 1828.* Appropriation of national funds to citizen "for informing against a certain pedlar vending merchandize without license." LCN 109.

158. *A Resolution passed on November 13, 1828.* Authorizing Nation to lease ferry and make improvements on the federal road. LCN 109.

159. *A Resolution passed on November 13, 1828.* Payment to reimburse citizen for "a pair of globes bought in New Orleans, with money contributed to the Cherokees, by the citizens of that city." LCN 109.

160. *A Resolution passed on November 13, 1828.* Salaries for public officials. LCN 110.

161. *A Resolution passed on November 13, 1828.* Payment for two individuals in lieu of "illegal fees collected from them, by direction of the Supreme Court in 1827."

162. *A Resolution passed on November 14, 1828.* Circuit courts to regulate "the rates of tolls, and ferriages at all turnpikes, toll bridges and ferries, belonging to individuals within the limits of the Cherokee Nation." LCN 96.

163. *A Resolution passed on November 14, 1828.* Increase in fine for citizens of Cherokee Nation convicted of employing U.S. citizens without permit. LCN 110.

164. *A Resolution passed on November 15 (?), 1828.* Persons prosecuted and convicted shall pay court costs. Provisions for boarding persons arrested for crimes. LCN 111.

165. *A Resolution passed on November 15, 1828.* Detailed provisions for decedent's property including wills and administration of estates. LCN 111–113.

166. *A Resolution passed on November 17, 1828.* Persons enrolling for emigration beyond jurisdiction of Nation "forfeit all rights, title, claim

and interest . . . as citizens . . . to the houses, farms or other improvements so left," and any citizen can "take and occupy for their own use and benefit" regardless of any provision made by emigrants. LCN 113.

167. A *Resolution passed on November 18, 1828.* Establishing circuit courts with jurisdiction over two district courts "to try and decide all cases, both civil and criminal, that come before them . . . and to call a Court, to try all criminals that may be arrested for murder." Procedures are set forth and duties of clerks in preparing record for appeal are outlined. LCN 102–104.

168. A *Resolution passed on November 18, 1828.* Expanding list of goods exempted from attachment or sale for debt to include sixty bushels of corn. LCN 113.

169. A *Resolution passed on November 19, 1828.* Business requirements of editor of the *Cherokee Phoenix* plus statement of additional duties as follows (1) "to withold . . . scurrilous communications which . . . excite and irritate personal controversies," (2) "not support or cherish . . . any thing on religious matters that will savour sectarianism"; (3) collect and publish as much original Cherokee material as possible; and (4) "have the manuscript laws printed in pamphlet form and attach to the printed laws" with index. LCN 114.

170. A *Resolution passed on November 17, 1828.* Provisions and specifications for construction of "a court house built at Echota, for the Supreme Court of the Cherokee Nation." LCN 114–115.

171. A *Resolution passed on November 19, 1828.* Appropriation of money for contingent expenses. LCN 115–116.

172. A *Resolution passed on November 19, 1828.* Increase in fine for violation of subpoena as witness from $25 to $100. Limit on number of witnesses to prove same point. LCN 116.

173. A *Resolution passed on November 22, 1828.* Procedure to fill vacancy in office of district sheriffs or constables. LCN 107.

174. A *Resolution passed on November 22, 1828.* Penalty for persons who "interrupt by misbehaviour, any congregation of Cherokee or white citizens, assembled at any place, for the purpose of Divine worship." LCN 107.

175. A *Resolution passed on October 15, 1829.* Treasurer's right to issue permits "to native citizens for the introduction of white men . . . into the Nation as mechanics &c. . . . suspended" until additional regulations are drafted. LCN 131.

176. A *Resolution passed on October 15, 1829.* Regulation of intermarried whites terminating citizenship status upon death of native Cherokee unless there is a child of this marriage. LCN 131–132.

177. A *Resolution passed on October 16, 1829.* Persons with buildings

on public square at Echota required to remove structures and additional building prohibited. LCN 132.

178. *A Resolution passed on October 16, 1829.* Appointment of person "to keep and take care of the public buildings of the Nation, in New Echota" who may "open the doors of the public buildings during recess of the . . . General Council and Supreme Court, to any minister or ministers, or any other person disposed to hold public worship." LCN 132–133.

179. *A Resolution passed on October 17, 1829.* Hiring repairs for Cherokee Council House. LCN 133.

180. *A Resolution passed on October 19, 1829.* A reprieve of Noochorwee of Aquohee "who had committed murder [is] discharged from the sentence of death . . . and placed under the protection of the laws . . . and any persons . . . who . . . mal-treat his body, or take away his life shall . . . experience the consequences of the law." LCN 133.

181. *A Resolution passed on October 21, 1829.* Limiting mechanics permits to one instead of five years with specific regulations and additional limitations. LCN 134–135.

182. *A Resolution passed on October 21, 1829.* Order of succession in case of removal, death, resignation or inability of Principal Chief and Assistant Principal Chief. LCN 135.

183. *A Resolution passed on October 22, 1829.* Appointment of translator to prepare "the journals of the two branches of the Legislative Council . . . for publication in the Cherokee language . . . weekly in the Cherokee Phoenix." LCN 135.

184. *A Resolution passed on October 22, 1829.* Recording "a law [which] has been in existence for many years but not committed to writing, that any citizen [who] shall treat and dispose of any land belonging to this Nation without special permission from the National Authorities . . . shall suffer death." Also creating state of outlawry subject to death for those who refuse to appear for trial. LCN 136–137.

185. *A Resolution passed on October 27, 1829.* Provisions for translation and publication of a pamphlet in Cherokee and English in parallel columns of a series of anti-Jackson essays from the *National Intelligencer.* LCN 136.

186. *A Resolution passed on October 27, 1829.* Collection provisions for debts owed the Nation. LCN 137–138.

187. *A Resolution passed on October 30, 1829.* Lease, repair and administration of roadways. LCN 138–139.

188. *A Resolution passed on October 31, 1829.* Provisions relating to citizens removing to Arkansas: (1) enrolled emigrants shall be treated as noncitizens; (2) sale of property to enrolled emigrants shall exclude seller from right to hold office as well as fine and lashes; (3) enrolled emigrants are intruders and must remove within 15 days. LCN 139–141.

189. *A Resolution passed on November 2, 1829.* Extension of act suspending poll tax and merchants tax "until the General Council shall deem it expedient to remove such suspension." LCN 139.

190. *A Resolution passed on November 2, 1829.* Procedures for holding elections. LCN 144–145.

191. *A Resolution passed on November 2, 1829.* Affirming rights of married women of the Cherokee Nation to own and dispose of property. LCN 142–143.

192. *A Resolution passed on November 3, 1829.* Additions to election law provisions. LCN 143.

193. *A Resolution passed on November 4, 1829.* Compensation for men employed by chief and executive council to enforce "law passed on the subject of intruders." LCN 143–144.

194. *A Resolution passed on November 4, 1829.* Additional pay for the editor of the *Cherokee Phoenix.* LCN 144.

195. *A Resolution passed on November 4, 1829.* Appointment of an assistant editor for the *Cherokee Phoenix* whose "duties shall be to translate all public documents from the English into the Cherokee language and all English news deemed useful." LCN 144.

196. *A Resolution passed on November 9, 1829.* Provisions for apprentices on the *Cherokee Phoenix.* LCN 144–145.

197. *A Resolution passed on November 9, 1829.* Appropriations to pay Kahetechee "to take good care of an old blind man, named Big Bear, at his house, and supply him with food, and wash his person and clothes, and keep him in a decent condition." LCN 145.

198. *A Resolution passed on November 9, 1829.* Instructions to National Treasurer to "dispose of all public gun-powder now on hand" and to determine money owed on lots at New Echota with provisions for collection. LCN 145–146.

199. *A Resolution passed on November 9, 1829.* Appropriation of funds for contingent expenses. LCN 146.

200. *A Resolution passed on November 10, 1829.* Provisions for costs of apprehending and guarding prisoners and for administration of courts. LCN 146–147.

201. *A Resolution passed on November 10, 1829.* Compensation for members of National Committee and Council. LCN 147–148.

3. Constitution of the Cherokee Nation

Formed by a Convention of Delegates From the Several Districts,
at New Echota, July, 1827

We, the Representatives of the people of the Cherokee Nation, in
Convention assembled, in order to establish justice, ensure tranquility,
promote our common welfare, and secure to ourselves and our posterity
the blessings of liberty; acknowledging with humility and gratitude the
goodness of the sovereign Ruler of the Universe, in offering us an
opportunity so favorable to the design, and imploring His aid and direction
in its accomplishment, do ordain and establish this Constitution for the
Government of the Cherokee Nation by the Treaties concluded with the
United States, are as follows, and shall forever hereafter remain unalter-
ably the same, to-wit: [Description, Article I, Sec. 1., omitted]

Sec. 2.—The sovereignty and Jurisdiction of this Government shall
extend over the country within the boundaries above described, and the
lands therein are, and shall remain, the common property of the Nation;
but the improvements made thereon, and in the possession of the citizens
of the Nation, are the exclusive and indefeasible property of the citizens
respectively who made; or may rightfully be in possession of them; Provided, that the citizens of the Nation, possessing exclusive and indefeasible
right to their respective improvements, as expressed in this article, shall
possess no right nor power to dispose of their improvements in any manner
whatever to the United States, individual states, nor individual citizens
thereof; and that whenever any such citizen or citizens of any other
Government, all their rights and privileges as citizens of this Nation shall
cease; Provided nevertheless, That the Legislature shall have power to
re-admit by law to all the rights of citizenship, any such person or persons,
who may at any time desire to return to the Nation on their memorializing

the General Council for such readmission. Moreover, the Legislature shall have power to adopt such laws and regulations, as its wisdom may deem expedient and proper, to prevent the citizens from monopolizing improvements with the view of speculation.

Article II.—Sec. 1.—The power of this government shall be divided into three distinct departments; the Legislative, the Executive, and Judicial.

Sec. 2.—No person or persons belonging to one of these Departments shall exercise any of the powers properly belonging to either of the others, except in the cases hereinafter expressly directed or permitted.

Article III.—Sec. 1.—The Legislative power shall be vested in two distinct branches; a Committee and a Council, each to have a negative on the other, and both to be styled the General Council of the Cherokee Nation; and the style of their acts and laws shall be.

"Resolved by the Committee and Council, in General Council convened.

Sec. 2.—The Cherokee Nation, as laid off into eight Districts, shall so remain.

Sec. 3.—The Committee shall consist of two members from each District, and the Council shall consist of three members from each District, to be chosen by the qualified electors of their respective Districts, for two years; and the elections to be held in every District on the First Monday in August for the year 1828, and every succeeding two years thereafter; and the General Council shall be held once a year, to be convened on the second Monday of October in each year, at New Echota.

Sec. 4.—No person shall be eligible to a seat in the General Council, but a free Cherokee male citizen, who shall have attained the age of twenty-five years. The descendants of Cherokee men by all free women, except the African race, whose parents may have been living together as man and wife, according to the customs and laws of this Nation, shall be entitled to all the rights and privileges of this nation, as well as the posterity of Cherokee women by all free men. No person who is of negro or mulatto parentage, either by the father or mother side, shall be eligible to hold any office of profit, honor or trust under this Government.

Sec. 5.—The electors and members of the General Council shall, in all cases except those of treason, felony, or breach of the peace, be privileged from arrest during their attendance at election, and at the General Council, and in going to, and returning from the same.

Sec. 6.—In all elections by the people, the electors shall vote viva voce. Electors for members to the General Council for 1828, shall be held at the places of holding the several courts, and at the other two precincts in each District which are designated by the law under which the members of this Convention were elected; and the District Judges shall superintend the elections within the precincts of their respective Court Houses, and the Marshals and Sheriffs shall superintend within the precincts which may be assigned them by the Circuit Judges of their respective Districts, together with one other person who shall be appointed by the Circuit Judges for each precinct within their respective Districts; and the Circuit Judges shall also appoint a clerk to each precinct.—The superintendents and clerks shall, on the Wednesday morning succeeding the election, assemble at their respective Court Houses and proceed to examine and ascertain the true state of the polls, and shall issue to each member, duly elected, a certificate, and also make an official return of the state of the polls of election to the Principal Chief, and it shall be the duty of the Sheriffs to deliver the same to the Executive; Provided nevertheless, The General Council shall have power after the election of 1828, to regulate by law the precincts and superintendents and clerks of elections in the several Districts.

Sec. 7.—All free male citizens, (excepting negroes and descendants of white and Indian men by negro women who may have been set free,) who shall have attained to the age of eighteen years, shall be equally entitled to vote at all public elections.

Sec. 8.—Each house of the General Council shall judge of the qualifications and returns of its own members.

Sec. 9.—Each house of the General Council may determine the rules of its proceedings, punish a member for disorderly behavior, and with the concurrence of two thirds, expel a member; but not a second time for the same cause.

Sec. 10.—Each house of the General Council, when assembled shall choose its own officers; a majority of each house shall constitute a quorum to do business, but a smaller number may adjourn from day to day and compel the attendance of absent members in such manner and under such penalty as each house may prescribe.

Sec. 11.—The members of the Committee shall each receive from the public Treasury a compensation for their services which shall be two dollars and fifty cents per day during their attendance at the General Council; and the members of the Council shall each receive two dollars per day for their services during their attendance at the General Council:— Provided, that the same may be increased or diminished by law, but no alteration shall take effect during the period of service of the members of the General Council, by whom such alteration shall have been made.

Sec. 12.—The General Council shall regulate by law, by whom and in what manner, writs of elections shall be issued to fill the vacancies which may happen in either branch thereof.

Sec. 13.—Each member of the General Council before he takes his seat shall take the following oath or affirmation, to-wit:

"I, A.B., do solemnly swear, (or affirm, as the case may be,) that I have not obtained my election by bribery, treats or any undue and unlawful means used by myself, or others by my desire or approbation, for that purpose; that I consider myself constitutionally qualified as a member of and that, on all questions and measures which may come before me, I will so give my vote, and so conduct myself, as may in my judgment, appear most conducive to the interest and prosperity of this Nation; and that I will bear true faith and allegiance to the same; and to the utmost of my ability and power observe, confirm to, support and defend the Constitution thereof."

Sec. 14.—No person who may be convicted of felony before any court of this Nation, shall be eligible to any office or appointment of honor, profit or trust within this Nation.

Sec. 15.—The General Council shall have power to make all laws and regulations, which they shall deem necessary and proper for the good of the Nation, which shall not be contrary to this Constitution.

Sec. 16.—It shall be the duty of the General Council to pass such laws as may be necessary and proper, to decide differences by arbitrators to be appointed by the parties, who may choose that summary mode of adjustment.

Sec. 17.—No power of suspending the laws of this Nation shall be exercised, unless by the Legislature or its authority.

Sec. 18.—No retrospective law, nor any law, impairing the obligations of contracts shall be passed.

Sec. 19.—The legislature shall have power to make laws for laying and collecting taxes, for the purpose of raising a revenue.

Sec. 20.—All bills making appropriations shall originate in the Committee, but the Council may propose amendments or reject the same.

Sec. 21.—All other bills may originate in either house, subject to the concurrence or rejection of the other.

Sec. 22.—All acknowledged Treaties shall be the Supreme law of the land.

Sec. 23.—The General Council shall have the sole power of deciding on the construction of all Treaty stipulations.

Sec. 24.—The Council shall have the sole power of impeaching.

Sec. 25.—Any impeachments shall be tried by the Committee;—when sitting for that purpose, the members shall be upon oath or affirmation; and no person shall be convicted without the concurrence of two thirds of the members present.

Sec. 26.—The Principal Chief, assistant principal Chief, and all civil officers, under this Nation, shall be liable to impeachment for any misdemeanor in office, but Judgment, in such cases, shall not extend further than removal from office, and disqualification to hold any office of honor, trust or profit, under this Nation. The party whether convicted or acquitted, shall nevertheless, be liable to indictment, trial, judgment and punishment, according to law.

Article IV.—Sec. 1.—The Supreme Executive Power of this Nation shall be vested in a Principal Chief, who shall be chosen by the General Council, and shall hold his office four years; to be elected as follows,—The General Council by a joint vote, shall, at their second annual session, after the rising of this Convention, and at every fourth annual session thereafter, on the second day after the House shall be organized, and competent to proceed to business, elect a Principal Chief.

Sec. 2.—No person, except a natural born citizen, shall be eligible to the office of Principal Chief; neither shall any person be eligible to that office, who shall not have attained to the age of thirty-five years.

Sec. 3.—There shall also be chosen at the same time, by the General Council, in the same manner for four years, an assistant Principal Chief.

Sec. 4.—In case of the removal of the Principal Chief from office, or his death, resignation, or inability to discharge the powers and duties of the said office, the same shall devolve on the assistant principal Chief, until the inability be removed, or the vacancy filled by the General Council.

Sec. 5.—The General Council may, by law, provide for the case of removal, death, resignation or inability of both the Principal and Assistant Principal Chiefs, declaring what officer shall then act as Principal Chief, until the disability be removed, or a Principal Chief shall be elected.

Sec. 6.—The Principal Chief, shall, at stated times, receive for their services,—a compensation—which shall neither be increased nor diminished during the period for which they shall have been elected; and they shall not receive, within that period, any other emolument from the Cherokee Nation, or any other government.

Sec. 7.—Before the Principal Chief enters on the execution of his office, he shall take the following oath, or affirmation; "I do solemnly swear (or affirm) that I will faithfully execute the office of Principal Chief of the Cherokee Nation, and will; to the best of my ability, preserve, protect and defend, the Constitution of the Cherokee Nation."

Sec. 8.—He may, on extraordinary occasions, convene the General Council at the Seat of Government.

Sec. 9.—He shall from time to time give to the General Council information of the State of the Government, and recommend to their consideration such measures as he may think expedient.

Sec. 10.—He shall take care that the laws be faithfully executed.

Sec. 11.—It shall be his duty to visit the different districts, at least once in two years, to inform himself of the general condition of the Country.

Sec. 12.—The assistant Principal Chief shall, by virtue of his office, aid and advise the Principal Chief in the Administration of the Government, at all times during his continuance in office.

Sec. 13.—Vacancies that may happen in offices, the appointment of which is vested in the General Council, shall be filled by the Principal Chief, during the recess of the General Council, by granting Commissions which shall expire at the end of the Session.

Sec. 14.—Every Bill which shall have passed both Houses of the General Council, shall, before it becomes a law, be presented to the Principal Chief of the Cherokee Nation. If he approves, he shall sign it, but if not, he shall return it, with his objections, to that house in which it shall have originated, who shall enter the objections at large on their journals, and proceed to reconsider it. If, after such reconsideration, two thirds of that House shall agree to pass the bill, it shall be sent, together with the objections, to the other house, by which it shall likewise be reconsidered, and if approved by two thirds of that house, it shall become a law. If any bill shall not be returned by the Principal Chief within five days (Sundays excepted) after it shall have been presented to him, the same shall be a law, in like manner as if he signed it; unless the General Council by their adjournment prevent its return, in which case it shall be a law, unless sent back within three days after their next meeting.

Sec. 15.—Members of the General Council and all officers, Executive and Judicial, shall be bound by oath to support the Constitution of this Nation, and to perform the duties of their respective offices with fidelity.

Sec. 16.—In case of disagreement between the two houses with respect to the time of adjournment, the Principal Chief shall have the power to adjourn the General Council to such a time as he thinks proper, provided, it be not to a period beyond the next Constitutional meeting of the same.

Sec. 17.—The Principal Chief shall, during the sitting of the General Council, attend to the Seat of Government.

Sec. 18.—There shall be a Council to consist of three men to be appointed by the joint vote of both Houses, to advise the Principal Chief in the Executive part of the Government, whom the Principal Chief shall have full power, at his descretion, to assemble; and he, together with the assistant Principal Chief, and the Counsellors, or a majority of them may, from time to time, hold and keep a Council for ordering and directing the affairs of the Nation according to law.

Sec. 19.—The members of the Council shall be chosen for the term of one year.

Sec. 20.—The resolutions and advice of the Council shall be recorded in a register and signed by the members agreeing thereto, which may be called for by either house of the General Council; and any counsellor may enter his dissent to the resolution of the majority.

Sec. 21.—The Treasurer of the Cherokee Nation shall be chosen by the joint vote of both Houses of the General Council for the term of two years.

Sec. 22.—The Treasurer shall, before entering on the duties of his office, give bond to the Nation with sureties to the satisfaction of the Legislature, for the faithful discharge of his trust.

Sec. 23.—No money shall be drawn from the Treasury, but by warrant from the Principal Chief, and in consequence of appropriations made by law.

Sec. 24.—It shall be the duty of the Treasurer to receive all public monies, and to make a regular statement and account of the receipts and expenditures of all public monies at the annual Session of the General Council.

Article V.—Sec. 1.—The Judicial Powers shall be vested in a Supreme Court, and such Circuit and Inferior Courts, as the General Council may, from time to time ordain and establish.

Sec. 2.—The Supreme Court shall consist of three Judges, any two of whom shall be a quorum.

Sec. 3.—The Judges of each shall hold their Commissions for four years, but any of them may be removed from office on the address of two thirds of each house of the General Council to the Principal Chief, for that purpose.

Sec. 4.—The Judges of the Supreme and Circuit Courts shall, at stated times, receive a compensation, which shall not be diminished during their continuance in office, but they shall receive no fees or perquisites of office, nor hold any other office of profit or any other power.

Sec. 5.—No person shall be appointed a Judge of any of the Courts before he shall have attained to the age of thirty years, nor shall any person continue to execute the duties of any of the said offices after he shall have attained to the age of seventy years.

Sec. 6.—The Judges of the Supreme and Circuit Courts shall be appointed by a joint vote of both houses of the General Council.

Sec. 7.—There shall be appointed in each District, under the Legislative authority, as many justices of the Peace as it may be deemed the public good requires, whose powers, duties and duration in office, shall be clearly designated.

Sec. 8.—The Judges of the Supreme Court and Circuit Courts shall have complete criminal Jurisdiction in such cases and in such manner as may be pointed out by law.

Sec. 9.—Each Court shall choose its own Clerks for the term of four years; but such Clerks shall not continue in office unless their qualifications shall be adjudged and approved of by the Judges of the Supreme Court, and they shall be removable for breach of good behaviour at any time, by the Judges of their respective courts.

Sec. 10.—No Judge shall sit on trial of any cause, where the parties shall be connected with him by affinity or consanguinity, except by consent of the parties. In case all the Judges of the Supreme Court shall be interested in the event of any cause, or related to all, or either of the parties, the Legislature may provide by law for the selection of three men of good character and knowledge, for the determination thereof, who shall be especially commissioned by the Principal Chief for the case.

Sec. 11.—All writs and other process shall run in the name of the Cherokee Nation, and bear test, and be signed by the respective clerks.

Sec. 12.—Indictments shall conclude, "against the peace and dignity of the Cherokee Nation."

Sec. 13.—The Supreme Court shall hold its session annually at the seat of Government to be convened on the second Monday of October in each year.

Sec. 14.—In all criminal prosecutions, the accused shall have the right of being heard, of demanding the nature and cause of the accusation against him, of meeting the witnesses face to face, of having compulsory process for obtaining witnesses in his favor; and in prosecutions by indictment or information, a speedy public trial by an impartial jury of the vicinage; nor shall he be compelled to give evidence against himself.

Sec. 15.—The people shall be secure in their persons, houses, papers and possessions, from unreasonable seizures and searches, and no warrants to search any place or to seize any person or things, shall be issued without describing them as nearly as may be, nor without good cause, supported by oath, or affirmation. All prisoners shall be bailable by sufficient security unless for capital offenses, where the proof is evident, or presumption great.

Article VI.—Sec. 1.—Whereas, the ministers of the Gospel are, by their profession, dedicated to the service of God and the care of souls, and ought not to be diverted from the great duty of their function, therefore, no minister of the Gospel, or public preacher of any religious persuasion, whilst he continues in the exercise of his pastoral functions, shall be eligible to the office of Principal Chief, or a seat in either house of the General Council.

Sec. 2.—No person who denies the being of a God, or a future state of rewards and punishment, shall hold any office in the civil department of this Nation.

Sec. 3.—The free exercise of religious worship, and serving God without distinction shall forever be allowed within this Nation; Provided, That this liberty of conscience shall not be so constructed as to excuse acts of licentiousness, or justify practices inconsistent with the peace or safety of this Nation.

Sec. 4.—Whenever the General Council shall determine the expediency of appointing delegates or other Agents for the purpose of transacting business with the Government of the United States; the power to recommend, and by the advice and consent of the Committee, shall appoint and commission such delegates or public agents accordingly, and all matters of interest touching the rights of the citizens of this Nation, which may require the attention of the government of the United States, the Principal Chief shall keep up a friendly correspondence with that Government, through the medium of its proper officers.

Sec. 5.—All commissions shall be in the name and by the authority of the Cherokee Nation, and be sealed with the seal of the Nation, and signed by the Principal Chief.

Sec. 6.—A Sheriff shall be elected in each District by the qualified electors thereof, who shall hold his office for the term of two years, unless sooner removed. Should a vacancy occur subsequent to an election, it shall be filled by the Principal Chief as in other cases, and the person so appointed shall continue in office until the next general election, when such vacancy shall be filled by the qualified electors, and the Sheriff then elected shall continue in office for two years.

Sec. 7.—There shall be a Marshal appointed by a joint vote of both houses of the General Council, for the term of four years, whose compensation and duties shall be regulated by law, and whose jurisdiction shall extend over the Cherokee Nation.

Sec. 8.—No person shall for the same offense be twice put in jeopardy of life or limb, nor shall any person's property be taken or applied to public use without his consent; Provided, That nothing in this clause shall be so construed as to impair the right and power of the General Council to lay and collect taxes. All courts shall be open, and every person for an injury done him in his property, person or reputation, shall have remedy by due course of law.

Sec. 9.—The right of trial by jury shall remain inviolate.

Sec. 10.—Religion, morality and knowledge being necessary to good government, the preservation of Liberty, and the happiness of mankind, schools and the means of education shall forever be encouraged in this Nation.

Sec. 11.—The appointment of all officers, not otherwise directed by this Constitution shall be vested in the Legislature.

Sec. 12.—All laws in force in this nation at the passing of this Constitution, shall so continue until altered or repealed by the Legislature, except where they are temporary, in which case they shall expire at the times respectively limited for their duration; if not continued by an act of the Legislature.

Sec. 13.—The General Council may at any time propose such amendments to this Constitution as two-thirds of each house shall deem expedient; and the Principal Chief shall issue a proclamation, directing all the civil officers of the several Districts to promulgate the same as extensively as possible within their respective Districts, at least nine months previous to the next general election, and if at the first session of the General Council after such general election, two thirds of each house shall, by yeas and nays, ratify such proposed amendments they shall be valid to all intents and purposes, as part of the Constitution; Provided, That such proposed amendments shall be read on three several days, in each house as well when the same are proposed as when they are ratified.

Done in Convention at New Echota, this twenty-sixth day of July, in the year of our Lord, one thousand eight hundred and twenty-seven; In testimony whereof, we have each of us, hereunto subscribed our names.

JNO. ROSS, Pres't Con.

Jno. Baldrige, Geo. Lowrey, Jno. Brown, Edward Gunter, John Martin, Joseph Vann, Kelechulee, Lewis Ross, Thomas Foreman, Hair Conrad, James Daniel, John Duncan, Joseph Vann, Thomas Petitt, John Beamer, Ooclenota, Wm. Boling, John Timson, Situwaukee, Richard Walker,

A. MCCOY, Sec'y to Con.

4. Thomas Jefferson to the Cherokee Deputies, January 9, 1809[*]

My Children, Deputies of the Cherokee Upper Towns.

I have maturely considered the speeches you have delivered me, and will now give you answers to the several matters they contain.

You inform me of your anxious desires to engage in the industrious pursuits of agriculture and civilized life; that finding it impracticable to induce the nation at large to join in this, you wish a line of separation to be established between the Upper and Lower Towns, so as to include all the waters of the Highwassee in your part; and that having thus contracted your society within narrower limits, you propose, within these, to begin the establishment of fixed laws and of regular government. You say, that the Lower Towns are satisfied with the divisions you propose, and on these several matters you ask my advice and aid.

With respect to the line of division between yourselves and the Lower Towns, it must rest on the joint consent of both parties. The one you propose appears moderate, reasonable and well defined; we are willing to recognize those on each side of that line as distinct societies, and if our aid shall be necessary to mark it more plainly than nature has done, you shall have it. I think with you, that on this reduced scale, it will be more easy for you to introduce the regular administration of laws.

In proceeding to the establishment of laws, you wish to adopt them from ours, and such only for the present as suit your present condition; chiefly indeed, those for the punishment of crimes and the protection of property. But who is to determine which of our laws suit your condition, and shall be in force with you? All of you being equally free, no one has a right to say what shall be law for the others. Our way is to put these questions to the vote, and to consider that as law for which the majority

* Thomas Jefferson, *The Writings of Thomas Jefferson*, XVI, 455–58.

votes—the fool has as great a right to express his opinion by vote as the wise, because it would be inconvenient for all your men to meet in one place, would it not be better for every town to do as we do—that is to say: Choose by the vote of the majority of the town and of the country people nearer to that than to any other town, one, two, three or more, according to the size of the town, of those whom each voter thinks the wisest and honestest men of their place, and let these meet together and agree which of our laws suit them. But these men know nothing of our laws. How then can they know which to adopt? Let them associate in their council our beloved man living with them, Colonel Meigs, and he will tell them what our law is on any point they desire. He will inform them also of our methods of doing business in our councils, so as to preserve order and to obtain the vote of every member fairly. This council can make a law for giving to every head of a family a separate parcel of land, which, when he has built upon and improved, it shall belong to him and his descendants forever, and which the nation itself shall have no right to sell from under his feet. They will determine too, what punishment shall be inflicted for every crime. In our States generally, we punish murder only by death, and all other crimes by solitary confinement in a prison.

But when you shall have adopted laws, who are to execute them? Perhaps it may be best to permit every town and the settlers in its neighborhood attached to it, to select some of their best men, by a majority of its voters, to be judges in all differences, and to execute the law according to their own judgment. Your council of representatives will decide on this, or such other mode as may best suit you. I suggest these things, my children, for the consideration of the Upper Towns of your nation, to be decided on as they think best, and I sincerely wish you may succeed in your laudable endeavors to save the remains of your nation, by adopting industrious occupations and a government of regular laws. In this you may rely on the counsel and assistance of the Government of the United States. Deliver these words to your people in my name, and assure them of my friendship.

Bibliography

I. Manuscript Materials

Alderman Library, University of Virginia, Charlottesville, Virginia:
Thomas Jefferson Papers.
Tracy McGregor Collection, Cherokee Documents.

Cherokee National Archives, Tahlequah, Oklahoma:
Prospectus for Cherokee Cultural Center.
Tribal Materials on loan to Oklahoma Historical Society.

Five Civilized Tribes Museum, Muskogee, Oklahoma:
Indian Agency Collection.
Tribal Materials of Cherokee Nation.

Georgia Department of Archives and History, Atlanta, Georgia:
Typescripts of Original Cherokee Documents.
Claims of Cherokee Depredations.

Georgia Historical Commission, Atlanta, Georgia:
Cherokee Microfilm Materials on Laws of Cherokee Nation.
Translation of unpublished Cherokee Mission Conference, 1819.

Harvard Law School Library, Cambridge, Massachusetts:
Cherokee Laws, Documents and Materials.

Houghton Library, Harvard University, Cambridge, Massachusetts:
Cherokee Mission Papers, American Board of Foreign Missions.

Indian Archives Division, Oklahoma Historical Society, Oklahoma City, Oklahoma:
Cherokee Tribal Records, District Court and Supreme Court Cases and Opinions. For a complete list see bound volumes on file in Oklahoma Historical Society, Cherokee Nation, prepared by Rella Looney, Indian Archivist. The Oklahoma Historical Society has over seven

239

hundred bound volumes and thirty filing case drawers of Cherokee manuscripts.
Grant Foreman Collection. Transcripts, Typescripts, and Vertical Files
Grant Foreman (ed.), "Indian and Pioneer Papers."
Journal of the Commissioner of Indian Affairs on Journey to the Cherokees and His Proceedings There, 1725.

Indian Heritage Association, Muskogee, Oklahoma:
Cherokee Documents Collection.
Cherokee National Records Microfilm Collection.
Gregory-Strickland Cherokee Field Notes.

Kilpatrick Collection, Tahlequah, Oklahoma:
Original Cherokee Language Materials.

Library of Congress, Manuscript Division, Washington, D.C.:
Alexander Longe, "A Small Postscript to the Ways and Manners of Indians called the Cherokees."
Papers of the Society for the Propagation of the Gospel.
Return J. Meigs, "Journal of Occurences in Cherokee Nation, 1801–1804."

National Archives of the United States, Washington, D.C.:
Letters Received by the Office of Indian Affairs. Cherokee Agency, East; Cherokee Agency, West; Cherokee Agency. Microfilm Publications.
Letters Sent By the Secretary of War. Microfilm Publications.
Records of the Cherokee Indian Agency in Tennessee, 1801–35. Microfilm Publications.

Newberry Library, Chicago, Illinois:
Buttrick Manuscript, Ayer Collection.
John Howard Payne Papers, Ayer Collection.

Northeastern State College, Tahlequah, Oklahoma:
Cherokee Collection.
W. W. Hastings Materials.
Stand Watie Papers.

Pierce Collection Law Office of Earl Boyd Pierce, Ft. Gibson, Oklahoma:
Collected Source Material on Cherokee History.
Records and Briefs in Selected Cherokee Cases.

Public Library, Muskogee, Oklahoma:
Grant Foreman Collection.

South Carolina Department of Archives and History, Columbia, South Carolina:
Journals and Records of Colonial South Carolina.

South Carolina Historical Society, Charleston, South Carolina:
Papers of Henry Laurens.

Records of the Lords Commissioners of Trade and Plantations.
Tennessee State Library and Archives, Nashville, Tennessee:
Cherokee Supreme Court Records, 1823–1835.
Thomas Gilcrease Institute, Tulsa, Oklahoma:
Cherokee Tribal Papers.
Grant Foreman Collection.
Letter to Brother John, William Fyffe, February 1, 1761.
John Ross Papers.
Wolf King's Answer to a Joint Talk, April 29, 1776.
University of Georgia, Athens, Georgia:
Cherokee Documents.
State Newspaper Collection and Index.
Vertical File Materials.
University of Oklahoma, Norman, Oklahoma:
Cherokee Documents in Phillips Collection.
Pardon Board Records of Cherokee Nation.
University of Tulsa, Tulsa, Oklahoma: Indian Law Collection.
Virginia Law Library, University of Virginia, Charlottesville, Virginia:
State Statute Materials.

II. Government Documents and Publications
A. Federal
Abel, Annie H. "Proposals for an Indian State, 1778–1878," *Annual Report of the American Historical Association for 1907*. Washington, D.C., Government Printing Office, 1908.
American State Papers: Indian Affairs. Washington, D.C., Gales and Seaton, 1832–1834.
"Cherokees." *Congressional Record*, 46 Cong., 3 sess., 781.
Cohen, Felix S. *Handbook of Indian Law*. Washington, D.C., Government Printing Office, 1942.
Commissioner of Indian Affairs. *Annual Report for the Year 1859*. Washington, D.C., Government Printing, 1860.
Fenton, William and John Gulick, eds. *Symposium on Cherokee and Iroquois Culture*. Washington, D.C., Government Printing Office, 1961.
Gilbert, William H., Jr. *The Eastern Cherokees*. Washington, D.C., Government Printing Office, 1943.
Kappler, Charles, ed. *Indian Affairs, Laws and Treaties*. Washington, D.C., Government Printing Office, 1903.
Kennedy, John F. *Public Papers of the Presidents: John F. Kennedy, 1963*. Washington, D.C., Government Printing Office, 1963.

Mooney, James. *Myths of the Cherokees*. Washington, D.C., Government Printing Office, 1897–98.

Mooney, James. *The Swimmer Manuscript*. Ed. by Frans Olbrechts. Washington, D.C., Government Printing Office, 1932.

Pilling, James Constantine. *Bibliography of the Iroquoian Language*. Washington, D.C., Government Printing Office, 1888.

Richardson, James D., comp. *A Compilation of Messages and Papers of the Presidents, 1789–1897*. Washington, D.C., Government Printing Office, 1896–99.

Royce, Charles C. *The Cherokee Nation of Indians*. Washington, D.C., Government Printing Office, 1887.

Swanton, John R. *The Indians of the Southeastern United States*. Washington, D.C., Government Printing Office, 1946.

United States Congress. *The Internal Feuds Among the Cherokees*. Sen. Doc. 298. April 13, 1846.

B. State

Acts of Alabama Passed at the . . . Annual Session of the General Assembly. 1825, 1826, 1827.

Acts of the General Assembly of the State of Georgia. 1826, 1834, 1836.

Codification of the Statute Law of Georgia. 1845.

Compilation of the Laws of the State of Georgia. 1831.

Digest of the Laws of the State of Georgia. 1822, 1831, 1837, 1851.

Hawkins, Benjamin. *Letters of Benjamin Hawkins, 1796–1806*. Savannah, Ga., Georgia Historical Society, 1916.

Kentucky Laws, 1821.

Laws of the Commonwealth of Massachusetts From 1780 to 1807. 1809.

Laws of the State of Maine 1821.

Laws of the State of New Hampshire 1828.

McDowell, William L., Jr., ed. *Documents Relating to Indian Affairs May 21, 1750–August 7, 1754* (Colonial Records of South Carolina, Series 2). Columbia, South Carolina Archives Department, 1958.

———. *Journals of the Commissioner of the Indian Trade: September 20, 1710–August 29, 1718* (Colonial Records of South Carolina). Columbia, South Carolina Archives Department, 1955.

Maryland Code 1829.

Public Statutes of Connecticut 1824.

III. Cherokee Publications

Act in Relation to Minerals. Tahlequah, Advocate Office, 1883.

Act Making Disposition of Estray Property. Tahlequah, Advocate Office, 1900.

Act of Union Between the Eastern and Western Cherokees, the Constitu-

tion and Amendments, and the Laws of the Cherokee Nation Passed During the Session of 1868 and Subsequent Sessions. Tahlequah, National Press, Edward Archer, 1870.

Act to Appropriate and Pay Certain Monies Out of Monies Arising From the Sale of the Cherokee Outlet to the Freedmen of the Cherokee Nation. Tahlequah, Advocate Office, 1896.

Act to Create a Joint Commission to Determine Claims to Citizenship of Freedmen Under the 9th Article of the Treaty of 1866. Tahlequah, Advocate Office, 1886.

Acts of the National Council Authorizing and Directing the Sale of Intruder Improvements. Tahlequah, Hawkeye Printers, 1897.

Acts of the National Council Authorizing and Directing the Sale of Intruder Improvements. Tahlequah, Sentinel Printers, 1898.

Acts of the National Council Authorizing and Directing the Sale of Intruders Improvements. Tahlequah, Advocate Office, 1900.

Amendatory Act. An Act to Transfer the Jurisdiction of the Supreme Court in Criminal Cases. Tahlequah, n.p., 1877.

Amendment to the Constitution of the Cherokee Nation, Adopted November 26, 1866. Washington, D.C., 1867.

Amendment to the Permit Law. Tahlequah, Advocate Office, 1892.

Annual Message to Hon. Chas. Thompson, Principal Chief of Cherokee Nation. Tahlequah, n.p., 1876.

Census Bill. Tahlequah, Advocate Office, 1896.

Cherokee Advocate. Tahlequah, Cherokee Nation, and Fort Gibson, Cherokee Nation. 1st and 2d series, 1844–1906.

Cherokee Messenger. August, 1844–May, 1846. Cherokee Nation, H. Upham, Baptist Mission Press, 1844–46.

Cherokee Phoenix. New Echota, Cherokee Nation, Georgia. 1829–1834.

Compiled Laws of the Cherokee Nation. Tahlequah, National Advocate Printers, 1881.

Constitution and Laws of the Cherokee Nation. St. Louis, R. & T. A. Ennis, Stationers, Printers and Book Binders, 1875.

Constitution and Laws of the Cherokee Nation. Parsons, Kans., Foley Railroad Printing Company, 1893.

Constitution and Laws of the Cherokee Nation: Passed at Tahlequah: Cherokee Nation, 1839. Washington, D.C., Gales & Seaton, 1840.

Constitution and Laws of the Cherokee Nation: Passed at Tahlequah, Cherokee Nation, 1839–51. Oklahoma City, Reprint Edition Published for the Cherokee Nation by Colorgraphics, 1969.

Constitution of the Cherokee Nation. Milledgeville, Ga., Office of the Statesman and Patriot, 1827.

Constitution of the Cherokee Nation: Formed by a Convention of

Delegates From the Several Districts. New Echota, Cherokee Nation, Ga., *Cherokee Phoenix,* 1828.

Council Bill No. 1. An Act Authorizing the Principal Chief in the Name, Stead, and Behalf of the National Council to dissent from Allowance per Mile for right of Way through the Cherokee Domain of the Kansas and Arkansas Valley Railroad. Tahlequah, Advocate Office, 1887.

Laws Cherokee Nation. Extra Session of 1884. Tahlequah, Advocate Office, 1884.

Laws Instructing the Several Revenue Officers of the Cherokee Nation. Tahlequah, Advocate Office, 1890.

Laws of Cherokee Nation. Tahlequah, Advocate Office, 1890.

Laws of the Cherokee Nation: Adopted by the Council at Various Periods. Knoxville, Knoxville Register Office, Heiskell & Brown, 1821.

Laws of the Cherokee Nation: Adopted by the Council at Various Periods. Tahlequah, Cherokee Advocate Office, 1852.

Laws of the Cherokee Nation: Enacted by the General Council in 1826, 1827 & 1828. New Echota, Cherokee Nation, Isaac Heylin Harris, *Cherokee Phoenix,* 1828.

Laws of the Cherokee Nation: Enacted by the General Council in the year 1829. New Echota, Cherokee Nation, John F. Wheeler, *Cherokee Phoenix,* 1830.

Laws of the Cherokee Nation: Enacted by the National Council at Their Annual Session A.D. 1841. Park Hill, Mission Press, John Candy, 1842.

The Laws of the Cherokee Nation: Passed at Tah-le-quah, Cherokee Nation, 1840–1843. Cherokee Nation, Baptist Mission Press, H. Upham, printer, 1844.

Laws of the Cherokee Nation: Passed at Tahlequah, Cherokee Nation, 1844–5. Tahlequah, *Cherokee Advocate,* 1845.

Laws of the Cherokee Nation: Passed at the Annual Session of the National Council, 1845. Tahlequah, Cherokee Advocate Office, 1846.

Laws of the Cherokee Nation: Passed at the Annual Session of the National Council, 1846. Tahlequah, National Council, 1846.

Laws of the Cherokee Nation: Passed at the Annual Sessions of the National Council of 1852–1853. Tahlequah, *Cherokee Advocate,* 1853.

Laws of the Cherokee Nation: Passed at the Annual Sessions of the National Council of 1854–1855. Tahlequah, *Cherokee Advocate,* 1855.

Laws of the Cherokee Nation: Passed by the National Committee and Council. Knoxville, Knoxville Register Office, Heiskell & Brown, 1821.

Laws of the Cherokee Nation: Passed During the Years 1839–1867. Com-

piled by Authority of the National Council. St. Louis, Missouri Democrat Printer, 1868.

Laws and Joint Resolutions of the Cherokee Nation: Enacted During the Regular and Special Sessions of the Years 1881–1883. Tahlequah, E. C. Boudinot, Jr., Printer, 1884.

Laws and Joint Resolutions of the Cherokee Nation: Enacted by the National Council During the Regular and Extra Sessions of 1884–1886. Tahlequah, E. C. Boudinot, Jr., Printer, 1887.

Laws and Joint Resolutions of the National Council: Passed and Adopted at the Extra and Regular Session of 1872. Tahlequah, John Doubletooth, Printer, 1873.

Laws and Joint Resolutions of the National Council: Passed and Adopted at the Regular and Extra Session of 1870. Tahlequah, National Printing Office, 1871.

Laws and Joint Resolutions of the National Council: Passed and Adopted at the Regular and Extra Sessions of 1871. Tahlequah, Frank J. Dubois, Printer, 1872.

Laws and Joint Resolutions of the National Council: Passed and Adopted at the Regular Session of 1876. Tahlequah, *Cherokee Advocate,* 1877.

Laws and Joint Resolutions of the National Council: Passed and Adopted at the Regular Sessions of the National Council of 1876, 1877 and extra session of 1878. Tahlequah, Cherokee Advocate Office, 1878.

Mineral Law. Tahlequah, Advocate Office, 1884.

Mineral Law. Tahlequah, Advocate Office, 1887.

New Jury Law. Tahlequah, *Cherokee Advocate* Office, 1892.

Notice of Township Commissioners. Tahlequah, National Printing Office, 1872.

Penal Law: An Act for the Protection of the Public Domain, and in Relation to Intruders Upon the Same. Tahlequah, *Cherokee Advocate* Office, 1878.

Penal Laws of the Cherokee Nation: Passed by the National Council and Approved for the Years 1893–1896. Tahlequah, Advocate Office, 1897.

Penal Laws of the Cherokee Nation: Passed by the National Council and Approved for the Years 1893–1896. Tahlequah, Sentinel Printers, 1898.

Resolution Establishing Police Force. Park Hill, Cherokee Nation, Mission Press, 1841.

Road Law. Tahlequah, Advocate Office, 1892.

Rulings of the Supreme Court of the Cherokee Nation. Tahlequah, Advocate Office, 1878(?).

Supreme Court Rules. Tahlequah, Advocate Office, 1877.

Treaties Between the United States of America and the Cherokee Nation From 1785. Tahlequah, National Printing Office, 1870.
Treaties of Cherokee Tribe. Tahlequah, n.p., 1884.

IV. Unpublished Studies

Ballenger, Thomas Lee. "The Development of Law and Legal Institutions Among the Cherokees." Ph.D. dissertation, University of Oklahoma, 1938.

Barnes, Margaret Louise. "Intruders in the Cherokee Nation, 1834–1907." Master's thesis, University of Oklahoma, 1933.

Beckett, Ola Lorraine. "The *Cherokee Phoenix* and Its Efforts In The Education of the Cherokees." Master's thesis, University of Oklahoma, 1934.

Beverage, Nancy. "The Keetoowah Society." Paper. University of Tulsa, 1969.

Burbage, Edward A. "The Legend of Zeke Proctor." Master's thesis, University of Tulsa, 1950.

Dickson, John Lois. "The Judicial History of the Cherokee Nation From 1721 to 1835." Ph.D. dissertation, University of Oklahoma, 1964.

Faulkner, Colleela. "The Life and Times of Reverend Stephen Foreman." Master's thesis, University of Oklahoma, 1949.

Fogelson, Raymond David. "The Cherokee Ball Game: A Study in Southeastern Ethnology." Ph.D. dissertation, University of Pennsylvania, 1962.

Fullerton, Eula E. "Some Social Institutions of the Cherokees, 1820–1906." Master's thesis, University of Oklahoma, 1931.

Gearing, Frederick O. "Cherokee Political Organization, 1730–1755." Ph.D. dissertation, University of Chicago, 1956.

Gray, Robert A. "The Southern Powder Keg: A Study of the Creek and Cherokee Nations, 1763–1796." Master's thesis, Western Reserve University, Cleveland, Ohio, 1950.

Milam, Joe B. "The Opening of the Cherokee Outlet." Master's thesis, Oklahoma A&M College, Stillwater, Okla., 1931.

Murphy, James Oakley. "The Work of Judge Parker in the United States District Court for Western District of Arkansas, 1875–1896." Master's thesis, University of Oklahoma, 1939.

O'Donnell, James Howlett, III. "The Southern Indian in the War of Independence, 1775–1783." Ph.D. dissertation, Duke University, 1963.

Richards, Arthur Lee. "The Distribution of Lands of the Five Civilized Tribes." Master's thesis, University of Chicago, 1922.

Roethler, Michael D. "Negro Slavery Among the Cherokee Indians, 1540–1866." Ph.D. dissertation, Fordham University, 1964.

Sheehan, Bernard W. "Civilization and the American Indian in the Thought of the Jeffersonian Era." Ph.D. dissertation, University of Virginia, 1965.

Smith, Benny. "The Keetoowah Society of the Cherokee Indians." Master's thesis, Northwestern State College, Alva, Okla., 1967.

Strickland, Rennard. "Cherokee Law Ways." S.J.D. dissertation, University of Virginia, Charlottesville, 1970.

Thomas, Robert K. "The Origin and Development of the Redbird Smith Movement." Master's thesis, University of Arizona, Tucson, 1954.

Tyner, Howard Q. "The Keetowah Society in Cherokee History." Master's thesis, University of Tulsa, 1949.

Uzzell, Minter. "The Cherokee Gold Rush in Georgia: A Forgotten Chapter in Indian Removal." Paper presented before a seminar in American history, Northeastern State College, Tahlequah, Okla., July 26, 1955.

Willis, William S. "Colonial Conflict and the Cherokee Indians, 1710–1760." Ph.D. dissertation, Columbia University, 1955.

V. Books and Pamphlets

Abel, Annie H. The American Indian as Slaveholder and Secessionist. Cleveland, Arthur H. Clark Company, 1915.

Adair, James. The History of the American Indians. London, Private Printing for E. and C. Dilly, 1775.

Alden, John Richard. John Stuart and the Southern Colonial Frontier: A Study of Indian Relations, War, Trade, and Land Problems in the Southern Wilderness, 1754–1775. Ann Arbor, University of Michigan Press, 1944.

Americus. "Characters," Annual Register . . . of the Year 1760, VI. London, J. Dodsley, 1790.

Apter, David E. The Politics of Modernization. Chicago, University of Chicago Press, 1965.

Ballenger, T. L. Around Tahlequah Council Fires. Oklahoma City, Cherokee Publishing Company, 1945.

Bartram, William. Travels through North and South Carolina, Georgia, East and West Florida, the Cherokee Country, the Extensive Territories of the Muscogules, or Creek Confederacy, and the Country of the Choctaws: Containing an Account of Those Regions, Together with Observations of the Manners of the Indians. New Haven, Yale University Press, 1958.

Bass, Althea. Cherokee Messenger. Norman, University of Oklahoma Press, 1936.

Berkhofer, Robert F. Salvation and the Savage. Lexington, University of Kentucky Press, 1965.

Blackwell, Jessie Dawson. *Families of Samuel Dawson and Polly Ann Rogers*. Tulsa, Okla. (?), Private Printing, n.d.

Boudinot, Elias. *An Address to the Whites Delivered in the First Presbyterian Church on the 26th of May, 1826*. Philadelphia, William F. Geddes, 1826.

Brown, John P. *Old Frontiers: The Story of the Cherokee Indians from Earliest Times to the Date of Their Removal to the West, 1838*. Kingsport, Tenn., Southern Publishers, Incorporated, 1938.

Bruton, Wilson Otto and William Christopher Norrid. *The Nutshell: Cherokee Constitution and the Laws and Rulings Bearing on the Autonomy of the Cherokee Nation Condensed In A Nutshell by Bruton & Norrid, Muldrow, Indian Territory*. Muskogee, Indian Territory, The Phoenix Printing Company, 1894.

Chroust, Anton-Hermann. *The Rise of the Legal Profession in America*. Norman, University of Oklahoma Press, 1965.

Corkran, David H. *The Cherokee Frontier: Conflict and Survival, 1740–62*. Norman, University of Oklahoma Press, 1962.

——. *The Creek Frontier, 1540–1783*. Norman, University of Oklahoma Press, 1968.

Corlett, William Thomas. *The Medicine Man of the American Indian and His Cultural Background*. Baltimore, Charles C. Thomas, 1935.

Crane, Verner W. *The Southern Frontier, 1670–1732*. Ann Arbor, University of Michigan, Ann Arbor Paperbacks, 1959.

Debo, Angie. *And Still the Waters Run*. Princeton, Princeton University Press, 1940.

——. *The Five Civilized Tribes of Oklahoma: Report on Social and Economic Conditions*. Philadelphia, Indian Rights Association, 1951.

Eaton, Rachel Caroline. *John Ross and the Cherokee Indians*. Menasha, Wis., Collegiate Press, George Banta Publishing Company, 1914.

Filler, Louis and Allen Guttmann, eds. *The Removal of the Cherokee Nation: Manifest Destiny or National Dishonor?* Boston, D. C. Heath and Company, 1962.

Flaherty, David H., ed. *Essays in the History of Early American Law*. Chapel Hill, University of North Carolina Press, 1969.

Foreman, Carolyn Thomas. *Indians Abroad*. Norman, University of Oklahoma Press, 1943.

——. *Indian Women Chiefs*. Muskogee, Okla., Star Printery, 1954.

——. *Oklahoma Imprints: 1835–1907*. Norman, University of Oklahoma Press, 1936.

Foreman, Grant. *The Five Civilized Tribes*. Norman, University of Oklahoma Press, 1934.

——. *Indian Justice*. Oklahoma City, Harlow Company, 1934.

——. *Indian Removal*. Norman, University of Oklahoma Press, 1932.

——. *Muskogee: The Biography of an Oklahoma Town*. Norman, University of Oklahoma Press, 1943.

——. *Sequoyah*. Norman, University of Oklahoma Press, 1938.

Foster, George E. *Se-Quo-Yah: The American Cadmus and Modern Moses*. Philadelphia, Office of Indian Rights Association, 1885.

Gabriel, Ralph H. *Elias Boudinot, Cherokee, and His America*. Norman, University of Oklahoma Press, 1941.

Gearing, Fredrick O. *Priests and Warriors: Social Structure for Cherokee Politics in the 18th Century. Memoirs of the American Anthropological Association*. Vol. 64, No. 5, Part 2, Memoir 93 (October 1962).

Gluckman, Max. *Politics, Law and Ritual in Tribal Society*. Chicago, Aldine Publishing Company, 1965.

Gregory, Jack and Rennard Strickland. *Cherokee Spirit Tales: Tribal Myths, Legends, and Folklore*. Fayetteville, Ark., Indian Heritage Association, 1969.

——. *Choctaw Spirit Tales: Tribal Myths, Legends and Folklore*. Muskogee, Okla., Indian Heritage Association, 1971.

——. *Creek-Seminole Spirit Tales: Tribal Myths, Legends, and Folklore*. Muskogee, Okla., Indian Heritage Association, 1971.

——. *Sam Houston With the Cherokees, 1829–1833*. Austin, University of Texas Press, 1967.

Gregory, Jack and Rennard Strickland, eds. *Hell On The Border*. Muskogee, Okla., Indian Heritage Association, 1971.

——. *Starr's History of the Cherokees*. Fayetteville, Ark., Indian Heritage Association, 1968.

Hagan, William T. *American Indians*. Chicago, University of Chicago Press, 1961.

——. *Indian Police and Judges: Experiments in Acculturation and Control*. New Haven and London, Yale University Press, 1966.

Hallum, John. *In Memorium Elias Cornelius Boudinot, 1835–1890*. Chicago, Rand, McNally & Co., 1891.

Hargrett, Lester. *A Bibliography of the Constitutions and Laws of the American Indians*. Cambridge, Harvard University Press, 1947.

——. *Oklahoma Imprints, 1835–1890*. New York, R. R. Bowker Company, 1951, for the Bibliographical Society of America.

Haywood, John. *The Natural and Aboriginal History of Tennessee*. Nashville, George Wilson, 1828.

Hoebel, E. Adamson. *The Law of Primitive Man: A Study in Comparative Legal Dynamics*. Cambridge, Harvard University Press, 1954.

Howard, A. E. Dick. *The Road From Runnymede: Magna Carta and Constitutionalism in America*. Charlottesville, University of Virginia Press, 1968.

Jacobs, Wilbur R. *Diplomacy and Indian Gifts*. Stanford, Stanford University Press, 1950.

———, ed. *Indians of the Southern Colonial Frontier: The Edmond Atkins Report and Plan of 1755*. Columbia, University of South Carolina Press, 1954.

Jefferson, Thomas. *The Writings of Thomas Jefferson*. Washington, D.C., Century Company, 1904.

Kilpatrick, Jack F. and Anna Gritts. *Friends of Thunder*. Dallas, Southern Methodist University Press, 1964.

———. *New Echota Letters: Contributions of Samuel A. Worcester to the Cherokee Phoenix*. Dallas, Southern Methodist University Press, 1968.

———. *Run Toward the Nightland: Magic of the Oklahoma Cherokees*. Dallas, Southern Methodist University Press, 1968.

———. *Shadow of Sequoyah: Social Documents of the Cherokees, 1862–1964*. Norman, University of Oklahoma Press, 1965.

Knowles, Nathaniel. *The Torture of Captives by Indians of Eastern North America*. Philadelphia, American Philosophical Society, 1940.

Llewellyn, Karl and E. A. Hoebel. *The Cheyenne Way: Conflict and Case Law in Primitive Jurisprudence*. Norman, University of Oklahoma Press, 1941.

Lumpkin, Wilson. *The Removal of the Cherokee Indians from Georgia*. New York, Dodd, Mead and Company, 1907.

McKenney, Thomas L. and James Hall. *History of Indian Tribes of North America*. Philadelphia, D. Rice and Company, 1865.

Malone, Henry Thompson. *Cherokees of the Old South: A People in Transition*. Athens, University of Georgia Press, 1956.

Masterson, V. V. *The Katy Railroad and the Last Frontier*. Norman, University of Oklahoma Press, 1952.

Maxwell, Amos D. *The Sequoyah Convention*. Boston, Meador Publishing Company, 1953.

Milling, Chapman J. *Red Carolinians*. Chapel Hill, University of North Carolina Press, 1940.

Nader, Laura, ed. *Law In Culture and Society*. Chicago, Aldine Publishing Company, 1969.

Nuttall, Thomas. *A Journal of Travels into the Arkansas Territory, During the Year 1819, with Occasional Observations on the Manners of the Aborigines*. Cleveland, Arthur H. Clark Company, 1905.

Owen, Narcissa. *Memoirs of Narcissa Owen, 1831–1907*. Washington, D.C., Private Printing, 1907.

Payne, John Howard. *Indian Justice: A Cherokee Murder Trial at Tahlequah in 1840*. Ed. by Grant Foreman. Muskogee, Okla., Star Printery, 1962.

Peckham, Howard H. *The Colonial Wars, 1689–1762*. Chicago, University of Chicago Press, 1964.

Pierce, Earl Boyd and Rennard Strickland. *The Cherokee People*. Phoenix, Indian Tribal Series, 1973.

Pierson, George W. *Tocqueville in America*. Garden City, Anchor Books, 1959.

Pound, Merritt B. *Benjamin Hawkins, Indian Agent*. Athens, University of Georgia Press, 1951.

Reid, John Phillip. *A Law of Blood: The Primitive Law of the Cherokee Nation*. New York, New York University Press, 1970.

Richardson, Albert D. *Beyond the Mississippi, 1857–1867*. Richmond, Virginia National Publishing Company, 1867.

Ross, Mrs. William Potter, ed. *The Life and Times of Hon. William P. Ross*. Fort Smith, Private Printing, 1893.

Schoolcraft, Henry Rowe. *Information Respecting the History, Conditions and Prospects of the Indian Tribes*. Philadelphia, Lippincott, Grambo & Company, 1853–1857.

Scott, Winfield. *Memoirs of Lieut.-General Scott, LL.D., Written By Himself*. New York, Sheldon & Company, 1864.

Simes, Lewis M. *Public Policy and the Dead Hand*. Ann Arbor, University of Michigan Law School, 1955.

Smith, James F., comp. *The Cherokee Land Lottery, containing a numerical list of the names of the fortunate drawers in said lottery with an engraved map of each district* . . . New York, Harper & Brothers, 1838.

Speeches on the Passage of the Bill for the Removal of the Indians, Delivered in the Congress of the United States. April and May, 1830. Boston, Perkins and Marvin, 1830.

Starkey, Marion L. *The Cherokee Nation*. New York, Alfred A. Knopf, 1946.

Starr, Emmett. *Cherokees "West", 1794–1839*. Claremore, Okla., Private Printing, 1910.

Stuart, John. *A Sketch of the Cherokees and Choctaw Indians*. Little Rock, Woodruff and Pew, 1837.

Timberlake, Henry. *The Memoirs of Lieut. Henry Timberlake*. London, Printed for the author, 1765.

de Tocqueville, Alexis. *Democracy in America*. Reeve-Bowen translation. Cambridge, Sever & Franois, 1864.

Van Every, Dale. *Disinherited: The Lost Birthright of the American Indian*. New York, William Morrow & Company, 1966.

Walker, Robert S. *Torchlight to the Cherokees*. New York, Macmillan Co., 1931.

Wardell, Morris L. *A Political History of the Cherokee Nation, 1838–1907*. Norman, University of Oklahoma Press, 1938.

Washburn, Cephas. *Reminiscences of the Indians*. Ed. by Hugh Park. Van Buren, Ark., Press-Argus, 1955.

Watts, W. J. *Cherokee Citizenship and A Brief History of Internal Affairs in the Cherokee Nation With Records and Acts of the United States Interior Department; Reports of Special Inspectors and Agents— Garland's Decision and Other Documentary Evidence*. Muldrow, Indian Territory, Register Print, 1895.

Wilkins, Thurman. *Cherokee Tragedy: The Story of the Ridge Family and the Decimation of a People*. New York, Macmillan Company, 1970.

Williams, Samuel Cole, ed. *Early Travels in the Tennessee Country, 1540–1800*. Johnson City, Tenn., Watauga Press, 1928.

——, ed. *The Memoirs of Lieut. Henry Timberlake*. Johnson City, Tenn., Watauga Press, 1927.

VI. Articles

Blackburn, Gideon. "An Account of the Origin and Progress of the Mission to the Cherokee Indians," *Panopolist* (1808), 325.

Brown, David. "Views of a Native Indian, as to the Present Condition of His People," *Missionary Herald*, Vol. 21 (1825), 354–55.

Brown, John P. "Eastern Cherokee Chiefs," *Chronicles of Oklahoma*, Vol. 16 (1938), 3–35.

Burke, Joseph C. "The Cherokee Cases: A Study in Law, Politics, and Morality," *Stanford Law Review*, Vol. 21 (1969), 500–31.

Chroust, Anton-Hermann, "Did President Jackson Actually Threaten the Supreme Court of the United States With Nonenforcement of its Injunction Against the State of Georgia?" *American Journal of Legal History*, Vol. 5 (January 1960), 76–78.

Corkran, David H. "Cherokee Prehistory," *North Carolina Historical Review*, Vol. 34 (1957), 455–66.

——. "Cherokee Sun and Fire Observances," *Southern Indian Studies*, Vol. 7 (1955), 33–38.

——. "The Nature of the Cherokee Supreme Being," *Southern Indian Studies*, Vol. 5 (1953), 27–35.

——. "The Sacred Fire of the Cherokees," *Southern Indian Studies*, Vol. 5 (1953), 21–26.

Crane, Vernon W. "A Lost Utopia of the First American Frontier," *Sewanee Review Quarterly*, Vol. 27 (1919), 49.

Davis, J. B. "Slavery in the Cherokee Nation," *Chronicles of Oklahoma*, Vol. 11 (December 1933), 1056–72.

Foreman, Carolyn Thomas. "The Light-Horse in the Indian Territory," *Chronicles of Oklahoma*, Vol. 34 (1956), 17–43.

————. "Military Discipline in Early Oklahoma," *Chronicles of Oklahoma*, Vol. 6 (1928), 140–44.

Foreman, Minta Ross. "Reverend Stephen Foreman, Cherokee Missionary," *Chronicles of Oklahoma*, Vol. 18 (September 1940), 229–42.

Foster, George. "A Legal Episode in the Cherokee Nation," *Green Bag*, Vol. 4 (1892), 486–90.

Fuller, Lon. "Positivism and Fidelity to Law—A Reply to Professor Hart," *Harvard Law Review*, Vol. 71 (1958), 642.

Garrett, Kathleen. "Darmouth Alumni in the Indian Territory," *Chronicles of Oklahoma*, Vol. 32 (1954), 123–41.

Gearing, Fred O. "The Structural Posses of 18th Century Cherokee Villages," *American Anthropologist*, Vol. 60 (1958), 1148–57.

Green, F. M. "Georgia's Forgotten Industry: Gold Mining," *Georgia Historical Quarterly*, Vol. 19 (1935), 93–111, 210–28.

Henderson, Archibald. "The Treaty of Long Island of Holston," *North Carolina Historical Review*, Vol. 8 (1931), 55–116.

Hoebel, E. A. "Law and Anthropology," *Virginia Law Review*, Vol. 32 (1946), 835–54.

Hoyt, Ard. "Brainerd Mission Journal," *Panoplist*, Vol. 15 (1818–1819), 42–43.

Johnson, Walter A. "Brief History of the Missouri-Kansas-Texas Railroad Lines," *Chronicles of Oklahoma*, Vol. 24 (1946), 340–58.

Kawashima, Yasuhide. "Review of *A Law of Blood*," *American Journal of Legal History*, Vol. 15 (1971), 157–59.

Kilpatrick, Jack and Anna G. Kilpatrick. "Record of a North Carolina Cherokee Township Trial, 1862," *Southern Indian Studies*, Vol. 16 (1964).

King, J. Berry. "Judge William Pressley Thompson," *Chronicles of Oklahoma*, Vol. 29 (1941), 3–4.

Malinowski, B. "New Instruments for Interpretation of Law—Especially Primitive," *Law Guild Review*, Vol. 2 (1942), 1–12.

Malone, Henry Thompson. "Return J. Meigs: Indian Agent Extraordinary," *East Tennessee Historical Society's Publications*, No. 28, 1956.

Martin, R. G. "*The Cherokee Phoenix*," *Chronicles of Oklahoma*, Vol. 15 (1947), 102–19.

Meriwether, Colyer. "General Joseph Martin and the Cherokees," *Southern History Association Publications*, Vol. 8 (1904), 443–50; Vol. 9 (1905), 27–41.

Mooney, James. "The Cherokee Ball Play," *American Anthropologist*, Vol. 3 (1890), 105–32.

Nader, Laura. "The Anthropological Study of Law," *American Anthropologist*, Vol. 47 (1965), 3.

Notes and Documents. "John Watt: A Name Engraved in the Cherokee Nation," *Chronicles of Oklahoma*, Vol. 44 (1966), 330–32.

Payne, John Howard. "The Green Corn Dance," *Chronicles of Oklahoma*, Vol. 20 (1932), 170–95.

Reid, John Phillip. "The Cherokee Thought: An Apparatus of Primitive Law," *New York University Law Review*, Vol. 46 (1971), 281–302.

Skarritt, Preston. "The Green-Corn Ceremonies of the Cherokees," *National Intelligencer*, April 4, 1849.

Strickland, Rennard. "Christian Gotelieb Priber: Utopian Precursor of the Cherokee Government," *Chronicles of Oklahoma*, Vol. 48 (1970), 264–79.

———. "History of Law, Environmental Values, and Social Change," *St. Mary's Law Journal*, Vol. 3 (1971).

———. "Idea of Ecology and the Ideal of the Indian," *Journal of American Indian Education*, Vol. 10 (1970).

———. "Redeeming Centuries of Dishonor," *University of Toledo Law Review*, Vol. 1970 (1970), 847–90.

——— and Jack Gregory. "Nixon's Indian Policy," *Commonweal*, Vol. 92 (1970), 432–36.

——— and James C. Thomas, "Most Sensibly Conservative and Safely Radical: Oklahoma's Constitutional Regulation of Economic Power, Land Ownership, and Corporate Monopoly," *Tulsa Law Review*, Vol. 9 (1973), 167–238.

Thompson, William P. "An Address Delivered Before the First Annual Meeting of the Oklahoma State Bar Association in 1910," *Chronicles of Oklahoma*, Vol. 2 (1924), 67.

———. "W. W. Hastings, 1868–1938," *Chronicles of Oklahoma*, Vol. 16 (1938), 269–70.

"Three Cherokees . . . to see The King Their Father," *American Scene Magazine*, Vol. 2 (1963), 6.

Wahrhaftig, Albert L. "The Tribal Cherokee Population of Oklahoma," *Current Anthropology*, Vol. 9 (1968), 510–18.

Williams, Alfred M. "Among the Cherokees," *Lippincott's Magazine*, Vol. 27 (February 1881), 195–203.

Witthoft, J. "The Cherokee Green Corn Medicine and the Green Corn Festival," *Journal of the Washington Academy of Science*, Vol. 36 (1946), 213–19.

Yadin, Uri. "The Proposed Law of Succession for Israel," *American Journal of Comparative Law*, Vol. 2 (1953), 143.

Index

Ward, Nancy: 73
Washburn, Cephas: 28–30
Washington, Pres. George: 51
Washington, Treaty of (1846): 6
Watie, Stand: education of, 122; law
  practice of, 124
Watts, W. J.: 116n.
Webber, Walter: 68
West, Nancy: 73
Western Cherokees: 4, 63, 67–68, 101,
  160
Whirlwind (Cherokee): 30
Whisky: 64–65, 149–50
White Path (Cherokee): 59, 76
Wills and trusts: see property
Wilson, W. C.: 122
Witchcraft: 28–30&n., 179; and law,
  183–86

Witt, Jackson: 124
Women, Cherokee: 22–23, 31; as court,
  26ff.; and office of "war women," 26;
  and commercial farming, 44; rights of,
  100–101; punishment by, 168; see also
  property
Women's Christian Temperance Union:
  172
Woodall v. Woodall: 161
Woodard v. Wilkerson: 164
Worcester, Samuel: 114; on slavery, 81–
  82; on Cherokee language, 106; on
  laws, 186; see also Worcester v. Georgia
Worcester v. Georgia: 8, 67; Cherokee
  reaction to, 78&n.
Wrosetastow (Cherokee chief): 55

Young, Roach: 156, 180